CRIMINALS AND FOLK HEROES

CRIMINALS AND FOLK HEROES

GANGSTERS AND THE FBI
IN THE 1930s

ROBERT UNDERHILL

Algora Publishing
New York

Library of Congress Cataloging-in-Publication Data —

Underhill, Robert, 1920- author.
  Criminals and folk heroes / by Robert Underhill.
      pages cm
  Includes bibliographical references and index.
      ISBN 978-1-62894-138-8 (soft cover: alk. paper)—ISBN 978-1-62894-139-5 (hard
cover: alk. paper) 1. Crime—United States—History—20th century. 2. Criminals—
United States—Case studies. I. Title.
      HV6783.U53 2015
      364.1092'273—dc23
                                    2015026715

Printed in the United States

For Sue—Beloved Daughter and Discerning Reader

Table of Contents

PREFACE

As the 1930s began, America was in the lowest depths of its greatest depression. Prices had hit bottom; homeless people were everywhere, sleeping in boxcars, tents, or cardboard cartons outside cities where hungry citizens lined up for bowls of soup or slices of bread. Estimates of the unemployed ranged from twelve to thirteen million. The shattered economy provided fertile soil for crops of thefts, robberies, murders, and kidnappings.

The Depression created a type of outlaw, fed by both need and greed. By 1930, in the East and in other large cities gangster syndicates from Prohibition Days still operated, but across the land and particularly in the Midwest, smaller bands held sway. Newspapers sometimes called the smaller groups *gangsters*, but they were different from the millionaire mobsters in metropolitan centers who reigned as feudal lords. Depression desperadoes were blue-collar criminals whose favorite targets were filling stations, grocery stores, and small town banks which dotted the plains and prairies of America's heartland.

The first five years of the third decade were noteworthy for several reasons. One significant change that occurred was emergence of cooperation among local, state, and federal police. Prior years had seen no coordination, and rivalries among the three entities made it easier for felons to escape capture. Citizens regarded robberies as affairs of the community and were to be handled by persons elected locally. State police were under-funded and relegated to such duties as licensing, traffic control, and monitoring public events. Adding to the cauldron of confusion was blatant corruption of police forces in several important cities in the Midwest. Through briberies and pay-offs, such amoral individuals made bank robberies and subsequent escapes easier.

The rise of the FBI is a second reason warranting special attention to the years between 1930 and 1935. Americans believed federal government had nothing to do with fighting crime: local police were expected to provide security and to apprehend criminals. The belief could be traced back to the U.S. Constitution and its provisions for states' rights.

The government in Washington, D.C., had set up the Division of Investigation as a branch of the Treasury Department, but the branch was miniscule, short of funding, and staffed by lawyers and accountants. Not until 1935 would this seminal agency be separated, named the Federal Bureau of Investigation, and under the aggressive leadership of J. Edgar Hoover have its crime detecting capabilities expanded and its agents permitted to carry guns. With new powers, the FBI set up its own laboratories for fingerprinting and the filing of criminal records, photographs, and related paraphernalia for crime detection. Moreover, the FBI could supply sheriffs all over the country with information on suspected routes of criminals, their records, pictures, fingerprints, and methods used in burglaries, kidnappings, bank robberies, or similar offenses.

Sensational kidnappings prodded Congress to fund the new agency, and its dedicated leader used every means at his command to enlarge its power. In March, 1932, the infant son of famed trans-Atlantic flier Charles A. Lindbergh was kidnapped and slain. Three months later, Congress passed a law dubbed the Lindbergh Act making it a federal crime whenever kidnappers crossed a state line. The law soon was expanded to put bank robbers in the same category, thus authorizing use of federal powers when banks were robbed and fugitives apt to flee across state lines.

A third reason for focusing on the years of 1930–1935 arises from respect regained by banks and financial businesses. By 1935 the monetary crisis had ended; the hardest times of the Great Depression were beginning to ease. Jobs were returning even though wages were still pitifully low. Some of the disdain which thousands of hungry and unemployed citizens had felt for banks and rich people was fading. Robbers and newspaper reporters had been quick to seize on such disdain by telling themselves, "After all, banks were robbers, too." The attitude fanned sentiments which painted bankers as the enemy and those who robbed them as "good ole country boys" driven to a life of crime by circumstances beyond their control.

The change in public beliefs was bolstered further by actions of the New Deal. Hundreds of American banks had collapsed during the initial years of the Great Depression. In the First Hundred days, Franklin Roosevelt's incoming administration engineered the Glass-Steagall Act which created the Federal Deposit Insurance Corporation. Under its authority the FDIC was given authority to insure bank deposits against loss in the event of a bank failure and to regulate certain banking practices. The Glass-Steagall Act followed by other New Deal measures helped stabilize the economy. Money was still hard to come by, but people were returning to jobs, and confidence in banks returning.

From thefts, robberies, and murders, the perpetrators gained loot and publicity. Reporters added interest by giving the criminals catchy nicknames: "Ma" Barker, "Creepy" Alvin Karpis, "Pretty Boy" Floyd, "Machine-Gun" Kelly, or "Baby-Face" Nelson. The monikers helped elevate cheap thugs into folk heroes. Many citizens looked on the small-time hoodlums with a sort of admiration and welcome diversions from woes of the Depression. The freelance criminals differed from disreputable big-city mobsters and syndicate racketeers. The freelancers seemed more like reincarnations of flamboyant former Wild West outlaws: Billy the Kid, Jesse James, and the Dalton gang. In truth, thugs of the early thirties seldom had long to enjoy happy, carefree days as they squandered booty from banks or businesses. Rather than glamour and luxury, their lives are little more than aimless odysseys forced upon them by their attempts to keep moving and one step ahead of the law.

Kidnappings especially helped create the modern FBI. By 1930, some desperadoes had come to believe that kidnappings paid more than bank robbing, and as tales of massive ransoms spread through underworld grapevines, kidnappings became more frequent. The year of 1933 brought 27 major cases, more than twice the number in any previous year.

Coming on the heels of the crime surge of the 1920s symbolized by Al Capone, kidnappings bolstered arguments for a federal police force. There was considerable argument over the need for a centralized force. On one side were reformers who argued that municipal authorities were often corrupt, ineffective, and unable to deal with mobile criminals who could cross state lines easily. Those who used that argument could supply plenty of evidence. Opposing them were alarmists and city authorities jealous of their turf, who alleged that a federal force was the first step toward an American Gestapo.

At its inception, the Federal Bureau of Investigation was made up of lawyers, accountants, and a few technicians. It was just what the name implied: *Investigation* not *enforcement*. In its infancy as a federal bureau, its members were not even permitted to carry guns. Not until late 1933 was the denial overturned, and on December 31st of that year, Wilbur Underhill, the Tri-State Terror, had the dubious distinction of being the first criminal ever shot by the new FBI.

(Let it be noted at the outset that no traceable evidence can be found that the present author is any more closely related to the infamous Wilbur

Underhill than are those who may read the book — although admittedly, the similarity of names helped lure the writer into his scribblings.)

Reporting crimes and criminals of the early 1930s is difficult for several reasons. One is that, frequently, crimes occurred at the same time in different places involving different personnel. Moreover, henchmen might hook up with several gangs. Another reason was the flood of rumors and fiction that engulfed leaders and related major happenings. A third is the competition between criminals and law enforcers, including internecine rivalries among federal officials, state, and local police—rivalries which were spiced with bald intrusions by newspapers and radio reporters.

From this kaleidoscope, writers in later periods can select only a few of the events and characters, omitting many and failing to include much supporting detail. Interested readers who want a fuller picture are encouraged to examine other histories or consult biographies of individuals who made the years between 1930 and 1934 so exciting.

Chapter 1. Wilbur Underhill—Tri-State Killer

An ambulance and a pair of passenger cars pulled up and parked in the main entrance of the municipal hospital in Shawnee, Oklahoma. Within minutes attendants wheeled out a stretcher on which lay a patient swathed in bandages. Stretcher and patient were loaded into the ambulance, and the three-vehicle caravan moved out to head southeast.

It was 8:30 A.M. on Saturday, January 6, 1934, and the 70 miles to McAlester would be the last ride 33-year-old Wilbur Underhill would take. He had been named Henry Wilber Underhill shortly after his birth on March 16, 1901, in the tiny town of Seneca in the southwest corner of Missouri, but early in his teens he changed the spelling to Wilbur, believing that spelling was more masculine.

Henry "Hank" Underhill, Wilbur's father, died in 1912 when the lad was 11 years old, and his mother, Almira, was left in Joplin to care for a brood of seven young children. It was almost an intolerable existence, for poverty tracked the family like a pack of hungry wolves. Almira took in washing, and she cleaned some of the finer residences in Joplin; yet without the help of her two daughters, Grace (25 years old) and Anna Lea (aged 15), the family could not have survived.

In her endeavors to keep the family intact, Almira could manage the girls but was unable to control the boisterous activities of three high spirited boys ostensibly living at home. The two older ones, Earl and Charles, were in their late teens and sometimes were away all night. Their younger brother Wilbur tried his best to keep up with them.

Even before he reached teen age, Wilbur played hooky, learned to hustle in the streets, swipe candy and small items, and when offered would swill rotgut whisky. He was a young, unreliable pupil at the Alcott school in Joplin when he suffered an accident. His mother and family members claimed the accident helped explain his erratic behavior.

A trash pit was next to the school building, and one day while Wilbur was rummaging through the pit someone threw a bottle out an upstairs window of the school. The bottle struck Wilbur on the head and fractured his skull. The injury put him down for a week, and loyal family members joined his mother to chorus that he was never the same afterwards but was agitated, temperamental, and given to violent outbursts.

He was 18 years old at the time of his first arrest when he was caught red-handed burglarizing a Joplin residence. Found in his possession was a gunnysack filled with identifiable silverware. Hauled before the court, a sympathetic judge warned the youth to mend his ways and slapped his wrists with a three-year suspended sentence.

The warning didn't take, and he was arrested again within the year, captured in a trap set up by local police. This time his crime was more serious.

A series of robberies had taken place in Lovers Lane—an area just west of Joplin. While couples parked in the isolated lane to indulge in their intimacies, a lone gunman would sneak up and announce, "This is a stick-up!" The intruder then would demand all the valuables from the startled couple and flee on foot.

Joplin police chose two of their own—a young male and a female of similar age—as decoys. One night while this pair was parked and whispering sweet nothings to one another, participating lawmen hid themselves in bushes nearby, ready to pounce on any stranger who appeared. An hour went by before a roughly dressed man holding a pistol crept up to the parked vehicle and ordered the couple to turn over their money and jewelry.

The hidden officers with guns drawn leaped out of the bushes, ran to the vehicle, and ordered the bandit to surrender. Instead, he turned and fired; his bullet barely missed one officer's head. An exchange of gunfire followed, and during it the robber fell to the ground with an audible "Damn!" The wound didn't keep him down, however, for he was able to rise and get away in the darkness.

A few days later, police were tipped off that a stranger was occupying an abandoned shack just inside the Newton County line. Cops moved in and found Wilbur Underhill suffering from a minor flesh wound.

Brought to the station, he was identified by the lawmen who had shot him and he was indicted for attempted highway robbery. His quick trial took place in Neosho, the Newton County seat, on October 13, 1920. The proceedings were brief, and after a guilty verdict was announced, Wilbur was sentenced to a two-year term at the Missouri State Penitentiary.[1]

The century old penitentiary and its work fields occupied 47 acres on a bluff in Jefferson City and was no bed of roses. Incoming prisoners were warned: "Do as you're told or take your punishment." Each cell had been built to house three men, but by the year Underhill arrived, the prison had more than 3000 inmates and each cell lodged six members. Among hardships suffered were poor food, brutal guards, gang violence, not enough ventilation in summer, and cold temperatures in winter.

Despite the jail's harsh conditions, Underhill managed to link up with confederates. His brother Earnest, seven years older, was behind bars in the same institution for selling booze or dope, and collecting gambling debts strong-armed style. From him and other seasoned cons, Wilbur learned more about burglary and bank robbing. A young rebel himself already toughened by gang fights and street brawls, within weeks after beginning his term, he was punished for gambling and knife fighting.

Prison records described him as thick bodied, rangy, and snaggle-toothed. He was six feet tall, weighed 175 pounds, had light sandy hair, gray eyes, and was missing two teeth in the upper left side of his mouth. His face showed a few moles and small scars. He went into the prison as a punk thief; released in December, 1921, he emerged better schooled in various crimes and ready to practice them.

Almira came to visit her jailed sons several times and, as she would do for more than a decade and a half, insisted they were not bad boys. They had been wronged by society; she put the blame on cops and their tactics for her boys' bad behavior.

Out of prison just before Christmas in 1921, Wilbur made a hasty visit to see his mother and sisters before going 50 miles southwest of Joplin into the very northwest corner of Oklahoma. Numerous lead and zinc deposits had been discovered there, and as a result the area had mushroomed with employment opportunities as established financiers and entrepreneurs came in to drill new mines and set up new businesses. Men seeking jobs arrived in droves to be followed by whores, gamblers, bootleggers, and dope peddlers coming to fleece wage earners from their funds. It was just the kind of environment Wilbur wanted.

He had no trouble finding a mining job in Picher, Oklahoma, a community thriving amidst the boom. After two weeks, though, the work began to pall on him; he knew there were easier ways to make a buck. Other toughs he met in pool halls and gambling houses were making it; why shouldn't he? Wilbur joined his newfound buddies in a few local burglaries around Picher, Hockerville, and Cardin before quitting the mining job and going back to Joplin with his meager funds.

Writers later would label the period the "Roaring Twenties"—a period rife with bootleg liquor that encouraged young men and women to jump the traces of traditional morality. The Prohibition Act made ever-present moonshining more profitable. Prices for wildcat whisky soared, and in the hill country of Oklahoma every community had its stills, sometimes barely hidden. Stills ranged from small ones on family farms to larger commercial operations; there were as many ways to brew the white lightning as there were men to make it.

It is worth noting a few reasons Wilbur Underhill never achieved the folklore status given to different criminals of the period. First, he was a forerunner when other news stories were more nationally important. Secondly, he was a yegg of the worst order with little to admire and no traits that would cause reporters to embroider his misdeeds with colorful monikers such as *Pretty Boy*, *Creepy*, or *Baby Face*. Thirdly, the Eastern establishment with its syndicated press association and multitude of reporters paid more attention to happenings in cities and eastern regions than to events or characters in Midwestern hinterlands.

One story which caught the attention of newspaper readers across the nation occurred in the late spring of 1924. The heinous crime and subsequent trial crowded Wilbur Underhill's bank robberies off the front pages.

Late in the afternoon of May 21, 1924, 14-year-old Bobby Franks was walking home from his school on the near south side of Chicago when Richard Loeb and Nathan Leopold, driving a rented Willys-Knight auto, stopped and asked him to come over to them.

Richard Loeb was 18 years old, the privileged son of a retired Sears Roebuck vice president. His partner Nathan Leopold was a year older, son of a millionaire box manufacturer, and like Loeb had been reared in an atmosphere of wealth and luxury. Each boy had his own car, his own checking account, more than ample funds to spend, and both were highly intelligent with intellects bordering on brilliancy. Loeb that spring had been recognized as the youngest graduate of the University of Michigan, and Leopold had enrolled to begin law studies at Harvard University in the fall.

That afternoon in south Chicago, Loeb asked the Franks boy to get into their car, saying they would take him home. Instead he killed the boy by hitting him over the head several times with a chisel. Then, with Leopold driving, the murderers went east to a marshland near the Indiana state line. They stripped Franks naked, poured hydrochloric acid over his body to make identification more difficult, and stuffed the corpse into a culvert nearby. The next morning, the parents of the murdered boy received a special delivery letter instructing them to secure $10,000 and await further orders; they never had to do it because the brutal and senseless crime had been committed carelessly.

A pair of horn-rimmed tortoise shell glasses was found near the body and were quickly identified as those sold recently to Nathan Leopold. Apparently they had slipped out of his pocket as he and Loeb were putting the corpse into the culvert. Also, the typewritten ransom note sent to the Franks was matched with a typewriter used by Leopold's law study group. Other damning evidence was given when the Leopold family chauffeur said he was certain the Leopold car, which both boys claimed they had used while driving around with girls the night the Franks boy was killed, had not left the garage on the day of the murder.[2]

Loeb and Leopold were arrested, and their families hired Clarence Darrow to defend them. Newspapers trumpeted that the noted Darrow was promised a million dollars if he could get the two culprits off free. Darrow persuaded the boys to change their initial pleas of "not guilty" to charges of murder and kidnapping to "guilty," thus insuring they would be given a hearing before a single judge rather than appearing before a jury certain to be incensed by lurid newspaper accounts.

The hearing took place in late August, and in his twelve-hour *tour de force* attempting to save his young clients from the gallows, Darrow presented the most eloquent attack on the death penalty ever heard in an American courtroom. His plea, mixing poetry and prose, science and emotion, hatred of bloodlust and love of man, persuaded the judge to grant the defendants life imprisonment rather than the death penalty.

Loeb and Leopold were moved to the penitentiary in Joliet and twelve years afterwards Loeb would be killed by razor slashes at the hands of another inmate (who was acquitted when he convinced authorities he was defending himself against Loeb's sexual aggressions).

Leopold taught in the prison schools, reorganized the prison library, and designed a system of prison education. After 34 years of confinement, he was released and migrated to Puerto Rico where he taught mathematics and did good work in hospitals and church missions before dying in 1971 at the age of 66.

Newspaper coverage of the sensational Loeb–Leopold case was so extensive it is no wonder that robberies by Wilbur Underhill in Missouri and Oklahoma went unnoticed except for items in local papers.

In the evening of December 14, 1922, armed with a .38 cal. Colt revolver, Underhill and a companion held up a filling station in downtown Joplin. The two of them took the employee and a patron as hostages and drove out into the country, where they forced their captives into a ravine and warned them against squealing. The next day, Underhill and his pal were arrested.

Underhill's trial came quickly, and convicted of burglary he was sentenced to five years of hard labor. To serve it, he was sent to the penitentiary near Jefferson City for the second time.

He was serving his third year when he and other inmates tunneled under a stage located in the prison's chapel, thereby gaining access to a sewer line leading to the Missouri River. Their break failed because, after wading through the underground line, the escapees found themselves blocked by heavy iron bars separating the sewer from the river.[3]

Earnest Underhill, oldest brother of Wilbur, was still behind bars in the State Penitentiary in Jefferson City, and in that June of 1925 brother Earl arrived after being sentenced to a five-year jolt for burglary. In March of the following year, George Underhill would join them to begin a two-year hitch given him for larceny. Almira Underhill in 1925 had four sons incarcerated in the same prison.

Authorities released Wilbur from the Missouri State Penitentiary in November 1926, and following the pattern in his first parole five years earlier, he first went back to Joplin and then to Picher, Oklahoma, where he found a job with the Eagle-Picher Lead Mining Company. There he met a 23-year old small time thief named Ike "Skeet" Akins.

The two of them quit their jobs in Picher and went to Claremont, Oklahoma, where Wilbur took up with Sarah Riddle, a floozy who knew her way around. Wilbur and Sarah married in a quick ceremony conducted by a Justice of the Peace. Aiken stayed near the newlyweds and went with them a month later to Tulsa.

Underhill and Aiken then began a splurge of minor thefts. First, they robbed a street car conductor in Baxter Springs, Kansas, not far away, taking from him several dollars, his watch, and a .41 cal. Colt revolver.

They pulled off several street muggings before the Christmas season of 1926 began. On December 12, Fred Smyth, 16 years old, was walking down the dark streets of one of the mining settlements when Underhill accosted him and demanded his money. The boy turned and tried to flee, but Underhill with a recently acquired revolver shot him, his bullet lodging deep in the right lung of the unfortunate boy. Hearing the shot and hullabaloo, neighbors rushed to the scene immediately, but the attackers were able to get away. An ambulance was called and Smyth survived but lay critically in the hospital for two weeks. However, in mug shots police showed him, he was able to identify Underhill as the thug who had shot him.

Underhill was not apprehended, and the following week he and Aiken hit the J. R. Roberts Grocery in Baxter Springs, the Milo Chew Drug store, and also knocked off a filling station on the state line between Kansas and Oklahoma. The two thugs stayed around Picher in various flop houses before Underhill met and began shacking up with Minnie Gregg, another bar hopping woman.

Meanwhile, the Eagle-Picher Mining Company, alarmed over the spate of robberies occurring on their properties, hired Deputy Joe Anderson to track down the culprits. A dogged pursuer, Anderson caught up with the robbing duo in Okmulgee, Oklahoma.

On Christmas Eve, the pair was seen loafing in front of the Phillips Drug Store and then doing the same at the Purity Drug Store a few blocks away. This store's owner, Ira Maynard, was at the cash register and his wife was taking inventory when two bandits entered, flashed their guns, and demanded money. The Maynards were handing the money to the robbers just as two teen-aged boys came into the store. When ordered to put up their hands, one of them, George Fee, refused, thinking it was some sort of prank, and started to walk toward the soda fountain. It was a mistake, for Aiken shot him, the .41 cal. bullet striking Fee in the arm and then passing into the trunk of his body. The bandits fled; an ambulance was called and rushed the wounded victim to the hospital where he died within an hour.

Deputy Joe Anderson had not been resting but was hot on the trail of Underhill and Aikens. Anderson followed when the two of them left Okmulgee and, traveling in a stolen car, went to Tulsa. Armed with "John Doe" warrants, Anderson collected aides from Tulsa police, found the hideouts of the two fugitives, and arrested them both. In searching the suspects, officers found a .41 cal. Colt, the same type of revolver used in the shooting of Fred Smyth and the slaying of George Fee, as well as a pair of other guns.

Ira Maynard from Baxter Springs and Rex Bell, the companion of the murdered George Fee, were called to Tulsa, and both were positive in identifying Underhill and Aiken as the bandits. Both were quickly escorted back to Okmulgee to face the charges.[4]

On January 26, 1927, Underhill and Aiken were given a hearing before a Justice of the Peace in Okmulgee, and the Justice ordered the pair to be held without bond and closed the hearing. Five days later, Underhill and three inmates sawed their way through the bars of their individual cells and made their way to the jail's main corridor on the fourth floor. Once there, the four escapees were able to lower themselves by means of a makeshift rope. On the ground, the quartet immediately split: Underhill and Aiken as one pair, and their fellow fugitives the other.

A huge posse was formed, and a manhunt got underway. The two inmates who had fled with Underhill and Aiken were captured soon, but there was no sign of Underhill or Aiken until February 5, when a taxi cab driver told authorities that two men matching their description had forced him at gunpoint to drive them to Fort Scott, Kansas.

In February, Skeet Aiken was arrested in Missouri after his vehicle had mired down. He first agreed to extradition to Kansas in order to avoid being sent to Oklahoma, where he would have to face murder charges, but skullduggery of some sort thwarted his hope. He was turned over to Oklahoma authorities, and while in the hands of guards taking him back to the Sooner State he managed to break free.

Leaving the car and the two deputies who had stopped it in a freezing rain, Aiken sped across an open field with the lawmen right behind him. When Aiken didn't halt, one of them shot him twice, both bullets hitting him in the head. He was dead before the summoned ambulance arrived.[5]

Within days, the Mystic Theatre in Picher was robbed by a rough-looking man matching Underhill's description. Constable George Fuller was alerted, and on the evening of February 13, accompanied by Robert O'Neal, he spotted a man fitting the description of the Mystic hijacker.

Fuller walked to within touching distance of the suspect before ordering him to raise his hands and turn around. At the same time, he handed a pair of cuffs to his companion O'Neal saying, "Cuff him."

Instead of obeying, the suspect whirled and with a pistol drawn from his shoulder holster smashed O'Neal in the face. Two shots followed, and O'Neal slumped to the sidewalk as the shooter bolted into a nearby alley. O'Neal was taken by ambulance to the town's hospital but expired on the operating table before the massive bleeding caused by his wounds could be stopped.

Lawmen hurried to the scene of the shooting, but the assassin was long gone, leaving no further evidence of the murder he had committed.

The next week a lone gunman robbed the Blue Mound Grocery Store located on the Oklahoma–Kansas state line just north of Picher. The same night, presumably the same thug robbed a filling station in the community; the owner of the station had no trouble identifying Underhill in the mug shots shown him.[6]

A climate of fear gathered over the district as law officers from Missouri, Oklahoma, and Kansas amassed to push the hunt for Underhill. Flop houses, pool halls, mining camps, and residences of his known molls were searched but to no avail. Wild rumors swept the area like one of its increasing dust storms. Newspapers began referring to Underhill as a real "Mad Dog" who ought to be shot to protect innocent citizens.

Eluding those on his trail, Underhill holed up in a boarding house until he could get out and hop a freight train going to Baxter Springs. From there he made it back to Joplin, where he slipped a note under his mother's door telling her he did not murder O'Neal, adding that most likely he would never see her again.[7]

The month of March 1927 was almost over before Underhill surfaced again. As the month was ending, Jimmie Johnson, Night Constable in Heavener, Oklahoma, was told that a stranger flashing a wad of dough was staying in the town's best hotel and squiring Lucille McDowell, the owner's daughter. Johnson had read a wanted poster from Okmulgee County and was curious enough to phone authorities there for a more complete description of Underhill. From information sent back to him, he was certain the stranger indeed was the notorious Underhill, wanted dead or alive. Rewards of $1,000 from Picher magnates and another $100 from Okmulgee County were offered for Underhill's capture. Those offers in the Depression years were enticement enough to set Johnson on his trail.

Johnson sought help from Deputy Sheriff Charles Crawford, and the two of them shadowed the stranger for nearly a week. In making their plans, they didn't really care whether their prey was taken alive or dead; the reward was to be the same, and they sure as hell weren't going to take a risk in capturing a thug like Underhill.

In the morning of April 20th, the two lawmen had positioned themselves in the stairwell of the England Hotel in Panama, Oklahoma, when Underhill and his lady friend came down the steps. The woman was first, and Underhill behind her was carrying a valise in one hand and a hatbox in the other. The two policemen pulled out their weapons, and Johnson shouted, "Hands up!"

Instead of complying, Underhill dropped the valise and threw the hatbox in Crawford's face, at the same time fumbling under his own coat. Johnson didn't wait; he fired his .38 cal. Colt, and the heavy slug penetrated Underhill's left forearm before entering his thigh.

The shot so stunned him that he stiffened and stood motionless, and while Johnson held the gun a few inches from his face, Crawford put the cuffs on their captive's wrists.

The officers didn't think Underhill's wound was as serious as he pretended, and both he and his girlfriend were taken to the police station for questioning. The woman said she was his wife but knew nothing about his "business" activities. Her answers satisfied the questioners, and she was released from custody.

Constable Johnson telephoned Okmulgee County Sheriff John Russell and told him he had Underhill in jail. In almost no time a delighted Russell along with Okmulgee County Attorney A. N. Boatman sped to Panama to pick up their prize.

In Panama, Johnson turned his prisoner over to Russell and Boatman and was given $100 along with the promise that his bid for the $1,000 reward would be heartily endorsed by both of them.

When Russell got Underhill back in the Okmulgee jail, a doctor was summoned and upon examination declared that the robber's wound was very slight—nothing really serious, yet Underhill complained constantly, saying he was in great pain, and repeatedly asked for towels, aspirin, blankets, and extra pillows.

Almira came to Okmulgee to see her son, and gave her usual plea to newsmen: Wilbur was innocent of any wrongdoing, and it was untrustworthy police who had put him on the run.

Sarah Riddle, Wilbur's paramour, came to Okmulgee, too, claiming she was his lawful wife. To complicate matters further, Otto McDowell, Lucille's brother, also showed up and insisted Wilbur had married his sister. Before that charge could be investigated or disputed, however, Otto was found inebriated and passed out in a hotel bedroom. Authorities sobered him enough to give him a bum's rush out of town.

Underhill's trial for the murder of George Fee during the Phillips Drug Store robbery began on June 1, 1927. Manacled by handcuffs and leg irons he was brought into the courtroom where his attorney immediately charged that his client had been treated harshly. Underhill played the role and was unchained for the rest of the proceedings.

The trial took a day and a half, during which numerous witnesses were called. Sarah Riddle claimed that both Underhill and Akens were with her in Tulsa the night George Fee was shot. Police officers gave contradictory evidence by testifying Underhill had told them he was in Picher, Oklahoma, the night Fee was murdered.

When Underhill took the stand, he began by complaining of brutality he had suffered at the hands of the police. Then he launched into an account of his childhood—an account so fictionalized it could have made the devil blanch. Underhill claimed he never had been given a chance to live decently like the honest citizen he wanted to be. Police had begun hounding him even as a youth, and it was corrupt, brutal, and dishonest cops who were responsible for any slight misdeeds he may have committed. And he swore he had not robbed the Phillips Drug Store and could not have been present when George Fee was slain.

The jury was not convinced and reached a unanimous decision in slightly more than one hour of deliberations. Returning to the courtroom, the verdict was handed to the judge, who after perusing it himself gave it to the clerk, asking her to read it: "Guilty as charged with a recommendation of life at hard labor."

The judge followed the jury's recommendation and sentenced Underhill to life at the Oklahoma State Penitentiary. Upon hearing the sentence, Underhill's white-haired, black-gowned mother, Almira, flopped in a dead faint. It was her second such spell during the trial. Authentic or faked, she revived and was taken back to her rooming house.

Underhill's legal troubles were not yet ended, for almost immediately Ottawa County officials asked the judge to turn him over to them so he could be tried for the murder of Earl Robert O'Neal during robbery of the Owl Drug Store in Picher, Oklahoma. The judge told them they would have to wait and file their request after Underhill reached the penitentiary.

On June 7, gates of the Oklahoma State Penitentiary in McAlester slammed shut on Underhill. Within days he connected with a vicious thug named Chester Purdy, acknowledged leader of a gang of thieves that had been burglarizing homes since 1925. Two police officers had been slain in different robberies, and early in 1927 Purdy and several of his fellow thugs were caught and charged with the slayings. All were given life sentences at hard labor.

After six months at the penitentiary, Underhill and his newfound crime partners tried to escape. He, Purdy, and two others got onto the building's roof by using hacksaws smuggled to them by a yegg on the outside. A guard spotted the convicts as they were getting ready to descend from the roof by means of bed sheets tied together. Tower guards fired a couple of rounds over their heads; the escapees halted and threw up their hands; their plan had failed.

Upon examination, authorities found the cons had civilian clothing, home-made shivs, and small cans of food stuff with them. Underhill was put in solitary confinement for a month. Later with habitual exaggeration, he claimed that he spent nearly half of his four years at "Mac" in solitary confinement, chained and beaten regularly by the hacks.[8]

On July 14, 1931, Underhill was a member of a road gang assigned to work on one of the state's highways. The men had been assembled and under guard were marching four abreast as they crossed a footbridge over a small stream. Unseen by the guard, Underhill managed to jump off the bridge and lie still in the water below until the contingent had marched past. Then he was able to get away and obtain civilian clothes. Donning them, he discarded his prison garb and made his way into the forested Ouachita Mountain Range, walking more than sixty miles on mountain trails to Wister, Oklahoma. His one-time wife Lucille McDowell lived in Heavener near to Wister, and whether he visited her or whether she helped him is unknown. At any rate, he soon hopped a freight train and got back to Joplin, Missouri.

Out of jail and out of funds, Underhill resumed doing what he knew best: robbing. No doubt he was accused of more robberies than he or any one person could commit, yet he was identified in enough burglaries and killings that reporters were not far wrong in dubbing him "The Tri-State Terror."

In the first week of August, 1931, a bandit whom Rhea Payne, cashier at the Midland Theatre in Coffeeville, Kansas, would identify as Wilbur Underhill pointed a handgun at her and took the night's proceeds of $220.

A day or two later, the Neely Cities Service Station was robbed by two men, one taller than the other, and in the robbery the owner of the station, William Neely, was shot and killed. The slaying of Neely, a community leader, encouraged authorities to set up roadblocks in which numerous citizens joined shotgun-holding deputies hoping to nab the pair, but their efforts were of no avail.

Witnesses would testify that the taller bandit was Wilbur Underhill; his companion was not identified. The accomplice was Frank Vance Underhill, Wilbur's nephew and son of his oldest brother Earl. Frank walked with a limp due to the infantile paralysis he had suffered when very young. His father Earl was in prison when his mother died, and the boy was put into the hands of other family members who moved to Kansas City. There in an attempt to avoid the stigma attached to the name *Underhill*, the teen-ager took the name Frank Vance.

Wilbur using the name Ralph Caraway bought a new Ford roadster in Wichita and registered it in Kansas receiving the license plate Kansas S-11674. Within a week of his purchase a Texaco filling station in Wichita was held up, and the 20-year-old attendant was made to lie face down in an alley while his assailants sped away in a Ford roadster.

Frank Vance was driving when the roadster was broadsided by another car which had sped through a stop sign. Both vehicles were badly damaged. Wilbur and Vance checked into a local hotel intending to wait there until the roadster was repaired. Wichita Police Office Merle R. Colver was making routine checks of hotels and boarding houses when Cora Brotherton, the woman at the desk of the Iris Hotel, told him a pair of strangers had just registered.

Colver decided he ought to check them out. While he was knocking on the door of the upstairs room where he had been told the strangers were lodged, a series of shots came from within. Moments later, Cora Brotherton at the registration desk and a couple of housekeepers were confronted by two men who had sprinted down the stairway. "There's been an accident," one of them shouted. "You'd better call the cops."

While Brotherton was on the phone calling, the two men hurried outside and disappeared. When police arrived, they found Officer Colver motionless on the floor. One bullet had struck him on the left side of his neck; another on the left side of his back shoulder before passing through his body to come out at the groin. Found at the crime scene were four steel-jacketed .45 cal. bullets: one in a mattress, another embedded in the dresser, and a third and fourth fell from Colver's corpse when the coroner rolled it over on its back. Underneath the body were several photographs, and on the back of two was scratched the name *Wilbur Underhill*. The photos were shown to Cora Brotherton, who was certain the older of the two men she had registered was the man in the photo shown her. A further search turned up the title to a Ford Roadster issued to Ralph Caraway of Cherryvale, Kansas.

Police immediately ordered an investigation into all garages and auto repair shops in the area, and soon discovered a wrecked Ford Roadster with 1180 miles on its odometer. All major roads leading out of town were guarded by hastily deputized officers or armed members of the American Legion or the Veterans of Foreign War. Ten hours later the pair of fugitives was found lying exhausted under a tree in a park a mile and a half from the scene of Colver's murder.

While Wilbur moaned, complained of great pain, and said he was dying, the suspects were hauled into the station. A doctor looked him over and found only a minor flesh wound, which was treated with Mercurochrome and a sterile bandage.

Wilbur and Frank were separated in the police quarters, and when the 19-year-old Vance was grilled, he quickly caved in. The gist of his confession was, "I didn't do it. Uncle Wilbur did.[9]

Cora Brotherton and the two maids were summoned, and all three positively identified Wilbur and Vance as the two men registered in Room #15 the morning of the murder and the same men who had come running down the stairs after shots had been heard.

Underhill was intensively questioned and responded by describing where he had gone and what he had done since his release from the Missouri State Penitentiary. Of course, he skipped mention of any robberies he had committed and said that he and his nephew Frank Vance had come to Wichita hoping to get jobs. Yes, they had registered at the Iris Hotel.

Asked to state in his own words what took place in the room he and Vance were sharing, Underhill unloaded with a long, rambling, and embroidered account:

> The officer came to the door, knocked, and said, "This is the police." Before I could unlock the door, he came on in . . . [he] started over to the other bed and I seen that he would find the pistol under the pillow; my being an escaped convict I couldn't stand the arrest, so I walked over and got the pistol just as he was reaching for it. . . . I told him to put his hands up; instead he started hitting me with his club. . . I fired one shot. . . . He kept grabbing me, and in the scuffle, I shot three more times. . . .

> We went on down the alley back of the hotel and got out to the edge of town. . . . Later in the evening two officers stopped us, and I started to walk away. . . I kept walking trying to get my pistol out of my coat pocket. . . this officer seen I was going for my gun, and he shot. The bullet hit me in the neck and caused my arm to go numb. The officer fired four or five more shots as I started running across the park. . . I fell down and was laying in some weeds when he ran up to me. They took me to the hospital, got my wound dressed, and then to the county jail and from there to the city jail.[10]

On the morning of August 17, Underhill and his nephew were led manacled from their jail cells to a courtroom in the county courthouse. Another hearing was set for Wilbur to take place on August 21, and the judge granted a delay for Vance's hearing as his attorney requested.

Evidence and testimonies against Underhill were overwhelming, and although prosecutors endeavored to add the killing of William Neely to the charges, their efforts failed. Wilbur would be tried here only for the slaying of Office Merle Colver. The State of Kansas didn't have a death penalty, and it made little difference to prosecutors who it was who had been killed as long as they could prove Underhill guilty of murdering someone in the state.

On September 4, 1931, Underhill was led into the courtroom and on advice from his attorney pled guilty to the murder of Officer Colver. The presiding judge sentenced him to serve the rest of his natural life at hard labor in the Kansas State Penitentiary in Lansing.

When Underhill arrived at the Kansas State Penitentiary, the institution was three-quarters of a century old. It had cells on blocks A, B,C, and D as well as a hospital, laundry, dining hall, punishment unit, recreation yard, baseball diamond, and various other facilities—all surrounded by a high stone wall with towers on each corner where armed guards watched the enclosed area twenty-four hours a day.

Authorities strove to make the prison as self-sufficient as possible by mining coal, making bricks, and operating a 2,000-acre farm just a couple of miles away. Due to overcrowding and understaffing, prisoners were not as closely supervised as they were at many state prisons. Drugs, including morphine and marijuana, were readily available, homosexual queens offered themselves, and fist fights in which home-made shivs might be used, were common occurrences. Incoming prisoners were designated third-class inmates with very few privileges; if they behaved, they could inch their way up to first class and be privileged to work under guards outside the prison walls.

Within a week after his arrival, Underhill had made contact with a group of hardened cons planning a break. However, a snitch learned of their plot and relayed it to the warden, hoping to gain favors. The perpetrators were identified, and Underhill was among the eight given solitary confinement. He spent two weeks in a small, dark, moldy cell furnished only with a slop bucket and water jug.

After this first solitary confinement, Wilbur wrote a letter containing instructions penned in what he thought was invisible ink (urine) for an accomplice to smuggle a gun to him. The ploy was discovered before the letter could be delivered, and again Underhill was sentenced to solitary.

He wrote numerous letters to his mother, his sister, and to attorneys asking them to seek his clemency, but their appeals were either rejected or ignored. A man convicted of two murders and suspected to have been involved in others was not likely to be granted leniency.

By the late spring of 1933, he knew appeals were useless. He approached "Big Bob" Brady, a lifer who worked in the prison's kitchen, and the two of them began forming an escape plan. They would have to have help, so they enlisted a trio of small time Oklahoma robbers—Jim Clark, Ed Davis, and Frank Sawyer. The plotters would need money—cash for guns, clothes, and fares, etc. Among the prisoners was Harvey Bailey, a St. Paul and Jazz Age yegg who had run with the Barkers and Alvin Karpis. Bailey, a lifer, had plenty of moneyed contacts and said he could get the needed operating funds. All six of the men involved in the plot were hardcore, habitual criminals.

They would make their move on Memorial Day when a baseball game was scheduled and the prison warden, Kirk Prather, was certain to be there watching. The plotters intended to capture him, seize other guards, and use them as bargaining chips to gain their freedom.

On May 30, 1933, the game was in the fifth inning, and Warden Prather was circulating among the prisoners and guards watching it. Jim Clark sneaked up behind him and wrapped a copper wire garrote around his neck cutting off his breathing while at the same time Harvey Bailey pushed a smuggled pistol against his spine and warned, "Do what we say or you're a dead man!"

Underhill took over control of the garrote allowing Prather to breathe, and with other conspirators following marched the captive down the line toward the tower. There he told Prather he would be shot unless he ordered the guards to throw down their weapons. The warden had no choice, for he knew Underhill meant business.

Other cons watching what was taking place asked Underhill if they could join in, and still holding the garrote and a pistol in Warden Prather's ribs he nodded assent.

The escapees gained access to the tower through a small door at its base, and then from the top of the tower used a rope to lower themselves to the ground outside. By this time the numbers had grown, and the group split up.

Underhill's bunch was the original six plotters as well as Warden Prather and two guards.

They were not yet free, and another guard had reached the tower and was able to fire a shot or two at them. One of his bullets struck Harvey Bailey just above his right knee shattering the bone. Underhill still held Prather in tow while Clark, Davis, and Sawyer dragged the wounded Bailey into the automobile of the Prison Farm Superintendent. The escapees knew that vehicle would be in the garage just outside the prison walls.

Clark took the wheel of the stolen auto, and Underhill still holding his gun against Prather's middle forced the warden to lie on the floorboard of the back seat. One of the captured guards was ordered to sit in the back seat and the other in the front between Davis and Clark. For the next four hours the fugitives and their captives drove country roads, changing vehicles when they commandeered another one. Finally, at a crossroads just outside Pyramid Corners, they stopped, and Underhill released Prather and the guards taken with him all unharmed.

The Memorial Day jailbreak made news for nearly every major daily paper in the country. Within days, Kansas Governor Alf Landon signed an executive order deducting six months off the sentence of every inmate in the prison explaining that although practically every prisoner had a chance to join the rioters only five did so, and he believed good behavior ought to be rewarded. Governor Landon also upped the reward for the capture of each of the six plotters (Underhill, Brady, Clark, Davis, Sawyer, and Bailey) dead or alive.

Over the next few weeks the six escapees were reportedly spotted in dozens of different locations; sometimes the conflicting reports put them in two places at the same time. Crimes at Pleasanton and Chetopa, Kansas, were added to Underhill's dossier when victims said they had recognized him as the man who had robbed or kidnapped them.

On June 1, 1933, the Bank of Chelsea, Oklahoma, was robbed of $2500; two days later a trio of strangers attempted to buy ammunition from a hardware dealer in Pawhuska close by, and the owner was positive in saying that Underhill was one of the strangers. In truth, Underhill was not involved in any of these, but that doesn't mean he wasn't continuing to rob, kidnap, and murder.

On June 17, 1933, lawmen had captured Frank "Jelly" Nash, a chubby, bald escapee from the federal penitentiary in Leavenworth, Kansas, and were returning him via a stop in Kansas City. Nash hardly looked like the vicious criminal he was. He first had been imprisoned in 1912 sentenced for life for murdering an accomplice. His sentence was commuted in 1918 to let him join the army. He fought in France, and not long after WW I was caught in an attempted robbery of a bank in Corn, Oklahoma. For this offense, he was given a second life sentence but was paroled in 1922. Joining a gang of thieves, he took part in Oklahoma's last train robbery. Convicted of mail robbery in 1924, he was sentenced to twenty-five years in Leavenworth and had escaped from there in 1930.[11]

Officials were glad to have the notorious lawbreaker "Jelly" Nash, in their hands at last and guarded him carefully because scuttlebutt warned them that his underworld pals might try to free the infamous Nash. They had reason for apprehension.

On June 17, 1933, two federal agents, Reed Vetterli and Ray Caffrey, and two officers from the Kansas City Police Department, were on the train station's platform when the Missouri Pacific rolled to a stop. Federal Agent Joe Lackey looked out and was relieved to see two confederates awaiting him and the convict he was bringing them.

Lackey went back to a drawing room in the train where Frank Smith, another federal agent, and Otto Reed, police chief from McAlester, sat with Nash between them. He had a big nose, wore an ill-fitting wig, and was dressed casually like a forty-five-year old businessman on vacation. His escorts were taking no chances, for he was handcuffed, and one of them had a firm grip on his belt from the rear.

Nash was led out of the train, through the station, and to Agent Caffrey's Chevrolet parked in the first row of the Plaza lot. The manacled Nash was put in the front seat; Lackey, Smith, and Reed squeezed into the rear, and Caffrey was walking around the front of his car so that he could climb in on the driver's side when suddenly a man with a machine gun appeared yelling, "Let 'em have it!"

Lead from three gunmen ripped into the lawmen and the Chevrolet. One officer, William Grooms, fell in the first volley; Caffrey was mortally wounded. In the back seat, Frank Hermanson from the Kansas City Police Department lay dead as did his chief, Otto Reed. Sprawled beside them was Ray Lackey with three bullets in his back.

Slumped on the floor of the front seat was the body of Jelly Nash, his wig askew and covered by blood as his head was literally blown apart by his would-be rescuers.[12]

The slaughter was quickly dubbed the Kansas City Massacre, and numerous persons testified they were certain Wilbur Underhill was one of the gangster gunmen. Subsequent testimonies and evidence would show that was one of many false reports.

Although after his escape from Lansing Underhill had resumed his pattern of robbing filling stations and small town banks, he could not possibly have been in all the places reported. The six escapees were suspected of murdering

Constable Otto Drake in Chetopa, Kansas, and then robbing a filling station in Miami, Oklahoma. A few days later, a half-dozen well-dressed men driving a new car robbed the bank at Chelsea. Four of the bandits entered the bank while two armed with shot guns stood guarding the door. Witnesses said they were sure Underhill was one of the men who entered the bank.

Underhill and his gang were accused also of robbing banks in Clinton, Oklahoma, and Canton, Kansas, during the month of July. In August, he, Brady, Clark, and Bailey allegedly took $6,024 from the Peoples National Bank of Kingfisher, Oklahoma. In September, Underhill and two unidentified accomplices hit the Peoples National Bank in Stuttgart, Arkansas. Witnesses said Underhill stood at the door with a machine gun in his hands while his pals scooped up more than $1,000 in bills from the till.

On October 9, Underhill and Ed Davis knocked off the bank at Tryon, Oklahoma, for $550. Next, on October 11, Underhill and three others carried out robbery of $1,000 from the International Bank of Haskell, Oklahoma, and were suspects in the theft of $14,000 from another bank, Citizens National Bank in Okmulgee, on November 2. He was the alleged perpetrator a week later when the First National Bank of Harrah, Oklahoma, was knocked off. The fall of '33 turned out to be the most active period in Underhill's disordered life.

Another event in his mottled career took place on November, 18, 1933. On that date and with confederates as best man and witnesses in Coalgate, Oklahoma, under his real name, Underhill married Hazel Hudson, nee Hazel Jarrett, sister of the Jarrett brothers, already notorious Oklahoma outlaws.

He took his bride and holed up with companions in the Cookson Hills. This heavily-timbered area a few miles southeast of Muskogee had been a hideout for bad men since the days of Jesse James and Belle Starr. It was wild, inaccessible country, honeycombed with caves and crisscrossed by chasms and gorges—24,000 square miles of wilderness speckled with scrub oak. Underhill used the sanctuary as cover and base of operations for his crime spree throughout the fall of '33.

The number of brazen robberies in Oklahoma attracted attention of the U. S. Department of Justice, not yet the Federal Bureau of Investigation, and that Department had put Ralph H. Colvin in charge of a task force made up of twenty-nine federal appointees, officers from the Oklahoma County Sheriff's Office, and several Oklahoma City lawmen.

A few days before Christmas, 1933, a snitch lured by increased rewards offered for information leading to Underhill's capture tipped off Colvin that the outlaw and his wife were staying at a residence in Shawnee, Oklahoma. At 2:00 A.M. on a wet, foggy morning in downtown Shawnee, Colvin told an assembled force, "We've got our man. Let's go get him." Then in order to protect against cross fire he gave explicit instructions as to where each man would be stationed.

Directly across the street from the targeted residence were three federal agents; on a porch of a house east of the prime residence were Deputies Bill Eads and John Adams; Oklahoma City Detectives Clarence Hurt, A. D. Bryce, and Mickey Ryan were assigned to cover the back of the home. All were armed with either a machine gun or shot gun; Officer Hurt also had a tear gas gun as well as his chopper.

Colvin and Hurt crept to a bedroom window of the targeted home, peeked in, and saw Underhill clothed only in long underwear standing at the foot of the bed; his wife scantily dressed sat on the edge of the mattress.

A dog started barking, and Underhill alerted strode to the window, looked out, and found himself staring into the eyes of Office Hurt, who immediately yelled, "This is the law, Wilbur. Stick 'em up!"

Instead of complying, Underhill wheeled and grabbed for an automatic Lugar pistol with an attached drum of 31 rounds lying on a convenient nightstand. Hurt reacted by firing a blast from his gas gun, the missile crashing through the screen and glass before hitting Underhill in the stomach. Colvin held the trigger down on his own machine gun, letting loose a fusillade of rounds that shattered a mirror and smashed the bedroom's walls. Hazel, Underhill's wife, dropped to the floor in a faint, a maneuver that probably saved her life.

Hurt would say later that Wilbur first fell to the floor, then jumped up and made it to the bathroom where he turned and opened fire toward the officers. Then he ran out the front door, and seeing him, Officers Bryant, Eads, Adams, and Stone began hosing down on him with shotgun and machine gun rounds. Hit hard by the volley, Underhill fell to the earth and lay still as the lawmen warily approached him. Suddenly he leaped to his feet and dashed madly into shadows between the two darkened houses.

He almost ran into Agent Colvin who, to use his own word, immediately "tattooed" the fugitive's back with a machine gun burst. To Colvin's astonishment, the horribly wounded Underhill kept running until he just disappeared. The Agent said afterward, "I don't know how he did it. The bastard just wouldn't stay down."[13]

The task force with its guns and flashlights immediately scattered throughout the neighborhood hoping to find him, but Underhill had vanished again. Agent Colvin called for bloodhounds, but those were kenneled in McAlester, a hundred miles to the south. When the dogs did arrive three and a half hours later, dawn was breaking and the hounds had just picked up the scent from a spot of blood when a police car roared in.

The two cops in it announced to the searchers that Underhill had just been brought to the City Hospital.

A motorcycle cop had been told by a friend, R. E. Owens, owner of a second-hand furniture store in Shawnee, that the badly wounded Underhill had stumbled in. Owens was an ex-con himself and had met Underhill when both were prisoners at McAlester. There was no collaboration, and Owens had been quick to notify police. Apparently, Underhill knew of Owen's establishment and was too badly hurt to go anywhere else.

When Colvin and other lawmen confronted Underhill in the hospital, he did not try to hide his identity. He was in a very grave condition when Colvin and other lawmen questioned him and on his deathbed talked a great deal. He confessed to robberies he had committed since Lansing, denying some of which he had been accused, and maintaining that neither he nor Harvey Bailey had anything to do with the Kansas City Massacre.

It was apparent to everyone who saw him that he was a dying man. Agent Colvin described some of his wounds:

> The wounds of Underhill, 13 in number, are as follows. One bullet struck him on the left corner of the forehead cutting off the top of his ear. . . Another wound entered his right side just above the liver and emerged through his spine tearing a jagged hole upon its exit. There was another wound through the right forearm. . . Several buckshot entered his back. . . .Other buckshot struck him on the left arm while more entered the right leg just below the thigh. . . . More buckshot hit him on the left leg on the inside just above the knee.[14]

Doctors at the City Hospital deemed Underhill's wounds too severe for survival; nevertheless, he was patched up and moved to a private, heavily-guarded room where he lapsed in and out of consciousness for 36 hours. On New Year's Day his condition was listed as critical and worsening. The next day doctors rushed him into emergency surgery in an effort to restructure what was left of his bladder.

On the morning of January 5, 1934, he rallied, sat up in bed, and asked his nurse how to get onto the highway. She reported the amazing change, and authorities immediately grew more apprehensive, fearing some sort of action was about to be taken by his gangster pals. Colvin wanted Underhill moved to a more secure location, and from Washington, D.C. the Director of Investigation J. Edgar Hoover agreed to his agent's request.

On Saturday morning, January 6, an ambulance accompanied by Colvin and two passenger cars containing a bevy of machine gun toting guards showed up to take Underhill to McAlester for safer keeping. On a stretcher, he was loaded carefully into the ambulance, which then pulled out, and was followed by the two passenger cars rolling their way to the McAlester prison.

Upon arrival there, Underhill was examined by the prison's physician, Dr. A. J. Munn, who expressed little hope that he could live. His diagnosis was right. At approximately nine o'clock that evening, Underhill lapsed into a coma which lasted for nearly two hours before he rolled to his right side and died. Only two hospital attendants were in the room with him. The psychotic thug—Tri-State Killer—with no moral scruples of any kind, passed into oblivion, January 6, 1934.

Chapter 2. The Barkers

The year of 1933 was an epochal one for the United States. The first day of the year came on Sunday, and the next morning, Franklin Delano Roosevelt completed his term as the 44th Governor of the State of New York, two months before he would take office as President of the United States. On Thursday in that first week of January, former President Calvin Coolidge, age 60, died at his home in Northampton, Massachusetts, while 3,000 miles west, construction was begun on a Golden Gate Bridge to be built over San Francisco Bay. On the last day of that opening month, the Lone Ranger made its debut on U.S. radio with notable use of *The William Tell Overture* as its theme song and catchy phrases like *"Quien Sabe?"*, *"Hi-Ho Silver,"* and *"Who was that masked man?"* During the next twelve months, dust bowls would cover more than a third of the nation; unemployment rolls would reach their highest, the Great Depression its lowest.

Citizens everywhere were affected by the nation's severe economic plight. A record total of 242 banks failed in that year. In mid-January after collapse of the American Trust Company of Davenport, Iowa, the newly-inaugurated Governor of the state declared a bank holiday, temporarily closing all banks within Iowa to prevent further withdrawals.

The State of Nevada had declared the first bank holiday on October 31, 1932; then consumer confidence rallied a bit after the fall's election of FDR. Yet the Iowa action was followed by more bank closings: Louisiana on February 3rd. and Michigan on the 14th. By March 4, 1933, Inauguration Day, half the 48 states had announced bank holidays, and two days later the new President declared a nationwide closure.

Newspapers and radios reported endless stories about business closings, family or individual plights, bread lines and soup kitchens in the cities. For diversions there were sports—the Yankees, prize fights, and the likes of Maggie and Jiggs, Etta Kett, Flash Gordon, or the Katzenjammer Kids in the funnies. And there were stories galore about crimes and criminals.

The battle against crime, random or organized, is a never-ending struggle. To paraphrase a newsreel chant then popular: *Crime*, like *Time*, *Marches On.*

Crimes had accompanied the nation's founding, and they worsened during military conflicts or economic depressions. Theft, murders, and black marketing were prevalent during the Civil War; WW I and the Prohibition Era encouraged illegal sales of scarce items as bootlegging with its associated thugs grew like weeds in an untended garden. Nefarious Al Capone, Chicago mobster, once said, "You can get further ahead with a kind word and a gun," before adding, "than with a gun alone."

At the beginning of the third decade of the twenty-first century, America was at its lowest point in economic doldrums. The mean national income had fallen by more than half since the stock market crash, and 13 million people were unemployed. Hundreds of families were homeless; numerous banks had failed or were tottering on the edge. Although crimes were occurring throughout the nation, the problem was most acute in the Midwest and Southwest. Many citizens considered Oklahoma a breeding ground for criminals and a dangerous territory for lawmen.

The 18th Amendment had been passed in the belief it would be a reform Act, but hopes backfired. The measure ordering a ban on sale, transportation, or exporting of alcoholic beverages was enacted by Congress in 1917 but had to be ratified before taking effect in January, 1920. By the opening of 1933, thirteen years later, it was obvious the Act was a failure. Incoming President Franklin Roosevelt had welcomed "wets" to his campaign and had vowed to nullify the Prohibition Act. He accomplished that in December of his first term when the Democratic controlled Congress passed the 21st Amendment legalizing the sale of alcoholic beverages. Repeal did reduce the crimes of bootlegging and hijackings, but murders and kidnappings continued to rise.

Train robberies had almost ceased at the turn of the century; criminals found easier pickings in bank hold-ups or kidnappings. By the time the 1930s began, new technology had outpaced the legal system. Faster, more powerful weapons such as the Thompson machine gun made criminals better armed than all but a few urban police forces. Wider use of automobiles was an even greater advantage, for with cars, robbers could speed away while local police were just getting into their vehicles.

Banks were particularly vulnerable because throughout the Hoover era they were held in scant esteem. Insurance nearly always covered a bank's losses in case it went down, but not losses of depositors, thousands of whom were ruined in the epidemic of bank failures. There was little shedding of tears by the general public, therefore, when banks were robbed.

Moreover, a bank robbery was a bonanza for newspaper reporters, editors, and readers. Reasoned and sound historical accounts were spiced with general portions of hearsay, exaggeration, and tall tales. The faltering economy made it easy for the public mood to think of these robbers with their colorful sobriquets as modern Robin Hoods acting to help the average citizen—a citizen who may have seen his life's savings wiped away in a bank's crash or in malfeasance by its owners. No small wonder that fact and fiction intertwined.

That certainly was the case of "Ma" Barker. She was born in the small town of Ash Grove, Missouri, in 1877, and christened Arizona Donnie Clark. Just before her sixteenth birthday, Arizona Clark—for unknown reasons called Kate—married George Barker. The couple had four sons: Herman, Lloyd, Arthur, and Fred. Kate was a plump, frowsy hillbilly who found pleasure in jigsaw puzzles and listening to Amos 'n' Andy on the radio. Her other interest was the welfare of her sons. Around 1915, George Barker fled the impoverished family, and Kate was left to raise the four boys by herself or with help from various male friends.

Each of the sons had a criminal career, and Kate, now "Ma," Barker, was reported to have condoned and partnered in their behaviors. Her son Herman committed suicide in 1927 by shooting himself after an hour-long gun battle with police. In the next year, Lloyd was incarcerated in the federal penitentiary at Fort Leavenworth, Kansas. Arthur "Doc" Barker was in the Oklahoma State Prison, and Fred doing time in the Kansas State Prison.

Ma Barker enjoyed luxuries her sons' robberies provided her, and a woman traveling across the land with an alleged husband and four sons proved to be excellent cover. Ma and her sons were joined by more hardened criminals, one of whom was Alvin Karpis, and for nearly a score of years, the Barker-Karpis gang terrorized the Midwest, robbing banks and killing dozens of people.

From the spree of robberies, kidnappings, and other crimes between 1931 and 1935, an image of Ma Barker as the gang's leader and mastermind emerged. Evidence would indicate later that although she knew of the gang's activities it was never shown that she participated in the actual commission of a crime.

Alvin Karpis, the gang's most notorious member, said,

> The most ridiculous story in the annals of crime is that Ma Barker was the mastermind behind the Karpis-Barker gang. . . She wasn't a leader of criminals or even a criminal herself. There is not one police photograph of her or set of fingerprints taken while she was alive. . .

she knew we were criminals, but her participation in our careers was limited to one function: when we traveled, we moved as a mother and her sons. What could look more innocent?[1]

The view that Ma was an abettor rather than an actual participant is corroborated by another nefarious bank robber, Harvey Bailey, who knew the Barkers well. In his autobiography he observed, "Ma Barker couldn't plan a breakfast, let alone a criminal enterprise."

Several students of the period have suggested that the myth of Ma Barker was encouraged by J. Edgar Hoover and his fledging Federal Bureau of Investigation in order to justify his agency's killing of an old lady.[2] Beyond such speculation, however, reports show that Ma was privy to the gang's activity but was not an active participant in the crimes her sons and their accomplices committed.

Chapter 3. Alvin "Creepy" Karpis

Alvin Francis Karpowicz was born August 10, 1907, in Montreal, Quebec. Canada. His parents, John and Anna Karpowicz, changed their name to Karpis in the 1920s, and it was under the name Alvin Karpis that their son gained notoriety.

John and Anna moved to Kansas and became naturalized citizens of the U. S. when Alvin was a young boy. Raised in Topeka, he was about ten when he started selling smutty pictures and running around with gamblers, bootleggers, and pimps.

He began his criminal career by stealing candy bars, knives, and small items from ten cent stores, gradually increasing the thefts before being arrested for stealing automobile tires when he was nineteen years old. For the burglary, he was sentenced to ten years at the State Industrial Reformatory in Hutchinson, Kansas, but managed to escape from there with a fellow inmate, Leonard De Vol.

The two went on a year-long spree of minor crimes before De Vol was arrested. Karpis came back to Topeka to live for awhile incognito with his parents. Then he moved to Kansas City, Missouri, where he was caught stealing a car.

He was sent back first to the Reformatory but being beyond teen years of age, he was transferred to the Kansas State Penitentiary at Lansing. During his imprisonment at that institution he fell in with an inmate, Fred Barker, one of Ma Barker's sons and a member of what newspapers were calling the "Bloody Barkers."

Abandoned by their father and growing up in an impoverished, share cropping family supported by a mother with questionable morals, all four Barker boys turned to robbing banks and killing with little provocation. Herman committed suicide after a 1927 shootout with police in Wichita; Lloyd was sentenced to

25 years in prison for mail fraud; Fred killed in a fusillade from G-men, and Arthur or "Doc" as he was called, sentenced to life imprisonment after murdering a night watchman.

The prison friendship between Fred Barker and Karpis was resumed in 1931 after both were paroled. Barker, living in Tulsa, Oklahoma, was a pal with a small group of other former convicts or parolees. Karpis joined this group, and soon he and Barker were the gang's leaders.

The Karpis-Barker gang became one of the most formidable collection of outlaws in the country, and they didn't hesitate to kill anyone who got in their way. Alvin Karpis had a photographic memory, and fellow gang members described him as "super-smart" because of his insistence upon planning every detail for an intended bank robbery or kidnapping.

Karpis and Fred Barker burglarized a clothing store in West Plains, Missouri, on December 19, 1931, and in the commission of that crime murdered a sheriff. The local newspaper reported the graphic details.

There had been several unsolved burglaries in the West Plains area. Late at night on December 17th, McCallon's Clothing Store was robbed of 2000 dollars worth of merchandise. Apparently the crooks entered the store through a back window after removing two metal bars. The stolen clothing had been carefully selected. The crooks were only interested in the latest fashions. The most expensive socks, ties, gloves, sweaters, and shirts were stolen. . . .

It was just before 9 A.M. on December 19, 1931, when a blue DeSoto sedan drove along East Main Street, pulling into the Davidson Motor Company. The men in the car needed two tires repaired. One of the mechanics started fixing the flats. Sheriff C. Roy Kelley had just finished his coffee and was walking into the post office across from the garage. While the flats were being fixed, the garage owner, Carac Davidson, noticed the men in the car were wearing clothes that looked like the merchandise stolen from McCallon's Store. Also, tires on the blue DeSoto made tracks similar to those found behind the building where the break-in had occurred. Quietly, Mr. Davidson slipped away and telephoned Mr. McCallon, asking him to come to the store to see if the men were wearing the stolen clothes.

When Mr. McCallon arrived at the garage, Sheriff Kelley was coming out of the post office. . . Just as the sheriff opened the car door, shots rang out. . . The two suspects knew they had been caught; one of them ran outside, reloading his pistol as he fled. Turning down an alley, he made his escape. Tires screeched as the blue DeSoto roared out into the street. The car hit the curb hard and bounced, causing the right rear door to swing open as the blue auto raced down the street.

. . . Sheriff Kelley was dead, shot twice in the chest and two more times in the left arm. Within days the blue DeSoto was accidentally found by a group of hunters. The car had been abandoned, and there were bullet holes in the back of it. . . . After checking license plates, police found that the car belonged to Alvin Karpis.[1]

For outlaws looking to lay low after committing a major crime, there were several places in the Midwest where they could find relative safety— for a price. Three most important hideouts were Joplin, Missouri; Hot Springs, Arkansas; and St. Paul, Minnesota. This last named metropolis was even worse in civic corruption than notorious Chicago where a criminal with enough money could buy sanctuary and enjoy a good life as long as he behaved and didn't interfere with whatever the mobs directed by Capone, Moran, and brethren gangsters ordered. The Green Lantern was St. Paul's premier criminal hangout—a saloon for safecrackers and bank robbers which "Creepy" Karpis called "my personal headquarters." The Lantern was turned over to Dillinger gang members Tommy Gannon and Pat Reilly in 1933, but closed not long after Dillinger's death in 1934.

After slaying Sheriff Kelley, Karpis and Barker had to hide out. One step ahead of the posse, they raced to the home of Herbert Farmer, a family friend who lived five miles south of Joplin, Missouri. Joplin was a haven for fleeing outlaws because it was a fair-sized town and only minutes away from the Kansas and Oklahoma state lines. Farmer advised the two fugitives to go to St. Paul, Minnesota, where a corrupt municipal police force had helped transform that quiet river city into a crime capital for the Midwest. In St. Paul, Karpis and Barker fell in with other gangsters who suggested that with the heat on for bank robbers, kidnapping would be easier and more lucrative.

Kidnappings did indeed flourish.. The year of 1933 saw 27 major cases, more than twice number of the previous year. Three months after the kidnapping and subsequent murder of Charles Lindbergh's infant son, Congress passed the Lindbergh Law (June 22, 1932), which made kidnapping a federal crime if the abductor or his victim had crossed a state border.

Karpis and Barker were persuaded that kidnapping would be easier than bank robbing, and within six months they committed two kidnappings. In June, 1933, they snatched William Hamm, owner of Hamm's Beer Corporation, and in January, 1934, they took wealthy banker Edward Bremer.

News of the Hamm kidnapping initially was withheld by officials in an effort to establish contact with the abductors and bring about their arrest. Within 48 hours, however, officials were convinced such contact could not be made, and they decided to make the seizure known.

The day following the seizure of Hamm, a headline in the *St. Paul Pioneer Press* blazed:

"WILLIAM HAMM KIDNAPED [*sic*];
$100,000 ASKED; PAY OR WE KILL HIM."

Under a smaller caption, the report continued:

> Taxi driver identifies Verne Sanke as the man who gave him the ransom demand for safe return of the St. Paul brewer. Victim in a postscript urges immediate payment. [2]

Negotiations began to unfold. First, William W. Dunn, Manager of Hamm's Brewery, received a phone call informing him of the capture. Next he was given a note delivered by a taxi driver stating that Hamm was being held for $100,000 ransom and that unless the money was paid, he would be killed. At the bottom of the note was a postscript with Hamm's signature urging immediate payment of the sum.

In the next three days, a series of notes with instructions came from the kidnappers. The money was to be put in one of the brewery's trucks to be driven by one man. The truck had to be entirely open so that it would be visible to other motorists and was to be driven to an area near Anoka, Minnesota, thirty miles north of St. Paul. There the driver was to turn onto a rural route for one mile and throw the bags containing the money alongside the dirt road.

Police kept out of the case at the earnest request of the Hamm family so that every opportunity could be given to meet the abductors' demands and to insure Hamm's safe return. Behind the scenes, however, the police had mobilized their forces to launch an intensive investigation the moment Hamm was freed.

Despite the family's desire for secrecy, details of the abductors' demands began leaking to the press. On June 19th, an article in the *New York Times* and attributed to the Associated Press had the caption: *RELEASE OF HAMM EXPECTED HOURLY.* The report continued to say the ransom request had been scaled down. The attorney for the Hamm family told reporters that payment of part of the demanded $100,000 had led Hamm's parents to believe he would be freed soon and unharmed. [3]

No matter what the amount of this payment, it worked, for within two days Hamm was released near Wyoming, Minnesota. As promised, he was unharmed, but unfortunately when police questioned him hoping to learn more about his captors, he claimed he knew little. He had heard their voices but had not seen their faces, having been forced to wear goggles with cotton between the lens and his eyes.

The Karpis-Barker gang was encouraged by the success of this caper. Not only did they get most of the ransom demanded but blame for the crime was put on others. The FBI arrested Roger Touhy, a bootlegger from Chicago, along with several of his confederates. Their trial was held in November, 1933, but when testifying, William Hamm couldn't verify that Touhy or any of his company had been his captors. In consequence, Touhy and his associates were acquitted.

Upon receipt of the Hamm ransom, Karpis flew to Reno, Nevada, but his share of the ransom went fast. After all, $100,000 split in fourteen ways didn't last long. According to a later FBI analysis, the largest portion of this ransom, nearly $25,000, went to two corrupt, cooperating detectives named Tom Brown and Jack Peifer. The six men who actually committed the kidnapping—Karpis, Fred and Doc Barker, Shotgun George Ziegler, Charles Fitzgerald, and Bryan Bolton—each got $7500.[4]

Short of funds, Karpis left Reno to return to the Midwest, and while hiding out in the Minneapolis area learned that on every Wednesday the Federal Reserve shipped the payroll for Swift and Company to a railway depot in South St. Paul. There two messengers would collect the bags of cash and then escorted by policemen walk around the corner to the post office and pick up more cash.

Karpis talked over a heist with his pal Doc Barker, and the two decided they would need more men for the job—at least four—two to collect the cash; one to watch the door for an unwelcome intruder, and a fourth to manage the "git"—a slang term for an accomplice in charge of the escape or getaway car, which meant learning the back roads for a tenth of a mile, knowing the time it took to reach recognizable landmarks, and having a fast car gassed up and ready with extra guns for the actual robbers.

Karpis and Barker recruited a couple of confederates, Bill Weaver and Chuck Fitzgerald, and these four men were armed and watching when the train pulled into the South St. Paul station at mid-morning on August 30, 1933.

Just as the robbers expected from their previous casings, two messengers took the money bags, and accompanied by armed police officers left the station to walk up an alley leading to the post office. One officer slipped behind the wheel of a marked police car parked in the alley while the other accompanied the messengers into the building.

A few moments later as the officer and the two messengers carrying more money bags emerged from the post office a black sedan drove up. Behind its wheel was Fred "Doc" Barker dressed in denim overalls. Another occupant of the sedan, Chuck Fitzgerald clad in a gray suit and with a pistol in hand, also jumped out.

Barker yelled, "Stick 'em up!" The officer complied at once, and when Barker ordered the messengers to throw down the money bags, they did as told.

Meanwhile, the officer in the police car, unaware of what was happening, started to back it onto the street in front of the post office. The car reached the corner where one of the robbers. Bill Weaver was standing. Weaver panicked and raising a sawed-off shot gun hidden by the newspaper he carried, he fired through the driver's window. The blast struck the officer in the head, knocking off his cap, and he slumped immediately, badly wounded. Karpis escaped and managed to get his companion, Chuck Fitzgerald wounded during the fracas, to a friendly doctor in Calumet City, a gritty suburb on the Illinois-Indiana border.

Less than a month after this caper, Karpis, two of the Barker brothers, and another confederate tried another heist—this one from the Federal Reserve Building in the heart of Chicago's financial district. It was a botched job, for after the bags of loot had been collected the four robbers—Karpis, Fred Barker and his brother Doc, along with Bryan Bolton, a fellow thug—got into a Hudson Terraplane that was parked and ready. Karpis was the driver and had planned the "git" carefully. Speeding north before veering left and heading west, he crossed the Chicago River Bridge but promptly crashed the Hudson into an oncoming coupe.

In the melee following the wreck, one police officer, Mike Cunningham a 35-year-old father of two, was shot by Bryan Bolton and died instantly. A bullet from Bolton's machine gun also ricocheted to strike Doc Barker in the hand. Nevertheless, he and Karpis commandeered a passing car, and helped by the two other thugs transferred the stolen bags and extra guns to the vehicle.

To cover their escape still further, they stole another auto and again transferred guns and loot into it before driving to a garage on the far southwest side of the city. There after shutting the doors of the garage they got started in opening the bags to share their plunder. Only then did they discover they had stolen five bags of U.S. mail!

At first both Barker brothers were furious, but by the next morning Fred had calmed down and said, "These things happen. It's not so bad; we didn't get any money, but more important, nobody left fingerprints on the damned Hudson."

The shoot-out in downtown Chicago was front-page news for several days. Slowly, more details were reported while a massive manhunt by local police and the FBI got underway. Detectives found several guns in the wrecked Hudson Terraplane but no fingerprints, and authorities believed the robbers had been a combination of Machine Gun Kelly, Verne Miller, and Pretty Boy Floyd.

By Christmas, 1933, Karpis was almost out of funds. He and Fred Barker decided another kidnapping would be more remunerative than a robbery.

They talked about choosing a victim in either Indiana or Chicago, but both those areas were dangerous because swarms of police were roaming over the region while searching for John Dillinger. The vicinity around St. Paul was more promising and one which Karpis and Barker knew best. Moreover, the Edward Bremer family was at least as rich as the Hamms.

By the opening week of 1934, Karpis and Fred Barker had talked five other thugs into joining them in kidnapping Edward Bremer, 37-year-old son of Adolph Bremer, millionaire owner of the Schmidt brewery. The recruits Karpis collected were: Shotgun George Ziegler, Bill Weaver, Volney Davis, and Harry Campbell from Tulsa.

For a week, Karpis and Fred Barker trailed Bremer, learning his habits and when he traveled alone. The best time to take him would be in the morning when he dropped off his nine-year-old daughter at school. Streets around her school were relatively quiet, and a getaway could be quick.

Karpis and Barker bought two new Buicks and outfitted them with radios, extra-strength heaters, and frost shields. Temperatures around St. Paul in January often dropped well below zero, and the last thing the kidnappers wanted was to have their escape car freeze up.

Just after nightfall on January 12, 1934, Karpis and Doc Barker were in the latter's Chevy en route to picking up their confederates when they spotted a patrol car with two policemen in it. While Karpis cradled a Tommy gun on his lap, Doc drove slowly around the neighborhood of brick apartments. Both could see from the rear view mirror that the police car was following them.

"What the hell are we gonna do?" Karpis asked.

"Only one thing to do," Barker replied. "That's stop 'em."

Barker stopped suddenly, and both he with his pistol and Karpis with his submachine gun jumped out and opened fire. Barker emptied his pistol, and Karpis fired all his 50-shot drum into the car. They couldn't see anyone sitting upright in the car, so they got back into their Chevy and drove off. The rest of that night they listened for radio reports of the encounter, but it was not until the next morning when Karpis bought a newspaper and read that the man he had machine-gunned was a Northwest Airline employee!

This man, Roy McCord, had returned home, and his wife told him she had seen a prowler in the area. Still in his aviator's uniform and wearing his peaked hat, McCord found a friend to help check out the neighborhood, and he had spied the car carrying Karpis and Barker. Seriously wounded in the shoot-out, McCord survived, and his companion was shaken but unhurt.[5]

During the Christmas holiday of 1933, the Karpis-Barker gang completed their plans to kidnap Edward G. Bremer, Jr. The prominent young Bremer from the Schmidt brewing family was president of the Commercial State

Bank in St. Paul and wealthy in his own right; the take from his kidnapping ought to be handsome.

The morning of January 17, 1933, was frosty in St. Paul. After breakfast, at 8:30 A.M., Bremer put his daughter Betty in his Lincoln sedan and drove to her school. After dropping her there and expecting nothing but another routine day, he continued driving toward his office when he stopped at the corner of Lexington Parkway and Goodrich Avenue.

As Bremer stopped, a black sedan carrying Fred Barker, Harry Campbell, and George Ziegler pulled in front of him. At the same time, another car containing Arthur "Doc" Barker, Volney Davis, and Karpis moved in behind Bremer's Lincoln blocking any kind of its passage.

Alarmed, Bremer opened the door on the driver's side of his Lincoln and attempted to escape only to be rewarded by pistol whippings from Doc Barker and a muttered, "Don't try to run or we'll kill you."

A subdued Bremer was shoved back into his car and had his eyes covered so that he couldn't see. Then the three cars in tandem drive slowly away and out into the countryside. The kidnapping had taken less than two minutes, and no one had witnessed it.

Bremer with his eyes still covered was taken to a house just outside Chicago in Bensenville where he was held for twenty-one days. Meanwhile a series of notes, newspaper ads, and telephone calls was exchanged between the abductors and Bremer representatives or family. It was a tense interval for captive and captors.

Unlike the previous kidnapping of William Hamm, the kidnappers this time had a victim who constantly complained: he was sick, uncomfortable, the food was bad, he was being mistreated; if released he'd help them choose another man far more wealthy. Bremer's grumblings got so bad that several times Fred Barker warned, "If you don't shut up, I'm gonna kill you." Doc Barker talked down his brother's murderous intentions by reminding him of the sizeable ransom they expected.

In the first week of February, following instructions from the abductors and despite protests from the FBI, a ransom of $200,000 was given to an intermediary, Walter Magee. The money was left on a dirt track near the small town of Mazeppa, Minnesota, and the next day Bremer was outfitted with new clothes and permitted to shave. Then he was blindfolded again, put in back of a car and driven to Rochester, Minnesota, where he was deposited in front of a downtown building and told to count to fifteen before moving or calling for help.

Karpis-Barker gang members were gleeful over success of the Bremer kidnapping, but this one would be their undoing. FBI investigators assigned by Director J. Edgar Hoover were given four five-gallon gasoline jugs and a funnel found on a road near Rochester. One can showed a traceable fingerprint. Despite the insistence of Karpis that gloves not be taken off during the refueling, Doc Barker had removed his and left a distinctive print on the can. This finding set the hunt off in earnest, and soon all of the gang was behind bars or dead.

Meanwhile, Alvin Karpis and his girlfriend Dolores Delaney traveled together registering under different aliases at hotels or tourist camps in Ohio, Indiana, and Iowa until the first week of December, 1934. Karpis by then was tired of traveling and keeping just one step ahead of the law. With some of the Bremer ransom money laundered and in his pocket he decided the best refuge would be Cuba. Accordingly, he and Delaney drove to Miami and upon arriving there checked into the El Commodoro Hotel. The next day they drove to Key West and boarded the S. S. *Cuba* for the six-hour cruise to Havana.

Karpis thought Havana would be the first place police might come looking for him, and with help from friends he rented a six-room beach house down the coast just outside the town of Veradero. He and Delaney spent an idyllic month there, sun bathing, beachcombing, fishing or playing cards while drinking rum and Coca-colas.

Fred and Ma Barker, irritable and cranky as ever, came to Veradero to spend a few days with them, and when Karpis drove Ma back to Havana from where she would take a steamer back to the mainland, he exchanged a $1000 bill at the Royal Bank of Canada. He was alarmed to note that some of the bills given him in the exchange were discolored. Checking their Federal Reserve numbers, he found they were from Minneapolis. He realized it was some of the Bremer kidnap money—money supposed to be in Venezuela or Mexico City. He had been double crossed, and immediately knew that FBI agents if not already in Cuba would be streaming there soon, searching for him.

Realizing that Cuba was no longer safe, Karpis with Delaney beside him drove to Havana, where he put his moll on a flight to Miami. He stayed overnight in Havana and the next morning boarded a ship for Key West. From Key West, he went by train to Miami where at the station Delaney was waiting.

In Miami, a gangster buddy, Willie Harrison, told him Ma and son Fred Barker were living in a house at Lake Weir in Florida. Karpis wired Barker to come to Miami, and there he and Karpis began talking about a hit on a bank in Cleveland, Ohio, but when Karpis told his pregnant girlfriend Dolores about going to Ohio, she pouted, reminding him that her baby was due in the next month but could come at any time.

Nevertheless, Karpis and Fred Barker continued planning for the Cleveland heist, and Fred on his own enlisted the aid of his older brother Arthur "Doc" Barker. Doc went to Chicago and was there preparing for the Cleveland caper, when FBI agents tipped off as to his whereabouts surrounded his apartment and captured him without a struggle. Locked away and questioned vigorously by federal agents, he clammed up and told them nothing. However, the agents located Bryan Bolton, an ally, who sang like a canary telling everything: who committed the Hamm and Bremer kidnappings and what had happened to the money. More important, a map in Bolton's possession informed authorities that Fred Barker and his mother were hiding out at Lake Weir in Florida. An armada of FBI agents descended on Ocala, the nearest town of any size to Lake Weir with the village of Oklawaha on its north side.

Federal agents surrounded the cottage hideout, and when he was ordered to surrender, Fred Barker opened fire. In the exchange of gunfire which followed, both he and Ma Barker were slain. In making the announcement of their deaths, Director Hoover of the FBI asserted without proof that the corpse of Ma Barker had a machine gun cradled in her arms.[6]

As was the case with most major crimes, rumors arose and spread. One tale that was popular for a time but later proved false was that after learning of the deaths of Ma and Fred Barker in Florida, Doc Barker sent word to Edgar Hoover that he intended to kill him for murdering Barker family members.[7]

Following his arrest, Doc was judged guilty of the Bremer kidnapping and imprisoned in state jails. By this time, Alvin Karpis was labeled by FBI and press as Public Enemy Number One. He left the Midwest and went to Atlantic City, New Jersey. The FBI learned of his hideout there and surrounded it in an attempt to capture him. However, Karpis and a companion Harry Campbell were able to shoot their way out and escape. Yet during the escape, Dolores Delaney, Karpis' girlfriend carrying an eight-months-old embryo, was hit in the thigh by a wild shot fired by Campbell.

Karpis found a late-model Pontiac with keys dangling from the ignition, and stealing that vehicle he and Campbell eluded police and raced out of the city. There had been no time to pick up Delaney, whose wound was treated by a friendly doctor. Karpis never saw her again, but in January of the following year when he was staying in a whorehouse in Toledo, he read in the newspapers that in Philadelphia, Delaney had given birth to a son—an infant turned over to Karpis' parents when Delaney herself received a five-year prison sentence for harboring Karpis and Campbell.[8]

Several weeks earlier while listening to a newscast by Lowell Thomas, Karpis learned that Pretty Boy Floyd was dead. He was still stewing over the death of that accomplice when another newscast informed him and other listeners that Baby Face Nelson had been killed at a shoot-out in Barrington, Illinois.

Karpis needed other accomplices, and in November, 1935, he teamed up with Freddie Hunter to rob a train when it stopped at Garrettsville, Ohio, forty miles northwest of Youngstown. The robbery was successful but netted only $34,000; Karpis had expected five times as much.

Karpis and Hunter then holed up for a time near Hot Springs, Arkansas, but when informants tipped off FBI agents about the hideout, the two fugitives hightailed it to Texas. Hunter had a girlfriend, Connie Morris, traveling with them, and knowing that FBI agents were hot on their trail, he and Karpis left Texas and drove to New Orleans where they rented an apartment. Agents learned Connie Morris carried a venereal disease that required frequent treatment, and by interviewing doctors in New Orleans they found the address of the rented apartment. Surveillance of the dwelling showed not only Hunter but Karpis as well coming and going into it. The FBI agent in charge wired Director Hoover in Washington so that he could come down and participate in the capture of this Public Enemy.

Hoover arrived to join the thirteen men Earl Connelly, the local FBI agent in charge, had gathered. The posse took up quarters in a vacant house across the street from the apartment, and when Karpis and Hunter came out of it to step onto the sidewalk they were confronted by men pointing guns at their heads.

There are varying accounts of the actual arrest. Hoover maintained he grabbed Karpis by the collar as he was trying to get at a rifle in the back seat. Hoover said he called, "Put the cuffs on him, boys." And after his order there was no resistance.

More than thirty years later Karpis published his autobiography and wrote, "I made Hoover's reputation as a fearless lawman. It's a reputation he doesn't deserve. . . I made that son of a bitch."

Karpis went on to add, "The story of Hoover the Hero is false. He didn't lead the attack on me; he waited until the coast was clear. Then he came out to reap all the glory."[9]

No matter how it happened, Karpis gave up with no resistance, and his capture helped cement Hoover's status as a national hero. Karpis was sentenced to life imprisonment and incarcerated at Alcatraz Island in San Francisco Bay. He gained a final bit of notoriety when it was announced he was the prisoner who had served the longest sentence at the prison.

Notwithstanding the original sentence of life imprisonment, Karpis was released on parole in 1969 and deported to Canada where he took up residence in Montreal. After four years, he moved to Spain where he died in 1979. First reports were that his death was a suicide—a belief nurtured when a bottle of prescribed sleeping pills was found in his apartment. The belief became questionable, however, when it was learned the prescription was for Nancy, his girlfriend who had left a week before his death.

So suicide was ruled out, and death certificates in Spanish when translated into English clearly report that he died of natural causes. No autopsy was performed, and the body of Alvin Francis "Creepy" Karpis lies buried in Spain.

Chapter 4. Charles A. "Pretty Boy" Floyd

"History," wrote François de La Rochefoucauld, French essayist of the classical period, "is the belief in falsehoods." The maxim was never more true than in tales surrounding figures such as Billy the Kid or Jesse James. Their lives had hardly ended before their careers were evolved into folk lore and songs.

In the first quarter of the twentieth century, as the nation grew, so did the number of crimes and criminals. The neurotic misfits of the 1920s, Richard Loeb and Nathan Leopold, were in jail, and the kingpin of mobsters, Al Capone, had been indicted by a grand jury for federal tax evasion and given an eleven-year jail sentence.

There were syndicates with enforcers and muscle men in the big cities, but across the country and particularly in the Midwest smaller gangs of bank robbers and kidnappers formed. Along with misdeeds came tales and regional recognition. Clyde Barrow and Bonnie Parker would draw widespread notoriety as a boy-and-girl stick up team, but the only outlaw attracting national attention in 1931 was Charles Arthur Floyd.

Floyd was born on a farm near Akins, Oklahoma in 1904. He had been a restless farm boy during his teen years, working for his father and occasionally with harvest crews. In adulthood, he was of moderate height, 5 ft., 8 in., with a good build, his upper arms powerful, his eyes gray, and his face moony and flat.

In November of 1907 Oklahoma had been admitted as the nation's 46th state, and since that time the number of its banks had grown steadily. Not all of those new ventures enjoyed good financial health. After WW I when foreign demand for American agricultural goods returned to more normal levels, rural banks were especially hard hit. The result was that prices for farm products tumbled. U.S. farmers could not come up with mortgage payments, so bankers in the affected areas failed to meet their obligations. Oklahoma was one of the states that suffered most. In just two years from 1921 and 1923, seventy Oklahoma banks failed—including the Sallisaw Bank and Trust Company in Floyd's hometown of Akins.

As a boy growing up in one of the dirt-road towns that dotted the hills of eastern Oklahoma, young Charlie Floyd had plenty of heroes. He was thrilled by the exploits of "Black Jack" Pershing, America's victorious general from WW I, by the career of the Manassas Mauler Jack Dempsey, the fleet-footed baseballer Ty Cobb, and the athletic Indian, Jim Thorpe. None of these idols, however, could match his adoration of Jesse James, a nineteenth century train robber whose reputation by the time of Floyd's boyhood had swelled out of all proportions; exaggerated tales about Jesse James spread faster than gossip at a church supper.

There was no equal to James in all of Charlie Floyd's boyhood idols. In his mind, James had not been a thief or murderer but a modern Robin Hood robbing the nefarious rich and giving to the deserving poor. Bankers and big business interests were the real criminals; James was a hero who fought against injustices. Folklore of the James brothers was as addictive to the growing Charlie Floyd as the corn stalk cigarettes he and other boys hand-rolled out beyond the town's cottonwood trees.

By the time he became a teen-ager, Floyd's formal schooling ended. In Oklahoma then, six or eight years of school was enough. Like his father, Charlie was expected to become a share-cropper, raising corn or cotton and boiling a little moonshine on the side. When the U.S. went to war in 1917, Charlie had picked up habits of stealing candy, pop, or small change from grocery stores or filling stations in Akins or in nearby towns, but otherwise he was a 13-year-old field hand laboring with his dad.

In the mid-1920s tenants worked as much as 80% of the land in several Oklahoma counties. Early in 1921, Charlie Floyd met 14-year-old Ruby Hardgraves. Vivacious and dark-haired with a trace of Cherokee blood, Ruby was three years younger than he but already dreaming of a life apart from being a barefoot daughter of one of the tenant farmers who had come to Oklahoma to grow cotton on other men's fields.

Sharecroppers like the Hardgraves eked out extremely meager livelihoods—worse off economically even than the Floyds. Sharecroppers lived in shacks unpainted and weathered and drove no sedans or trucks. They usually managed to raise their own chickens and grow their own vegetables, had their own tobacco, and swilled their own whisky, but it was a hard life—a life that bred disregard for rules while nurturing strong notions of self reliance.

When Charlie and Ruby first met both were wild kids full of desire. Ruby's Cherokee eyes, sun-kissed hair, and swivel hips enchanted Charlie, and during the winter and spring of 1923 and 1924 they spent more and more time together, making love every chance they got.

As soon as Ruby found out she was pregnant, the two of them got a marriage license in Sallisaw and were married there in a simple ceremony on June 28, 1924, a hot, sweltering day. Both dressed in their best clothes, and Ruby carried a bouquet of fragrant home-grown blossoms. Their son, named after the famous prize fighter and whom everyone would call by his middle name, Charles Dempsey Floyd arrived at the very end of December in that same year.

Even when Floyd did find a job, the wage was pitifully low, so the young parents had to scrounge for pennies. But everyone was suffering. The hard times helped create disdain for money lenders and jealousy toward rich people. Bank robbers were quick to seize upon such popular sentiments to justify their own crimes, for it was just like many citizens said, "After all, banks were robbers, too." Bankers were the enemy as far as poor folks were concerned; bank robbers were *good-ole country boys* driven to a life of crime by circumstances beyond their control.

For six months Floyd lived the role of a hard-working father and dutiful husband, but shortly after his first wedding anniversary, restlessness struck. He was tired of chopping cotton, mixing mash, cutting piles of wood needed to keep the home fires burning, or selling a jug of moonshine for one of the farmers who had cooked the mash somewhere out in the woods. Besides, older men had come home from what was being called the Great World War and had brought with them tales of foreign lands, big cities, bawdy women, and escapades that fired the imagination of the virile youth.

Floyd laid down his hoe, packed his grip, told Ruby he would send her money, then set out to see the world. He went westward, sleeping in haylofts, bathing in creeks, and drinking at a farmer's pump. He hired out as a field hand where his thick arms and well-muscled shoulders were suited for pitching hay, shucking corn, or shocking wheat.

He was not yet a veteran criminal. True, he had been arrested at the age of 18 for stealing $3.50 from the local post office, but all this was petty stuff to a young man as dissatisfied and ambitious as Charlie. He made brief visits to Tulsa and Oklahoma City, but it was Wichita which held special attractions for him.

Wichita, Kansas, once a wide-open cattle town, had grown into a bustling flour-milling and meat-packing center in the Sunflower State. By the time Floyd reached it, petroleum deposits and aircraft factories had brought new wealth to the former cow town.

When Floyd took up residence in Wichita, one of its most notorious characters was John Callahan, a sly, corpulent Irishman and the best known "fence" for a ragged army of bootleggers. Callahan could dispose of anything— jewels, autos, bank securities, or whisky—and as a result of such talents, every sneak thief, burglar, or bank robber in the Midwest found a way to link up with him. Criminal historians would describe Callahan as a modern-day Fagin—an adult who tutored youths in ways of crime and lawlessness.[1]

Floyd fell under the influence of Callahan, along with other young men ready to step over the brink and fall into the criminal abyss. One of those men was a young tough named Fred Hildebrand; he and Floyd soon became pals.

There may have been other crimes before the robbery which began Floyd's rap sheet, but the first one on it occurred in the late summer of 1925. In the second week of September in that year a trio of armed men in St. Louis robbed couriers of $11,929 in payroll funds bound for the Kroger Grocery and Baking Company. A week later Floyd and Hildebrand showed up back in Sallisaw. Both were smoking four-bit cigars, wearing new suits, and Floyd was driving a late-model Studebaker. A deputy sheriff who had known him as a youth was suspicious. The deputy summoned the Police Chief and the two of them trailed the Studebaker before pulling it over for a stop. Examination found on the suspects two rolls of money, with a thousand dollars in each roll. The money was still in yellow paper wrappers stamped with the name *Tower Bank of St. Louis.*

Floyd and Hildebrand were charged with robbery and were returned to St. Louis for trial. During the questioning, Floyd clammed up and confessed nothing, but Hildebrand broke down and implicated Floyd as well as a third accomplice. A Kroger Company courier also testified that Floyd was one of the three bandits and remembered him as "a young fellow, about twenty or twenty-two, with a round kind of *pretty* face."[2]

It was not the first time Floyd had been called *pretty*, and he didn't like the appellation. As his notoriety arose, various tales would surface as to how the name came about. The most common version is that Beulah Baird, a dark-haired prostitute in Kansas City, used it when she placed a stein of beer before him and sat down by his side saying, "Hello, *pretty boy*. Where did you come from?"[3]

Indicted for the Kroger Store robbery, Floyd was held in the St. Louis jail for several months before December 8, 1925. By then he had decided to change his plea to guilty and take his medicine. He hardly blinked when the judge said, "I hereby sentence you to five years at the state penitentiary in Jefferson City, Missouri."

At the time Floyd began serving his sentence, the Big House at Jefferson City enclosed more than thirty acres and held three thousand inmates with more arriving daily. Life for the prisoners there was harsh and cruel. The standard work day was twelve hours; flogging was common punishment, and misbehaving inmates were given ice baths, the sweat box, or locked up with a ball and chain. Really hard-core *cons* were put in the hole, given a thin mattress, and fed a steady diet of bread and water.

In the Jefferson City penitentiary, Floyd first was assigned to kitchen labor but later worked in the machine shop and also outside the gates on one of the prison's farms. Guards said he was an average inmate. The assistant deputy warden Charles Hargus reported:

> He was intelligent. . . That doesn't mean he was a model prisoner. He would steal things like most convicts, but he didn't go out of his way to hunt trouble. Floyd seemed to have a desire to be let alone more than anything else. He kept to himself, went quietly about his tasks, and showed no disposition to be a troublemaker.4

Paroled in 1930, Floyd went to Kansas City. Police there had been alerted that an ex-con probably would be returning to his home stomping grounds and were waiting. Floyd was watched, followed, and probably was "harassed by the bulls" as he later claimed. He was picked up twice on vagrancy charges and questioned about highway robberies but was able to convince the court of his innocence in both cases. For some reason, he went to Pueblo, Colorado, where despite a plea that he was looking for work, he was fined fifty dollars and sentenced to sixty days in jail. Floyd's record was mounting fast; within two months after his release from the Missouri State Penitentiary, he had been arrested three times.

During his imprisonment at Jefferson City, Ruby had divorced him and with their son Dempsey had moved in with Bradley Floyd, Charlie's older brother, who was a dependable oil field hand living with a wife and four sons in the boom town of Earlsboro, Oklahoma.

Floyd's favorite hangout in Kansas City was the home of Sadie Ash, an infamous madam with three grown sons, Walter, William and Wallace. Walter's wife was Beulah Baird, and her sister Rose was a girlfriend to Wallace Ash. Both William and Wallace Ash were on police lists as suspects in the city's network of illegal activities, including gambling and peddling of narcotics.

Floyd had teamed up with Willis Miller, a thug six years younger than he but already a killer. The two of them frequently came to the Ash residence together. Floyd wanted to take up with Beulah, and Miller chose her sister Rose. The men had to be careful though because the Wallace brothers were suspected to be snitches for the police, and both had obvious criminal leanings.

Police in Kansas City had been told to be on the lookout for Floyd and Miller, and whenever or wherever a robbery occurred in the area, the two were blamed. Some of the reports may have been true, for the two men spent lavishly and had no recognizable income. Yet it would have been impossible for them to commit all the crimes attributed to them, for several were carried out at the same time in spots too far apart for even the fastest cars to travel.

Feeling police heat, Floyd and Miller retreated eastward. On February 5, 1930, in Sylvania, Ohio—a suburb in the northwest corner of Toledo—a Studebaker sedan with Michigan license plates pulled up and parked in front of the Farmers and Merchants Bank. One man remained in the car behind the wheel, and the other four climbed out to enter the bank. Once inside, one of them called out, "This is a stick-up, and we mean business!"

Each of the bandits had a pistol in hand as he intimidated patrons and herded employees behind the cages back toward the vault. The chief cashier, John C. Iffland, realized what was happening, and he instinctively slammed shut the vault's door and spun the dial on its front, activating a time clock, which meant that the vault holding tens of thousands of dollars could not be opened until the next day. When he and another cashier gave that news to the robbers, one of them was so infuriated he slugged Iffland, knocking him to the floor.

Someone on the sidewalk outside had witnessed what was going on inside the bank and had immediately phoned the police. The town siren began its wail, and upon hearing that warning, the bandits scooped up whatever cash they could find in the tellers' cages and rushed out the front door, climbed into the waiting Studebaker, and took off.

Police and a fire truck tried to follow the Studebaker, but couldn't match its speed. However, the cops did get close enough to note the license plate. The numbers were traced, and a few days later acting on tips from informants, a police squad raided a joint in Akron where Floyd and his pals were playing cards.

The raiding party consisted of Sergeant Kovach from the vice squad along with Herbert Michaels and Arthur Possehl—all in plain clothes—and Policeman Harlan F. Manes in uniform. Two men and two women were arrested, and as Manes was attempting to put the cuffs on one of the culprits, the man pulled out a gun, pushed Manes away, and shot him point-blank. With that shot, the two male suspects raced away, and Manes, seriously wounded, was rushed to the Akron hospital.

The next day a larger cadre of police surrounded and entered another home known to be a bandits' hangout. There they arrested James Bradley, who gave his name as Bert Walker, and dragged Floyd out from under a bed. Both men were brought before the dying Manes in the hospital, who said that Floyd was not the man who shot him. When Bradley (aka Bert Walker) was brought in, Manes quickly identified him as his assailant.

Manes died, and Bradley went to trial for his murder. Upon conviction, Bradley was sentenced to death, and died in the electric chair in November, 1930.[5]

Floyd was kept in the Toledo jail for six months until December 10, 1930, the day he was to be transferred from Toledo to the state prison at Columbus. For the trip, he was handcuffed to another prisoner and put on the train with two sleepy deputies as guards. Halfway to their destination, Floyd got permission to go to the train's bathroom where he opened its small window and jumped out, landing in a small embankment covered with rocks and winter stubble.

Three years later, Joe Packo, one of the two men assigned to guard Floyd and two other prisoners on the train, gave his account of Floyd's escape.

> We got on the train about five o'clock that night after searching the prisoners and cleaning them up for the trip. . . Floyd wanted to go to the lavatory all the time, but we wouldn't let him. When the train stopped at Trenton to pick up passengers, he asked us again, and we finally told him he could go after the train started. . . I was handcuffed to another prisoner named Nathan King. . .

> Danielak (the other guard) went to the end of the car and the door to the lavatory, where he could catch them if they tried to break out. They hadn't been inside more than ten seconds before we heard a window crash. I pulled the cord that stopped the train, and then hauled my prisoner with me to the end of the car. Danielak stepped into the lavatory and found King standing alone with the handcuffs dangling at his side. The window was smashed. Floyd was gone. [6]

The other two prisoners were held; the train stopped and the guards got out to search for the escapee. They were unsuccessful as Floyd remained hidden in deep grasses nearby. After the guards gave up and the train pulled away, slowly and carefully he began sneaking his way toward Kansas City.

In March of 1931, the bodies of William and Wallace Ash were found in a ditch just across the Missouri border into Kansas. Their days of crimes and suspected "snitching" to police were over. They had been killed in execution style: bullet wounds from close range in the back of the head, and the corpses pitched face downward into the mud of the ditch.

Police immediately suspected Floyd and Willis Miller because of their involvement with Beulah and Rose. Miller, already on the lam for robbery and murder, and Floyd, too, had good reason to leave the Kansas City area in a hurry. Within a couple of weeks after the Ash brothers' bodies were found, he and Miller showed up in northwestern Ohio together with two lady friends.

In mid-April, Floyd, Miller, and their two women were spotted in Bowling Green, Ohio, driving a late-model sedan with Missouri license plates. Merchants were suspicious of the strangers and alerted the police who tailed the car for nearly a week. On April 16, 1931, just as the four suspects were about to enter a department store, the cops drove up, stopped their car, and two officers got out to walk toward the couples.

Floyd was first to see the police coming, and he yelled to Miller, "Look out! Cops!"

Miller whipped a .45 cal. pistol out of his shoulder holster and fired a single shot. The two policemen then drew their own weapons and began shooting. Floyd drew his own pistol and fired several rounds, one of which struck Officer Ralph Castner in the abdomen. Castner, seriously wounded, fell to the pavement but from his prone position kept firing. During the fusillade, pedestrians on the street ran for cover while Miller took a bullet in the stomach before collapsing dead on the street.

As soon as the gun battle began, the two sisters ran from the scene, but in their flight Beulah was struck in the head by a stray bullet, seriously wounding her; Rose was unscathed.

Floyd's survival instinct took over, and he dashed down an alley toward the street where their car was parked. He was followed by the Chief of Police who had been unable to catch up but had managed to note the license plate number on the sedan as Floyd drove it away.

The license number was traced and found to have been issued to a Ruth Saunders in Missouri—a 23-year-old woman in Kansas City arrested twice on beer raids but never convicted. In part because of this name, the first newspaper accounts of the confrontation in Bowling Green were filled with inaccuracies: the dead Miller identified as "Clarence Saunders," the wounded Beulah was called "Wanetta Ross," and her sister Rose was "Ruth Saunders." The fugitive who escaped was believed to be "Ted Shea" of St. Louis.

Two days later a fresh wire service dispatch corrected the mistakes and gave a more accurate summation:

Bowling Green, Ohio—

Willis (Billy the Killer) Miller, known to police in several Middle Western cities as a desperado, is dead, two of his girl companions are under arrest and a second gunman is hunted today in the aftermath of a fight with the police. . .

One of the two girls, who gave her name as Beulah Baird, 20-year-old. Kansas City, divorced wife of Walter Ash, slain in Kansas City a month ago, was picked up near Miller's body, a bullet in her skull. She is in serious condition. . . The second gunman, listed here as Clarence Saunders, Kansas City, was suspected by police of that city as being Charles Arthur Floyd, a pal of Miller wanted in connection with the slaying of Wallace and William Ash. The Ash brothers were thought to have been killed because of their rivalry with Floyd over the two Baird sisters.[7]

Throughout the State of Ohio a manhunt for Floyd got underway, but the searchers were unsuccessful. Police speculated that he was being hidden by gangsters in Toledo, Youngstown, or Akron, and paid them with money gained from his previous robberies. Authorities in Wood County, the county seat for Bowling Green, offered a $1000 reward for his capture and warned that "extreme caution should be used when approaching Floyd as he was armed and would not hesitate to shoot."

On the evening of July 20, 1931, police in Kansas City came close to capturing him. Acting on tips, a squad raided a suspected north-side liquor warehouse. In it were nine men seated around a table, taken by surprise when police broke down the door and entered with guns drawn. One of the culprits started to protest over the intrusion but shut up as soon as an officer zapped him on the head.

The smell of alcohol permeated the room, and Floyd feigned drunkenness as he rose and weaved toward the door.

"Hey! You know who that fella is? It's that Pretty Boy Floyd character," shouted one of the raiders.

Floyd immediately drew his pistol and an exchange of gunfire commenced. Explosions from police revolvers and automatic pistols were deafening, and in the melee Floyd was able to get out the door and make it to his Plymouth sedan parked nearby.

Five men were shot in the fight. One suspect who tried to escape was hit by a shotgun blast and died instantly. Policeman Joe Anderson suffered a minor wound, apparently struck by a glancing bullet that struck him in the abdomen. Clarence Reedy, a detective, was wounded in the neck, and M. P. Wilson, a young man from Alabama who had nothing to do with the raid, was found lying in the street with a wound in his stomach.

The most seriously wounded was Detective Curtis Burks, hit in the stomach causing paralysis from the waist down. Four of the wounded men recovered, but two days after the fracas, Curtis Burks died. His death set police off in high dudgeon, searching for a killer who had slain one of their own. Murdering hoodlums like the Ash brothers was bad enough, but killing an officer of the law was absolutely intolerable. Pretty Boy Floyd had to be caught.

On the run by 1932, Floyd might yet have drifted into obscurity if it had not been for the shootout at Union Station in Kansas City. There was no direct, single path that led to that disaster where five men lost their lives and others were wounded. Instead there were twisted trails, multiple events, and overlapping careers all jumbled in a tangled mess making a background for the tragedy.

One of the principals was Frank "Jelly" Nash. Born in Indiana, Nash when a child had been taken with his parents to Oklahoma where he had started his criminal career as a small-time thief. His first serious run-in with the law came in 1913 when he and a companion robbed a Sapulpa, Oklahoma, store of almost a thousand dollars; Nash then murdered his partner and kept all the loot for himself.

He was caught and given a life sentence to be served in the Oklahoma State Penitentiary. When World War I came along, the glib Nash was able to talk his way out of the pen so that he could enlist in the army. Instead of becoming a soldier, however, he resumed his career in crime. He joined with several gangs, one of which was led by Al Spencer and had as a member the nefarious Wilbur Underhill. The gang robbed stores mainly but in 1923 held up a train and from that robbery stole twenty thousand dollars in Liberty Bonds. That theft was a federal offense, and Nash fled to Mexico. He was caught in El Paso and sentenced to twenty-five years at the federal prison at Leavenworth, Kansas.

Nash so smooth talking that he could sell a double bed to the Pope, became a trustee at Leavenworth, and one day he simply walked away. He succeeded in getting to Chicago, where he set up an illegal beer parlor, managed slot machines, and robbed banks with the Karpis-Barker gang. By the opening of the 1930s, Jelly Nash was one of the most wanted criminals in the country.

In June, 1933, he was in Hot Springs, Arkansas, posing as a wealthy businessman from Chicago. He was in a cigar store, drinking beer, and talking with several other men when police acting on a tip he was there, pulled up in front of the store and waited for him to come out. When he did, he was alone; a trio of policemen with guns drawn approached him saying, "You're under arrest. Come with us."

They escorted him back to their car with its driver still behind the wheel, and after getting the unresisting Nash inside the vehicle they ordered him to take off his hat and toupee. Sure enough! They had captured the infamous bald bank robber Frank "Jelly" Nash.

His capture set off a series of underworld long-distance calls, one of which went to Verne Miller, a big-time gangster with a speckled past that included county fair parachute jumping, WW I hero, county sheriff, imprisonment for embezzling, bootlegging, bond-breaking, and bank robbing as a member of the Karpis-Barker gang.

Miller, a friend to Nash, sought help from fellow gangsters in Minnesota, first telephoning the Barker brothers in St. Paul, but they were busy with the kidnapping of the wealthy brewer William A. Hamm Jr. Next, Miller set up a meeting with Johnny Lazia, local crime boss of Tom Pendleton's corrupt Kansas City regime. Lazia said he didn't want any of his lieutenants or subordinates involved, but he suggested that Miller contact two gunmen, Charlie Floyd and Adam Richetti, who were visiting a whorehouse on Holmes Street.

Miller took the advice, met Floyd and Richetti, and persuaded them to join him in an effort to free Frank Nash. For all of the men involved, it seemed like a good idea. Miller would get the men he needed; Lazia and his crew would not be directly involved but would be doing a favor for a couple of outside strong men. In the future he might need to call upon them for repayment. Floyd and Richetti would be paid handsomely in cash from Miller and would have earned respect from the powerful crime boss of Kansas City.[8]

The opening months of 1933 were ones marked by more major crimes than can be enumerated, but a few relating to characters portrayed in this book are worthy of mention.

In the first week of that year, the First National Bank in Cleveland, Texas, was robbed of $1200, and the crime was charged to Pretty Boy Floyd. Six days later three men robbed the bank at Ash Grove Missouri, of $3,000, and again Floyd was suspected along with two members from the Barrow Gang.

In April the Barrow Gang while attempting to escape murdered Detective Harry McGinnis and Constable J. Wesley Harryman in Joplin, Missouri, and Floyd was reported as one of the suspects.

At the end of May, eleven convicts, including Harvey Bailey, Wilbur Underhill, and "Big Bob" Brady staged a mass breakout from a state prison in Lansing, Kansas, taking the warden and two guards as hostages—all three were later released unharmed. The U.S. Bureau of Investigation reported that guns used in the escape were supplied by Bailey's friend, Frank "Jelly" Nash.

In early June, the Barrow Gang wrecked their escape car after a robbery near Wellington, Texas, and Bonnie Parker was badly burned. The criminals made it to a nearby farm where they shot one woman in the hand, took the family as hostages, and escaped by kidnapping two law officers later released unharmed.

In the three days between June 15 and June 18, the Hamm kidnapping played out when Alvin Karpis aided by Fred and Doc Barker captured the brewery kingpin and held him before releasing him unharmed after a $100,000 ransom was paid.

On June 16, Pretty Boy Floyd and Adam Richetti kidnapped Sheriff William Killingsworth at Bolivar, Missouri, and abandoned his car near Clinton in the same state. Then stealing another car and taking its driver hostage, they drove to Lee's Summit just south of Kansas City and released their captive unharmed.

Thus Floyd and Richetti were easily available in KC when Verne Miller came calling, asking for help in rescuing Frank Nash from the police.

Early on the morning of June 17, 1933, Miller, Floyd, and Richetti got into Miller's dark-green 1933 Chevrolet coupe and drove to Union Station in downtown KC, where they parked in front of the station's huge doors. Floyd entered and went to the vacant office of the Travelers Aid Society. With no one around, he sat in a chair there until shortly before seven o'clock when Mrs. Lottie West, a case worker for the Aid Society, came in. She asked the stranger if she could help him, but he said nothing, simply rose and walked out. Interviewed later, West said she thought he had been very rude, and when shown pictures of several suspects, she picked out one of Floyd, saying she was certain he was the stranger in her office that morning.

The train from Little Rock pulled into the station on time, 7:15 A.M. Two FBI agents from Oklahoma City, Joe Lackey and Frank Smith, together with Otto Reed, Police Chief of McAlester, Oklahoma, had been assigned to deliver Nash to KC. The three men had Nash in their middle when they got off the train and walked down the stairwell into the lobby where two municipal policemen, Frank Hermanson and W. J. "Red" Grooms, were awaiting them. With them were two special agents from the Kansas City FBI office, Raymond J. Caffrey and the Special Agent in Charge, R. E. Vetterli.

The seven lawmen with Nash in handcuffs poorly covered by a handkerchief exited the station and started toward Caffrey's two-door Chevrolet. The lawmen had agreed to use it in transporting Nash to Leavenworth rather than an official vehicle in order to avoid attention. Caffrey unlocked the right door of his Chevrolet; officers Lackey, Reed, and Smith climbed into the back, and upon insistence from Caffrey, Nash was put in the front seat next to the driver. Caffrey then shut the door and began to walk around the car so he could enter the left door and drive. Officers Grooms, Hermanson, and Vetterli were standing slightly to the right of the front hood when the firing began.

Floyd had moved out from his stance behind another car, and raising his machine gun he shouted just before pulling the trigger, "Put 'em up! Up! Up!"

At about the same time, Verne Miller and Adam Richetti stepped from behind a third car, and Miller yelled, "Let 'em have it. Let the bastards have it."[9]

The lawmen were caught unaware but Grooms, upon recovering, drew his gun and got off two hurried shots, one of which struck Floyd in the shoulder. As the gangsters blazed away with machine guns and a sawed-off shotgun, victims began falling. The first was Hermanson, whose head was half blown away by a shotgun blast. Grooms was killed by machine gun fire, and both corpses lay on the pavement their bodies almost touching one another.

Agent Vetterli had a flesh wound in the arm and chose to duck back into the station and call for help. Shots whistled around him as he ran for the station's doors, reaching them without being hit again.

Special Agent Ray Caffrey fell to the ground, mortally wounded by a shotgun slug to his right temple. He would die en route to the hospital.

Upon realizing that an attempt was being made to free him, Nash started to slide left below the steering wheel, but several machine gun bullets stitched through his torso and pelvis; his head snapped back as his blood spewed over the seats, and his toupee fell askew.[10]

The other three men in the Chevrolet were helpless because its windshield was shattered by gunfire. In the back seat, the wounded Lackey dropped to the floor where he was hit again by two shots. With machine gun bullets at the base of his spine and a revolver bullet in his pelvis, he was in terrible anguish but would survive although never be able to work or walk again.

His companion, Frank Smith, drew his own gun, and heard the firings and the bullets spattering before he, too, dropped to the floor, playing dead. He was lying prone and immobile when almost immediately Chief Otto Reed, who had been sitting beside him, was slain by machine gun bullets and fell dead atop him.

Pandemonium reigned as bystanders fled in every direction; taxi drivers ducked to the floor of their cabs, and cars collided as the gangsters made a quick getaway. Less than two minutes had passed since the shooting began. Five men were dead: Nash and four officers; two others had been wounded; only Agent Smith was unhurt.

Special Agent Vetterli wired a Western Union telegram to his superior in Washington soon after the debacle ended:

DIRECTOR, U.S. BUREAU OF INVESTIGATION, WASHINGTON, D.C

OTTO REED, CHIEF POLICE MCALESTER, OKLAHOMA, SPECIAL AGENTS FRANK SMITH AND LACKEY WITH FRANK NASH WERE MET UNION STATION THIS MORNING AT SEVEN FIFTEEN A.M. BY AGENTS VETTERLI AND CAFFREY AND TWO

LOCAL DETECTIVES. NASH WAS TAKEN TO CAFFFREY'S AUTOMOBILE IN FRONT OF UNION STATION WHEN UNKNOWN PARTIES BELIEVED FOUR ALTHO DEFINITE NUMBER UNKNOWN OPENED UP WITH SUBMACHINE GUNS KILLING TWO LOCAL POLICE OFFICERS CHIEF REED FRANK NASH AND SHOOTING CAFFREY FATALLY IN HEAD LACKEY SHOT RIGHT SIDE NOT BELIEVED FATAL FRANK SMITH ESCAPED UNINJURED VETTERLI NIPPED IN LEFT ARM LICENSE NUMBER OF SHOOTING CAR OBTAINED DOING EVERYTHING POSSIBLE

VETTERLI.[11]

Hoover, Director of the FBI, incensed upon learning of the five deaths, announced that the whole affair was nothing less than a coordinated attack upon legitimate law forces set up by civilized society.

After making their getaway, Floyd, Miller, and Richetti holed up for a day with one of Miller's girlfriends. She fixed them meals and tried to dress Floyd's shoulder wound. A day or two later Miller hunted up Johnny Lazia and told him they needed a doctor for Floyd and a car to get out of the city. Lazia supplied both, and on June 19, Floyd, Miller, and Richetti were in a Buick sedan safely out of Kansas City and on Highway 40 driving east toward St. Louis.[12]

Within days the slaughter at KC had been publicized in newspapers throughout the nation, and interest rose higher when the Bureau of Investigation in Washington identified Verne Miller, Charles "Pretty Boy" Floyd, and Adam Richetti as the killers. The outrageous act of shooting down law officers in broad daylight enraged many citizens who formerly had been sympathetic to crooks who they believed robbed the wealthy and gave to the oppressed.

As time went by, however, versions of the event began to differ, and questions about motives and character arose. Most readers accepted the theory that the raiders wanted to free Frank Nash, one of their own. Others speculated that the raiders were from rival gangs who wanted to silence a crony who knew too much and was a loudmouth.

Some readers with altruistic perceptions of Charles Floyd maintained he simply could not be one of the crazed killers described by Hoover, agents, and witnesses. The picture was blurred more when the KC police received a note dated June 19, 1933, sent from Springfield, Missouri:

Dear Sirs:

I—Charles Floyd—want it made known that I did not participate in the massacre of officers at Kansas City.

Charles Floyd[13]

Some police believed the note and signature were genuine; others scoffed and reiterated their faith in the sworn testimonies of agents and witnesses. The note's authenticity was never settled.

The Kansas City Massacre as it soon was called gave rise to a flurry of sightings of Floyd, Miller, and Richetti reported to have been in various places throughout the Midwest. In Floyd's home town a cobbler told authorities that Floyd had visited him and asked to get some shoes resoled; a Tulsa couple claimed that on the same evening they had been kidnapped by Floyd and Richetti and held until dawn until their captors had fled in the victims' automobile; the proprietor of a tourist camp near Wichita said that after a domestic fight his wife had hired Floyd "to beat him up," and he had a broken rib as proof; Missouri newspapers reported that Floyd was the suspected robber of a bank in Seneca; several persons in Tulsa insisted they saw Floyd delivering bootleg liquor to a host at a downtown party.

Such were the rumors but not fact, for both Floyd with his sweetheart Beulah Baird and Adam Richetti coupled with her sister Rose had gone east and taken up quarters in Buffalo, New York.

Verne Miller had split from the entourage and gone to New York City. His hopes for joining one of the New York gangs there didn't pan out, and he retreated to Chicago. His career was about to end, for fellow criminals, aware that police from several states as well as the Federal Bureau of Investigation were close on his trail, wanted nothing to do with him.

The naked body of Verne Miller was found on November 19, 1933, in a drainage ditch near Detroit. It was a brutal gangland execution; the corpse was bound with clothesline around his arms and legs; his skull had been crushed by blows from a blunt instrument; his tongue and cheeks had been punctured probably by an ice pick, and he had burn scars over his torso.

Investigators learned that Miller had been surprised by four underworld figures while he was steaming in a Louisville bathtub, killed him there, and transported the corpse hundred miles north to the Detroit drainage ditch.[14]

Floyd and Richetti with their two molls hid for a year in a drab neighborhood in Buffalo, New York. Charlie Floyd and Beulah Baird took the names of Mr. and Mrs. George Sanders; Richetti and Rose became Mr. and Mrs. Ed Brenner. The four kept to themselves; there were no friends, no parties with outsiders, no callers, and little mail except a rare letter from one of Floyd's relatives back in Oklahoma.

After a year the virtual isolation in the cramped New York apartment began taking its toll. Charlie in particular had cabin fever, and besides that, funds were running low. He had become an avid newspaper reader especially interested in the flood of crimes the tabloids reported.

He may have liked the notoriety given him for various capers and didn't seem to mind when some were falsely attributed to him. He did protest against the most heinous ones and was incensed by the kidnapping of the Lindbergh child. After Richard Bruno Hauptmann was captured and finally executed, Floyd said he was glad that "damned perpetrator" had been caught.

On October 20, 1934, Floyd and Richetti, with their two live-in women, left Buffalo and drove through Pennsylvania before crossing into Ohio. Then they turned south heading toward Wheeling, West Virginia, where Richetti had relatives. At the city limits of Wellsville, four miles below East Liverpool, the pavement was wet and slippery. Floyd lost control of the car, and it skidded into a telephone pole.

They managed to push the vehicle back onto the highway, but both Floyd and Richetti knew it couldn't go far without being repaired. They coaxed the women into driving the damaged car to Wellsville to find a mechanic. Then the two women were to drive back for the two men who would be camped on a hillside.

As night came on, the women had not yet returned, and Floyd and Richetti on the hillside were cold and uncomfortable. They gathered leaves and twigs and started a small fire. A nearby farmer seeing the smoke came out, found and questioned the two men, whom he thought were tramps. Floyd was wearing a suit with no tie!

The farmer was suspicious and went home where he called a neighbor. The two of them summoned the town's police chief, a feisty fellow named John H. Fultz.

Fultz deputized two men loafing around the station, and the three of them went out to investigate. Fultz was armed, carrying a .38 cal. police special. He accosted Richetti but as soon as he started questioning him, Floyd admonished, "Don't talk to him. He's a cop."

Richetti whipped out a .45 cal. automatic at once and pulled the trigger, but with no shell in the chamber, the gun didn't fire. Fultz yanked out his own weapon and got off a shot or two when Richetti began running toward nearby timber. Fultz followed him, and when he got close enough that no one could miss, Richetti stopped, raised his hands, and said, "I give up."

As Fultz was putting handcuffs on Richetti, Floyd pulled a Thompson machine gun from beneath their blankets by the fire. The two deputies were trying to capture Floyd, but he fired a couple of bursts from the Tommy gun wounding one of the deputies in the shoulder. The other fired a blast from his shotgun and dived for cover.

Floyd disappeared into denser parts of the forest. When the three officers took the manacled Richetti and left the area, he was nowhere to be seen. Pretty Boy Floyd had escaped again.

Floyd trudged farther through the hills and came upon a farm where a 25-year-old, George MacMillen, was working on a car. MacMillen, hard up for cash, agreed that for ten dollars he would drive his own Model T and take Floyd to Youngstown.

En route to Youngstown, MacMillen was directed to stay on back roads, but he got very apprehensive when Floyd identified himself and exposed the big gun in his shoulder holster. MacMillen deliberately flooded the engine of the Ford until it stopped. At the time, they were in front of a farm owned by 60-year-old James Baum. Floyd was able to talk Baum into driving them in his own 1929 Nash the remaining few miles into Youngstown.

Fultz had delivered his captive Richetti to jail and had gathered more deputies ready to join him in renewing the chase for Floyd. The new aides were George Hayes, armed with a revolver, and Charlie Patterson, who carried a shotgun. The three of them set up a roadblock near a bridge on a highway leading toward Youngstown, and stopped all cars, allowing only one at a time to pass.

A big tan Nash approached but stopped, apparently when the driver saw the roadblock. The car turned around and sped away from the blockage. The three lawmen, with Hayes driving, went after it. As he came closer to the Nash, Hayes started holding down his horn, endeavoring to get the Nash stopped. It did not stop, and Floyd fired a shot or two from its back window. Patterson in the pursuit car was hit by flying glass, but the bullets passed over his head.

The Nash finally stopped and three men got out. They didn't halt when the law officers called for them to do so—just kept running away. The lawmen fired, and some of Patterson's buckshot hit Jim Baum in the thigh. Floyd had used Baum and MacMillen as shields before he ran into an open area, crossed it, and entered the thick Spencer woods.

Deputy Hayes told Patterson to watch Baum and MacMillen while he went for more help. He amassed a posse of at least a hundred men, armed with .22 rifles, old Mausers, shotguns, or weapons of any sort and returned to the scene of action. The posse searched the area the entire next day, but Floyd was gone. He had escaped again!

Melvin Purvis from the Federal Bureau of Investigation was in Cincinnati at the time, and upon learning of the chase for Floyd he immediately cabled Director Hoover asking for permission to join in the hunt. Hoover agreed; Purvis went to West Virginia to join with the Fultz forces, but once there he used an assumed name, hoping to avoid undue publicity. The internecine struggle between the federal bureaucracy and local police surfaced again.

The issue was not new. For years, many persons held to a belief that the federal government should have nothing to do with fighting crime, except in a few narrowly defined circumstances. The belief, according to a host of legalists, went back to the U. S. Constitution and its provisions for states' rights. Those provisions, they argued, meant that only state and local governments could mount major efforts to stifle crime. An important expansion of federal crime-fighting power came in 1932 with enactment of federal kidnapping statutes, after the abduction and murder of the twenty-month-old son of aviator and national hero Charles Lindbergh.

Out of the cauldron brewing controversy between national and local police authority, new laws were passed giving increased power to the federal government. In July, 1933, the Division of Investigation was created and merged with the Prohibition Bureau; two years later the Division would be separated and named the Federal Bureau of Investigation.

Melvin Purvis, federal officer in Ohio in that October of 1934, wanted Police Chief John Fultz to turn the captured Richetti over to him, arguing that Richetti could then be tried for the more serious murders at the Kansas City Massacre. Fultz responded that Richetti "had wounded one of my men, and I'm going to prosecute him." Furthermore, he resented the subterfuge used by Purvis in giving a false identity.

About two dozen federal agents from Pittsburgh, Cleveland, Detroit, Louisville, New York, Chicago, and Indianapolis were ordered to the scene where they joined with Ohio State Police and local forces throughout eastern Ohio in setting up roadblocks on all bridges across the Ohio River.

As dawn broke on the morning of October 22, the manhunt for Floyd was still underway. Around ten o'clock that morning, an unshaven and dirty Charles Floyd showed up at the farmhouse of Robert Robinson. The stranger said he was very hungry, so Robinson's daughter fixed him a sandwich. The man implored Robinson to drive him to Youngstown, but Robinson refused. The stranger got on the road again and started walking.

In a couple of miles, he reached the farm of Mrs. Ellen Conkle, a widow living alone. Her brother, Stewart L. Dyke, was husking corn in a field within sight of the house. Without identifying himself, Floyd told the widow he had been hunting squirrels or rabbits and had gotten lost. Mrs. Conkle was suspicious of a man who said he hunted squirrels at night, and she saw that instead of a rifle or shotgun he had a pistol in a shoulder holster. Nevertheless, she fed the visitor a dinner of pork chops, potatoes, rice, and coffee with doughnuts and pumpkin pie for dessert—the last meal Charles Floyd would have.

After eating, he went out into the yard and climbed into a Model A Ford. He was fiddling with something under the dashboard when Stewart Dyke came up.

Floyd quickly said, "I was hunting and got lost. Your sister said you might take me to the bus line."

The two men exchanged a few remarks, but Dyke could not be persuaded to drive to the bus line; however, he finally did agree to drive the stranger to Clarkson, eight miles north on State Highway 7.

Fearing that she might telephone a warning, Floyd insisted that Mrs. Conkle go with them. She dutifully got in the back seat and Dyke got in behind the wheel. Floyd sat next to him, but just as Dyke began to back up and onto the drive, Mrs. Conkle called their attention to two cars approaching the farmstead.

Floyd unsheathed his gun and said, "They're looking for me." He swore before ordering Dyke to drive over to a nearby corn crib. There he jumped out and with pistol in hand ran behind the crib.

Officers piled out of the two police cars, and yelled to him, "Come out or we'll shoot."

Instead of obeying, Floyd raced the other way in a zigzag pattern across an open corn field toward the woods. He carried his .45 pistol and once or twice glanced back over his right shoulder, neither firing nor slowing his haste.

Then Police Chief Hugh McDermott and Melvin Purvis gave simultaneous orders: "Let him have it."

At least fifty shots echoed—from rifles, shotguns, revolvers, and machine guns. Purvis fired his own .38 cal. special. Under such a fusillade at that range, hardly anyone could miss.

Floyd was hit numerous times. First in the forearm probably by a rifle bullet. Then a .45 slug entered below his left shoulder and lodged in the rib cage in the upper left of his chest. That one shattered his eighth rib and took away part of his lung. Another bullet struck on his left side; the two bullets had crossed, each nicking his heart. He staggered only two or three steps before he fell, arose, and fell again to roll over on his back.

He was barely alive when agents asked, "Are you Pretty Boy Floyd?"

"Yeah," was his whispered reply. "I am Charles Arthur Floyd."

He lived only long enough to swear more at the officers and say, "I'm going; I'm going." Then at 4:25 P.M. on October 22, 1934, fifteen minutes after he had been shot, Charles Pretty Boy Floyd died.[15]

CHAPTER 5. LESTER GILLIS—"BABY FACE" NELSON

Pretty Boy Floyd made good newspaper copy for months, and whenever newspaper accounts of him ebbed, there were graphic accounts of the exploits of other criminals: "Baby Face" Nelson, "Machine Gun" Kelly, Homer Van Meter, a Hoosier robber named John Dillinger, Ivan "Buck" Barrow, and his younger brother Clyde, who brought along a 20-year-old misfit from Texas named Bonnie Parker.

The flood of crimes gave vigor to the federal agency charged with monitoring them. J. Edgar Hoover characterized the massacre at Kansas City as "a challenge to law and order and to civilization itself," adding that his agency was ready to undertake a war on crime. Supporters backed him up, saying that the KC Massacre had shown that crime bosses read his words and picked up the challenge; criminals were going to bring down the flag of decent government.

Added to public umbrage was growing awareness of corruption in the ranks of municipal police in many cities. Hoover's Bureau profited from the unrest, for his agency was given more funds by Congress along with far wider authority. The additional monies allowed expansion, sophisticated equipment, radios, bullet proof vests, and weapons—machine guns, revolvers and shotguns which matched those already in the hands of experienced crooks.

One target for the Bureau's weapons was Lester Joseph Gillis, who as an adult was better known as Baby Face Nelson. He was born December 6, 1908, in a red brick townhouse in Humboldt Park four miles northwest of Chicago's downtown Loop and was the seventh child of Joseph and Marie Gillis, two former Belgians who had come to America fifteen years earlier.

As the baby in the family, Lester Joseph was pampered and doted upon by his four sisters. Also, his mother, a former school teacher, built high hopes for her little boy with his blond hair, apple-cheeks, and beguiling smile.

At the age of six, Lester's parents enrolled him in a public school; his first three years in it were uneventful, but by the age of nine his parents were told Lester was not attending regularly. His mother moved him to a nearby Catholic school, but results were the same. He would attend for a few months, and then truancy would set in. His parents tried other Catholic schools, but the pattern continued. The boy was well-behaved in the classroom, but he wasn't there often enough. Either he wasn't challenged or was basically a dissatisfied youth.

Humboldt Park, where Lester Gillis grew up, was center piece of an area known locally as The Patch. The Patch was made up of middle-class working families mainly with Irish and Italian ethnic backgrounds and with a sprinkling from other groups. Most boys in the Patch were older than Lester, but he gained their acceptance by his daring and combativeness, readiness for a fight with any bigger or heavier tough.

Automobiles and guns fascinated young Lester, and around July 4, 1921, when he was thirteen, the attraction brought him his first brush with the law. He and a pal were in the latter's garage admiring a new car the friend's father had bought, when Gillis saw a revolver resting in the side pocket of the car's front door.

The two boys took the weapon and went outside the garage where Lester said, "Let's fire a shot or two." By this time a couple more boys had joined them. It was near the Fourth, and the neighborhood already was crackling with the sound of firecrackers. Who would notice an extra bang or two?

Lester's pal put a tin can on a fence post, and the boys got ready for the demonstration. Lester won rights for the first shot. Taking careful aim, he pulled the trigger. One of the boys alongside him screamed and put both hands on his own face. The bullet had fragmented when it hit the fence post and ricocheted to strike the friend.[1] Lester's mother paid the injured boy's hospital bills, but a few days later when all the boys were given a hearing in the juvenile court, Lester Gillis was judged guilty and sentenced to twelve months in the Cook County School for Boys.

At the reformatory, the Superintendent and his wife grew fond of the cherub-faced, well-behaved lad, and he was given privileges, one of which was an occasional visit to his parents; the only restriction was that he had to be back at the reformatory every night. Most often, after a few hours with her son his mother would accompany him back to the prison. On one of those days, he and his mother were on a street car which stopped within a couple blocks of the reformatory. Another boy also being returned was alongside them. Lester flashed his beguiling smile and said, "Mama, you don't need to get out of the street car. We know the way, and we'll walk the couple of blocks ourselves."

His mother believed him, kissed him goodbye, and watched the two youths start their walk. The next morning she received a telephone call from the Superintendent telling her that Lester and the other miscreant had not returned.

The two thirteen-year-olds hatched a hazy hope of going to Florida and stole a car but got only as far south as Cicero when out of gas and money they simply abandoned their vehicle and returned to the reformatory.

Lester served a full year in the reformatory, and upon his release his mother enrolled him in another parochial school, hoping he had learned his lesson and would complete his education without further problems.

It was not to be, for Lester already was running with an older and rougher crowd which included adults who had moved into serious crimes such as burglary and mugging. He was still a scrawny teen-ager but was accepted because he had developed a knack for siphoning bootleg beer from a pipe in the back of speakeasies. He would collect the brew, put it in pails, which he then would carry and sell to workmen on various construction sites.

His fascination with automobiles had not abated, and with other accomplices he might "borrow" a car, take it for a joy ride, and return it when the gas needle showed almost empty. He didn't think of the episodes as "stealing," but car owners did, and his luck ran out on October, 1922, when he was arrested and charged with automobile theft. Found guilty, he was sentenced to eighteen months at the Illinois State School for Boys at St. Charles.

Released on probation in April, 1924, Lester returned home, and for a short time delighted his mother by helping with daily chores, including showing her the way he had been taught to make beds in the reformatory. His parents had invested their savings in a small café which soon fell into bankruptcy, and that failure led his father's drinking habits to worsen.

It wasn't long before household chores became too boring for the lad, and he resumed association with old friends from the Patch. One of these was Jack Perkins, who was making money stealing car parts and sometimes the entire vehicle. It took little coaxing to persuade Lester to join him, and in September, 1923, the two were caught in a stolen car. Lester's arrest was enough to cause the courts to revoke his parole, and he was sent back to the state school at St. Charles.

Again in the reformatory Lester was a model inmate. At fifteen, he had reached his full height of 5 ft., 5 in. At Christmas time, he was granted a few days off to go home and attend his father's funeral, who sodden with drink, had committed suicide. That event and witnessing his widowed mother's bereavement may help explain Lester's near total abstinence from alcohol.

In July, 1925, he was granted another parole from St. Charles, and he returned to stay for a short time with his mother. In the middle of the Roaring Twenties, Chicago was a gangster's paradise. Prohibition had transferred mobsters into millionaires, and crime bosses divided the city into territories ruling them like ancient warlords. The bosses would solicit "torpedoes" or "enforcers" from neighborhood gangs; the Patch was an especially productive source for such hoodlums.

One Patch member already into big time crime when Lester Gillis first met him was Vincent Gibaldi, who would be known by various aliases but chiefly as "Machine Gun" Jack McGurn after he had become one of Al Capone's chief lieutenants. Gibaldi was a North Side thug before being picked by Capone as an aide and had been one of the gunmen carrying out the notorious St. Valentine's Day Massacre in 1929.[2]

Gibaldi was flashy, cocky, and a snappy dresser when Gillis met him in 1925, and the paroled youngster quickly adopted him as a role model. Lester Gillis envisioned himself as a future successful gangster but was still a clumsy amateur. Almost a year from the date of his last arrest, he again was caught stealing an automobile. Authorities offered him a deal if he would give them names of accomplices, but he refused, and in October, 1925, he was sent back to St. Charles. Seventeen years old, he began serving another sentence in the reformatory.

In June of the next year, Gillis received his third and final parole from the state institution. He quickly linked up with pals from the Patch, and nine months later was arrested again—this time for breaking into a repair shop and stealing automobile tires. The partner arrested with him pled guilty and avoided jail by paying a hefty fine. When Lester's case came to court, his mother appeared in his behalf, made an eloquent plea for leniency toward her 18-year-old son, and he was given a year's probation.

He got a job driving a truck and making deliveries for the Commonwealth Edison Company, and remained an employee there for a year and a half. It was the longest legitimate job of his life. His only problems with the law were several speeding tickets only three of which ever went to traffic court. His mother Mary complained that local police were hounding him and attempting to pin every neighborhood crime—burglary or stolen car—on him. She maintained "that police pushed him over the line into a definitely anti-social life."[3]

Gillis's year of probation ended in mid-March, 1928. By that time he had resumed running with lawbreaking cronies. He and two pals, Albert Van de Houton and Jack Perkins, set up a still in Evanston, but their enterprise lasted only a few months because a man they employed to oversee the mill and cook the mash stole the largest part of the alcohol leaving them almost no profit.

Some time in that spring, Gillis met Helen Wawrzyniak. The family name was difficult to pronounce and hard to spell, so it later was changed to Warwick. Helen then was just 15 years old, small and raven-haired with a soft, milky complexion and sapphire blue eyes. Already swivel-hipped and properly curved, Lester fell for her immediately.

How the two met is unknown, but soon they were inseparable. She was a clerk at Goldblatt's Department Store where Lester visited her so often that the management warned her to keep her boyfriend away. The warning didn't take, and the inevitable happened; by September, Helen was pregnant. Without saying a word to family or friends, the couple eloped to Valparaiso, Indiana, where they married on October 28, 1928. Lester gave his age as 21, and his bride subtracted five years from her date of birth. For a year and a half, the newlyweds lived with Helen's sister Julie and her husband in Chicago, and in April 1929, Helen gave birth to a son whom they named Ronald Vincent Gillis.

Two months before the baby's birth, the St. Valentine's Day Massacre occurred. The carnage inflicted at that event shocked the public, and the wholesale slaughter of seven men there brought international infamy to Chicago's already unsavory image.

No evidence was ever discovered that linked Gillis to the Massacre, but investigators agreed that his pal from the Patch, "Machine Gun" Jack McGurn, had been one of the gunmen.

As the year of 1930 began, Chicago had no rival as the crime capital of the Midwest, and robberies of three prominent families titillated the reading public while frustrating police investigators.

The first such break-in was on January 6, when Charles M. Richter, Vice President of Consolidation Magazine Corporation, and his wife were accosted in their home on Lake Shore Drive by five intruders who took away more than $25,000 in cash and jewelry.

Two weeks later the same gang, if police were to be believed, struck again. This time it was the home of Stuart J. Templeton, a wealthy attorney living in the upscale suburb of Lake Forest. Neither Templeton nor his wife was at home that late afternoon, and the four robbers aimed their revolvers at two maids before escorting them to the master bedrooms which were then ransacked. The thieves left with rings, bracelets, and other jewelry estimated to be worth more than $5,000.

The two thefts were just sixteen days apart, and Chicago's elite society put pressure on the municipal police force to make arrests. Two months passed with few leads and no arrests, but there were no other significant heists. Police assumed the gang had left the Windy City. Wealthy residents sighed with relief and felt a little safer.

Then in the early afternoon of March 31, two men came to the door of the Lottie (Brenner) von Buelow mansion on Sheridan Road along the lakefront on the city's North Side. The strangers said they were census takers, and when told that Mrs. von Buelow was not in but would return by five o'clock, the men said they would return. The two accompanied by a third man did come back at the appointed time, and when admitted the three intruders whipped out pistols, tied up Christopher Gross, Lottie's brother-in-law, and forced Lottie to show them around the house.

In her bedroom, they discovered a wall safe and demanded that she open it. Lottie demurred, insisting that her former husband had installed the safe and hadn't given her the combination. One robber cursed her, tied her to a chair, and repeatedly waved his pistol in her face threatening further violence.

Then a commotion downstairs arose and Enrique von Buelow, a fake count who had married Lottie for her wealth, came in the door. He, too, was accosted and tied up quickly. The upstairs burglar had bound Lottie von Buelow to a chair, and hearing voices and clamor below he hurried down the stairs carrying the plunder he had collected from the dressing rooms.

There was more swearing and a few hasty comments before one of the robbers said, "We've got what we came for. Let's go."

The bandits left, and after a few minutes, Lottie von Buelow was able to free herself and call the police. But the thieves were long gone, and it took hours before she was able to itemize the stolen jewelry. In addition to cash and watches, the robbers escaped with a $40,000 pearl necklace, a $3,500 diamond ring, a lavaliere with 28 diamonds valued at $3,500, a $5,000 diamond bracelet, four pairs of diamond earrings, a $3,000 pendant, another worth $1,200, and three gold chains each valued at $300. [4]

For a few months, Gillis enjoyed a leisurely life with his wife and son although he got bad news in the last week of June when his accomplice "Machine Gun" Jack McGurn was stopped by police and arrested for carrying a concealed weapon.

A year earlier Gillis had taken up with Stanton John Randall and Harry Lewis Powell. Randall on parole after spending ten years in an Ohio prison for murder was twice the age of Gillis by this time being known as Nelson. Powell, a relative newcomer to the criminal coterie, had worked in a jewelry store and convinced his compatriots that he knew a lot about diamonds and other gems.

Nelson's wife Helen was pregnant again, and gave birth to a baby girl on May 11, 1930. With a wife and two children, Nelson's expenses rose, and by early fall he was running out of cash. His job at a Standard Oil station simply didn't pay enough, and he decided to pull another caper.

Itasca, Illinois, was a suburb a few miles from Cicero where Lester and Helen, who had introduced themselves to neighbors as Mr. & Mrs. George Nelson, were living, and Nelson cased the suburb's State Bank before deciding it was an easy mark. He couldn't pull the stunt by himself and had no trouble persuading Powell and Randall to join him.

Soon after the bank opened at 9:00 A.M. on October 3, a pair of well-dressed young men entered, and one thrust an automatic pistol into the face of the unsuspecting cashier. "This is a stick-up," Harry Powell said. "Step back and don't do anything foolish."

The second man, smaller in size, jumped over the railing and waving a .45 pistol herded two other employees together before ordering them both to lie face down on the floor. Nelson stood guard over the two of them while Powell searched the tellers' cages, putting whatever cash he found in a white pillowcase brought along for that purpose.

The robbers forced the cashier to open the vault and then quickly stuffed all the cash they could find into the pillow case. Carrying their loot while emerging from the vault, they had to pass the two employees lying on the floor. One of these, Emma Droegemueller, got a good look at the smaller of the two men and later recalled, "He had blond hair and the bluest eyes I've ever seen. I always wondered how anyone so innocent looking could rob us."

The robbers raced outside and climbed into a dark red sedan which a driver behind the wheel had parked and kept the motor running. The vehicle sped north disappearing on Irving Park Boulevard without anyone getting so much as a glance at the license plates. The robbery netted Nelson, Powell, and Randall a good haul—$4,678—four times the average annual wage of a working man in 1930.[5]

Three days later, Mary Walker Thompson, wife of Chicago Mayor "Big Bill" Thompson, was held up and robbed by three men as she came out of her apartment on Sheridan Road. The description she gave police matched ones given of the robbers at Itasca, especially when she said that the smaller man looked so innocent and had a "baby face."

The moniker got further boost a month later when Nelson and an accomplice attempted a bank hold-up at Plainfield, Illinois. The venture failed because unknown by the robbers, the tellers' cages had been reinforced by bullet-proof glass. Again, the bank employees said that one of the bandits was small and had a "baby face."

Nelson did somewhat better on November 22nd when he, Stanton Randall and a newcomer named Harry Lewis robbed the State Bank in

Hillside, Illinois. Their take for this heist, however, was only $4,000, which didn't last long when split three ways.

They tried to get more the next day by robbing a tavern on the southern outskirts of Chicago. The deed went awry when employees and patrons resisted. Three women were killed and three other persons wounded. Arrested several years later, Stanton Randall confessed to being one of the robbers and insisted that Nelson had been the gang's leader.

Nelson was on a killing spree, for within three days another tavern hold-up occurred, this one on Waukegan Road north of Chicago. Edwin Thompson was killed, and one of the robbers was captured. The captive told police Nelson was the other bandit and the actual killer.[6]

In January, 1931, Nelson was arrested in his apartment in Cicero, and six months later in July when his case for armed robbery was heard, he was sentenced to the State Prison at Joliet. While he was serving that sentence, investigators could search for evidence that would warrant indictment for other serious suspected crimes.

The stratagem paid off, for while in jail at Joliet, Nelson was indicted and brought to trial for another bank robbery—one that had taken place before his arrest. Found guilty of robbing a bank in Wheaton, Illinois, an additional one to twenty years was added to his sentence. Two days after being sentenced in this latter case, he was in the process of being transferred from Wheaton back to Joliet, but an accomplice from the outside had managed to slip him a pistol. How the slip was made is unknown, but with the weapon, Nelson overpowered his guards and escaped. The "baby face" killer was on the loose again.

He kept a low profile for nearly a year and a half; at least there were no confirmed reports of his participations in any crimes. In August, 1933, however, he teamed up with Eddie Bentz and Earl Doyle. Nelson and Bentz had met while both were hiding out in Long Beach, Indiana. While at Long Beach, they planned a robbery of the Peoples Savings Bank in Grand Haven, Michigan.

First, the desperadoes needed more weapons, so Nelson drove to San Antonio, Texas, and finding a gunsmith there purchased two machine guns and a couple of pistols modified to his liking.

The robbery on August 18, 1933, did not go smoothly, for armed guards and witnesses were able to thwart the trio's schemes. The driver of the bandits' getaway car parked just outside the bank panicked when he saw a police car approaching. He drove away in a hurry, leaving Nelson, Bentz, and Doyle inside the bank. In the exchange of gunfire which followed, Earl Doyle was captured. Yet Nelson and Bentz made their getaway, escaping with a loot of $30,000.[7]

In the last week of January, 1934, radio news cackled with reports that the notorious bank robber John Dillinger and a couple of his cronies had been arrested in Tucson, Arizona. Baby Face Nelson listened to such reports and expressed surprise that "a bunch of hick cops in a two-horse town" had managed to capture a gang with the smarts of Dillinger.

Nelson was in California where his wife Helen had been admitted to the hospital in Vallejo because of a complicated miscarriage in her third pregnancy. Nelson had plenty of cash; he bought a new Hudson sedan in San Francisco and registered it using another alias, this time Jimmie Rogers. He obtained California license plates for the Hudson and stayed a month in the Golden State making numerous telephone calls or sending messengers to gangland friends back in the Midwest.

At the end of February, 1934, with his wife Helen beside him he motored leisurely back to St. Paul. There he arranged a meeting with Eddie Green, Homer Van Meter, and Mickey Conforti. The four outlaws discussed a range of targets. Following instructions telephoned by Nelson while in California, Green had cased three banks: one in South Dakota and two in Iowa. Then Van Meter had visited each of them, sketching diagrams of their interiors and making maps for getaway routes.

The first caper for this assembly of ruffians—an assembly that police and reporters would call the Second Dillinger Gang—was robbing the Security Bank and Trust Company in Sioux Falls, South Dakota. Two of the men, most likely Nelson and Green, bought a new green Packard sedan from a dealer in downtown St. Paul, and the next day, Nelson drove it to a repair shop often used by gangland friends. He bolted a pair of Kansas license plates to the car's front and rear and asked the mechanic to check it out, making certain it was in tip top shape.

On the day the Packard was in the repair shop, a Hudson sedan with California license plates cruised up and down streets in St. Louis Park, a suburb of Minneapolis. Two residents there, Ted Kidder and his wife Verna, were driving home from a birthday party when a car with two men forced them to the side of the road. Angered, Kidder got out and went over to the men in the Hudson which also stopped. An altercation broke out, and to the horror of Verna, sitting back in her own vehicle, one of the men in the Hudson whipped out a pistol and fired three shots into the chest of her husband. Kidder fell to the ground and was dead by the time his wife reached him; the Hudson raced away. The murder was never officially solved, although late in 1934, Fatso Negri, a member of the Nelson–Dillinger gang, testified that Nelson on several occasions boasted that he had gunned down that bastard in St. Paul. [8]

On the day the Kidder affair occurred, John Dillinger made his escape from the Lake County Jail in Crown Point, Indiana, and by prearrangement went to Minneapolis to team up with Nelson who was there with three other thugs: Homer Van Meter, Tommie Carroll, and Eddie Green.

A day or two after his arrival, Dillinger followed this quartet of criminals who piled into the checked out Packard and drove 235 miles southwest to Sioux Falls, South Dakota. While Van Meter and Carroll shot pool, Nelson and Green took another look at their intended target.

The bank they meant to rob occupied the entire first floor of a huge granite building, and from this second casing, Nelson learned that Van Meter's and Green's earlier diagrams were very accurate, including everything—cages, offices, vault areas, even rest rooms.

Shortly before ten o'clock on the morning of March 6, 1934, a dark green Packard with Kansas plates drove up and parked in front of the Bank. Five men wearing long overcoats and four carrying bulky objects beneath their coats got out of the car and entered the bank.

Nelson entered first, followed closely by Green and Carroll; Dillinger and Van Meter waited until the getaway car had moved to a more favorable spot. Inside the bank, Nelson took a machine gun from under his coat and brandishing it in the face of Bessie Dunn, working at a Savings Desk, said, "This is a stick-up. Lie down; don't move, and you won't get hurt."

Van Meter and Dillinger were just coming in the doors, shouting and waving their weapons. Don Lovejoy, another bank teller, was standing within reach of the alarm button and was able to push it, setting off a bell which clanged throughout the robbery. Moments after Lovejoy hit the alarm, Nelson punched him in the face and then, waving his machine gun, strode over to the stenographers' tables and ordered them all to lie on the floor.

The robbers' plans then began falling apart. While Nelson was ordering everyone to lie on the floor, at the other end of the bank's lobby, Green was telling people to raise their hands and turn toward the doors. Van Meter and Dillinger, coming in, found everyone staring at them. Van Meter barked, "Move back toward the walls," while Nelson shouted, "Get your hands down, and move back from those damned windows."

Green had singled out Fred Anderson, another teller in the bank, and had forced him to unlock the door to the money cages. Dillinger put a gun into the back of Bank President C. R. Clarke and marched him over to the vault. Unable to open it, Clarke called Robert Dargen, another employee, to do so. With the vault opened, Dillinger handed Clarke a white sack and instructed, "Put all the dough in it, and do it damned quick."

Nelson had climbed atop a marble counter and kept his machine gun leveled as he watched what was going on. Van Meter, the only bandit with a pistol, aimed it continually around the encircled employees, warning, "If any one of you wants to get killed, just make a move."

Like a magnet, the bank's alarm had drawn police, pedestrians, merchants, shoppers, and reporters. The first policeman to reach the scene arrived while the robbery was still taking place, and one of the thieves, Tommie Carroll, shoved the muzzle of a machine gun into the cop's ribs, disarmed him, and ordered him to join the other captives. A policeman in another car drove up, and this man, too, was subdued and forced to join the herded employees.

Motorcycle Patrolman Hale Keith off-duty but in uniform roared up, parked his bike, and with a hand on his holstered revolver ran toward the bank. Nelson had moved from the marble counter and looking out the windows saw Keith coming down the sidewalk. Nelson fired a burst from his machine gun blasting a cluster of holes through the plate glass windows before striking Keith. The officer fell, severely wounded by a bullet in his abdomen, another in his thigh, a third in his upper right arm, and a fourth in his right wrist.

Minutes after the gang's departure, Keith was rushed to a Sioux Falls hospital, given blood transfusions, and was able to survive his wounds.

Reaching the Packard, the bandits climbed inside, but not before Nelson chose six hostages and ordered them to stand on the car's running boards. As the car pulled away, the windows were kept open and the bandits reached out to grab hold of the ladies and to say, "Don't be afraid; we won't hurt you."

The overloaded Packard had not gone far before steam and smoke began gushing from under the hood. The driver stopped; hostages were ordered off the running boards, and Nelson, Dillinger, and Carroll spread roofing tacks across the pavement hoping to delay pursuers. Four of the women were ordered to get into the car and sit on the laps of the gangsters. The other two hostages from the running boards were left standing on the curb as the Packard headed south.

After a few miles it stalled again, and the gangsters commandeered a Dodge, and by zigzagging over miles of back roads were able to elude pursuers. That night under the cover of darkness they slipped back into the city of Minneapolis. [9]

After gunning down the patrolman, Nelson swaggered back to help guard the captives while Van Meter and Dillinger were collecting loot from the vault. Nelson picked out a dozen captives and then using them as human shields, the four bandits with their guns leveled at the victims marched the procession out of the bank and over to the Packard where a driver was sitting behind the wheel and keeping the motor running.

The heist at Sioux Falls netted the bandits $46,000, but that had to be split six ways. To divvy up the cash, the five bandits and their driver met in Green's Minneapolis apartment, and each participant got something less than $8,000. A week later the same gang robbed the First National Bank in Mason City, Iowa.

The month of March can bring raw, biting winds, and snow to the community in north central Iowa—one of the most arable sections in the state claiming to have one-fourth of the Grade A land in the country. As might be expected, the First National Bank was prosperous and looked to be easy pickings.

In midmorning on March 13, Van Meter and Green drove their large blue Plymouth to a hamlet just south of Mason City, where a late model Buick with Indiana license plates was waiting. In the Buick were five accomplices: Nelson, Dillinger, Carroll, John "Red" Hamilton, and a fifth man never identified.

All seven men climbed into the Buick. Each man except the driver was wearing a bulky, steel reinforced vest and had a sub-machine tucked inside his long overcoat, so the car was crowded. Carroll was the driver, and he parked the Buick near the rear corner of the bank, the barrel of his .351 rifle ready to poke through the window.

The other men got out and stationed themselves according to plans previously adopted. Van Meter took up a post in front of an adjoining drug store, and Nelson went to an alley running behind the bank. The other four bandits entered the bank, waving their machine guns and yelling to the 31 employees and customers to "hit the floor."

"Red" Hamilton tried to capture Willis Bagley, the bank's president, but Bagley managed to make it to an office and slammed the door in Hamilton's face. Frustrated and maddened, Hamilton fired a burst through the door, the bullets missing Bagley by inches.

Above the office to which Bagley had retreated was a newly-installed steel cage shielded by bullet-proof glass. From inside the cage, Tom Walters, another bank employee, watched the havoc below—first in disbelief. Then realizing what was going on, he grabbed a tear-gas gun stacked in the cage, pushed the barrel through an opening slit, and fired. One of the gas pellets struck Green, and from behind the counter, Hamilton yelled, "Get that son of a bitch with the tear gas!"

As had happened at Sioux Falls, a crowd of onlookers had begun gathering outside the bank; some observers pressed closer thinking they were watching a mock robbery being filmed for a stage crew in town.

In the alley behind the bank, Nelson saw a man approaching and he hollered for him to stop. When he didn't, Nelson fired a burst from his machine gun, several bullets striking but not killing the man. Nelson came over, searched him, and found papers identifying him as the school's secretary. "Stupid son of a bitch," Nelson said to the bleeding victim. "I thought you were a cop."

Inside the bank, Dillinger, Hamilton, and Green were gathering all the cash they could—mainly stacks of one dollar bills—and collecting a dozen employees to use as hostages. They forced this group outside into the near-freezing temperature where Nelson and Van Meter with their machine guns were holding a few individuals.

Police began arriving, but were stymied and could not get close or fire their weapons because of the throng of bystanders held at bay. From a window on the third floor of the bank building, Judge John C. Shipley saw the hostages menaced by guns in the hands of Nelson and Van Meter, and coming out the bank were three more robbers. The middle-aged judge had a pistol in his desk drawer, and with this weapon he took careful aim at one of the robbers. His bullet caught John Dillinger in the right shoulder and spun him around.

At the vault, Harry Fisher, assistant cashier, had diverted Hamilton from larger cash by doling out one dollar bills. He had been forced to start on five dollar ones when Green poked his head in and shouted to Hamilton, "We're pulling out."

Hamilton responded immediately, leaving Fisher and more than $157,000 still in the vault. From his third floor window, Judge Shipley fired again, his bullet this time hitting Hamilton in the shoulder. Hamilton was able to join other members of the gang, however, as they piled into the Buick—four members in the back seat, Green and Van Meter in front, and Carroll behind the wheel.

Still surrounded by hostages, the gunmen ordered three of the women to get into the car; others were to stand on the running boards. The loaded car crept away at about ten miles per hour. At the outskirts of the town, Carroll tried to accelerate, but the women on the running boards couldn't maintain their grasps, so he stopped, and they were let off to stand by the road in the freezing cold.

Carroll drove a few miles farther, stopped again, and let the women in the car get out. Meanwhile, Nelson scattered roofing tacks on the highway to delay the police car that was giving chase.

It was almost midnight by the time the bandits got into St. Paul, where with the aid of a crony, the wounded Hamilton and Dillinger were driven to the office of Dr. Nels Mortensen, a prominent Minneapolis doctor who maintained close ties with Midwestern gangsters. Having been shot, both

Hamilton and Dillinger needed medical attention. Dr. Mortensen cleansed and treated the pair's wounds and was paid well for his services.

When the robbers got together to divide the $52,000 plunder, each of the seven participants got an equal share of $7,600. [10]

Four days after the Mason City heist, Nelson put his wife, son, and mother into the Hudson and left Minneapolis. He drove slowly and it was March 20 before he reached Reno, Nevada. He and his troupe stayed there three days before going on to San Francisco and then to his sister Leona's home in Bremerton, Washington.

At the beginning of April, Nelson felt it was time to move again, so he and his wife Helen packed up and drove away, leaving Mary, Nelson's mother, to tend for Ronald, his five-year-old son, who also would remain in Leona's home. Father and son would never be together again.

In the first week of March, 1934, a coterie of crooks gathered around Nelson holed up in Chicago. Among the crooks was John Dillinger, just having made his sensational escape from the Crown Point jail in Indiana.

Whether Nelson or Dillinger planned the rendezvous in Wisconsin is unknown, but no matter who the architect, at the beginning of April most of the gang showed up at Little Bohemia, a secluded tourist lodge in Manitowish Waters, Wisconsin. Given tips that the gang was going to assemble there, FBI agents led by Melvin Purvis, were sent immediately from Chicago, the nearest big city. Without much planning and without asking for help from local authorities, the agents attacked the lodge where Nelson, Dillinger, Van Meter, Hamilton, and Carroll together with wives or girlfriends were staying.

Dillinger, Van Meter, and Hamilton escaped through the back of the lodge, which was unguarded, and made their way north on foot through woods and past a lake to commandeer a car. Carroll was not far behind them. The four made it to Manitowish, stole a car, and drove without being apprehended back to St. Paul.

Nelson, who with his wife Helen had been in a cabin apart from ones housing the other criminals, returned the fire from Purvis and his squad before retreating into the main house of the lodge. From there, Nelson slipped out a back door and fled in the opposite direction to emerge from the woods ninety minutes later a mile away from Little Bohemia.

He stole a car, invaded a home, and took the man and wife living there as hostages. Nelson had his custom-converted .45 automatic with its fore grip for the left hand making it virtually a sub-machine gun pistol, and with that weapon as enforcer he ordered his captives to drive him out of town. As they were preparing to leave, another car carrying two federal agents and a local constable pulled alongside them. The agents were W. Carter Baum and Jay Newman; the constable was Carl Christensen.

Newman, driver of the federal car, was just getting out when Nelson surprised them all by firing his automatic. His first burst killed Baum with three shots in the neck, and other bullets wounded Christensen and Newman.

Nelson then got into the FBI car but had driven it less than 15 miles before a tire went flat. Unsuccessful in trying to change it by himself, he wandered on foot into the woods and took up residence with a Chippewa family in their cabin for several days before making a final escape by means of another stolen vehicle.[11]

Three of the women traveling who had accompanied the gang to the Wisconsin hideout were captured inside the lodge and charged with harboring and abetting criminals.

There was a hiatus of more than two months before the Nelson gang made the headlines again. On the morning of June 30th, Nelson, Van Meter, and three accomplices robbed the Merchants National Bank in South Bend, Indiana. Two of the three accomplices were Joseph "Fats" Negri, an associate of Nelson's from California, and Jack Perkins, an old friend from boyhood days in the Patch; the third was never identified.

When the robbery began, Howard Wagner, a policeman directing traffic outside the bank, saw what was happening and drew his gun to move toward the bandits. Van Meter, stationed to guard outside the bank, saw him approaching with his gun in hand. Van Meter fired at once, his bullets striking Wagner in the chest and killing him instantly.

A local jeweler named Harry Berg, holding a pistol, came into the bank where Nelson was collecting cash. Berg shot at Nelson several times, but his bullets were ineffective because of the bullet-proof vest Nelson was wearing.

The robbers emerged from the bank with sacks containing $28,000 and were shielded by three hostages held at gunpoint before them. Several more policemen had arrived and fired into the emerging group, wounding a hostage and grazing Van Meter in the head. He would recover, but the wounding of a hostage and several bystanders aroused further public concern and stepped up the search for Nelson.

During the month of July, the manhunt for him was intense, but Baby Face and his wife had fled to California where they met up with John Paul Chase, a man who would remain with Nelson and who returned to Chicago with him.

In the middle of July, Nelson, Chase, and a few cronies were meeting at a favorite spot when two Illinois state troopers, Fred McAllister and Gilbert Cross broke in. Nelson fired quickly with his converted "machine gun pistol," and the gangsters made their getaway. Although wounded, both troopers survived, and when arrested and brought to trial months later, Chase identified Nelson as the shooter.

Dillinger was shot and killed by FBI agents on July 22 in Chicago. A month afterwards on August 23, 1934, Van Meter was slain by police in St. Paul, leaving Nelson as the sole survivor of the so-called "Second Dillinger Gang."

The final lap in Nelson's criminal trek began with the death of an accomplice, Eddie Green. Green, a short, slim, scowling man with a pock-marked face, squinty eyes, and thin lips, had served prison terms in Iowa and Wisconsin before he joined Nelson and other criminals in the Twin Cities.

In 1934, Green was living with Bessie Skinner, age 36 and mother of a 19-year-old son. Acting on tips given by other informants, FBI agents were watching and waiting for Green when in late afternoon of April 3. he returned to his apartment. Who fired first became a matter of dispute, but a burst of five shots from one of the agents felled Green. He dropped to the floor, one slug having torn through the back of his skull and another smashing into his right shoulder. A police ambulance was summoned and rushed him to a hospital while his live-in moll Bessie was taken into custody.

In the hospital, Green died slowly, lasting eleven days during which he often was delirious or heavily sedated, but he had occasional moments of lucidity in which he named gangster pals without disclosing their whereabouts. Police got their information from Bessie, who under relentless questioning turned canary. She not only filled in blanks left by her delirious lover but added pages of insight into workings of the Twin Cities underworld, adding details about the deceased Frank Nash and Verne Miller, fingering other members of the Barker–Karpis gang, and recounting many of the activities which Nelson, Van Meter, Hamilton, Dillinger, Carroll, and others had carried out. She said everyone called Hamilton "Red" rather than John, and Van Meter was variously just Van or Wayne.

Bessie told investigators that in the gang there was always a little man known to her only as "Jimmie." He had light hair and complexion, and she knew he had a wife named Helen. Jimmie, she said, often traveled with Helen, their two children, and Jimmie's mother. When shown Nelson's photo, Bessie said she was positive he was the man usually accompanying her husband in his nefarious escapades; her testimony sent FBI agents much farther along on the trail of Baby Face Nelson.

For three months, Nelson, usually accompanied by his wife and John Paul Chase, drifted west to cities including Sacramento and San Francisco in California and Las Vegas and Reno in Nevada. FBI interest focused on one of his former hideouts—Lake Como Inn at Lake Geneva in Wisconsin. It was believed he might return to spend the winter. When Nelson and Chase did return on November 27, they came face to face with unprepared FBI agents. Both Nelson and agents were so surprised that no shots were fired, and Chase spun his vehicle around so quickly that he and Nelson could speed away safely.

In Chicago, Nelson stole a late model Ford V8 and with Helen and Chase as passengers drove 50 miles northwest reaching the wealthy suburb of Barrington. There he caught sight of a sedan containing two FBI agents: Thomas McDade and William Ryan. Agents and outlaws simultaneously recognized each other, and after several U-turns, Nelson wound up in pursuit of the agents' car. He and Chase fired at the agents, shattering their windshield and causing Agent McDade to skid his car into a field. The two lawmen with weapons drawn got out and crouched behind their auto ready to fight it out with their pursuers.

However, Nelson and Chase had stopped, and the FBI learned later that one of Ryan's shots had punctured the radiator of Nelson's Ford V8 and that another car, a Hudson containing FBI Agents Sam Cowley and Herman Hollis, had joined the pursuit.[12]

Nelson's V8 lost power due to the punctured radiator, and he swerved into the entrance of Barrington's North Side Park. Cowley and Hollis stopped their vehicle and huddled behind it in protection from the shots coming from Nelson and Chase. The gun battle was witnessed by more than two dozen bystanders attracted by noise and confusion.

Helen Gillis following frantic instructions from her husband ran into the adjoining field before looking back. When she did that, she saw Nelson wounded but firing his modified .351 rifle so fast the agents thought it was a machine gun. From the other side of the V8, Chase also was shooting at the officers.

Six bullets from Agent Cowley's submachine gun hit Nelson in the chest and stomach, and pellets from Agent Hollis's shotgun struck him in the legs. Hollis possibly already wounded moved toward better cover behind a telephone pole but was killed by a bullet to his head.

Nelson was able to crawl to the agents' Hudson, where Chase and Helen came to lift him into the car. Chase then drove as fast as possible to Wilmette nearby. Agent Hollis was dead by the time assistants got him to a hospital, and Cowley lived long enough to undergo surgery before dying of wounds similar to ones that had struck Nelson.

Chase was desperate, and the only possible help he could think of in the vicinity was Father Phillip Coughlan. Like the majority of Nelson's friends and associates, Coughlan was a product of Chicago's West Side, where a goodly share of Irish lads became hoodlums, cops, or priests. He had chosen the third route and had ministered in parishes in Missouri and Oklahoma. Then in 1929, he had been installed as chaplain at the Oak Park Hospital.

Father Coughlan's duties often involved contact with numerous gangland characters, including bootleggers and members of the Touhy gang. Several times his relations with known criminals had brought him to the attention of the church, but in each instance he was able to talk his way out of trouble by assuring superiors that his dealings with disreputable figures were strictly of a spiritual nature. Critics alleged he was partial to Irish whisky and the only spirits involved were the ninety-proof variety that gangsters passed to him.

Entering Wilmette, Chase with Helen in the back seat endeavoring to comfort her badly wounded husband drove to 1155 Mohawk Road, the home of Father Coughlan's sister. Father Coughlan was there, and although Helen and Chase pleaded with him to provide a refuge for Nelson, the priest refused. It was his sister's home, he protested, adding that her eight-year-old son was present and that his sister was preparing for a bridge meeting there later in the evening.

Father Coughlan did consent to lead them to a safer location, although he would say later that he had no specific place in mind. His immediate objective was to get them away from his sister's home. With that in mind, he helped Helen and Chase maneuver Nelson back into the Hudson. They put Nelson in the passenger's seat; Helen got in back, and Chase slid behind the wheel.

Father Coughlan then went to his own car, a Ford coupe, and backed it out into the street. He drove north on Ashland Avenue while the Hudson with its three occupants trailed behind him. After a few blocks, Chase suddenly made a U-turn and accelerated the Hudson so fast the good Father couldn't keep up.

Chase, Helen, and perhaps even Nelson believed Coughlan was leading them into a trap, so they decided to ditch him. On Sixteenth Street, a very weakened Nelson told Chase to drive down an alley. Chase did that and soon reached a red two-car garage in front of a gray stucco cottage.

"A friend in there might help us," Nelson whispered. "Ask him to come out."

Chase knocked on the door, and a tall man in his late thirties answered. The man agreed to follow Chase back to the Hudson, and when the man saw the bleeding Nelson inside it, he said, "Why, it's Jimmy."

The two men with Helen following, carried Nelson into the cottage. Once inside, they put him in bed, and Helen did all she could to stop the bleeding and make him comfortable. She cut the bloody clothing away from his body, stuffed cotton into the bullet hole in his stomach and the gaping wound exit wound in his back, then covered both wounds by wrapping his waist with a long strip of cloth torn from the bed sheet.

Nelson muttered that his pain was easing and that he was feeling numb. Helen could only clench his hand and wait for the end.

On November 27, 1934, at 7:30 P.M., Lester Joseph Gillis, better known as Baby Face Nelson, a vicious, strutting psychotic who killed without a conscience, died in bed with his wife sitting beside him.

Tabloids and Hollywood glorified his misdeeds, but responsible authorities reported that he and another cop-killer, Clyde Barrow, during their careers had slain more than 50 police officers.[13]

Chapter 6. Buck and Blanche Barrow

One of the greatest disasters ever to strike the United States occurred in September of 1900 when a hurricane with winds estimated at more than 145 miles per hour made landfall in the city of Galveston, Texas. Coming in years well before accurate weather forecasting and well in advance of more modern hurricane protection, the storm exacted a toll of human lives usually given as 8,000. It would take years before Texas could recoup losses from the tragedy.

And as the century opened, there were other happenings. The year of 1901 saw William McKinley inaugurated on March 4 as the nation's 25th President and to have him assassinated six months later by an anarchist named Leon Czolgosc. The first Memorial Day was celebrated on May 30; the first auto license plate in the country was issued in New York for a fee of $1.00, and in the same state a man was arrested for playing golf on Sunday. In Texas discovery of oil beneath the state's barren, worthless topsoil would touch off unimaginable changes, and from faraway Paris, France, came a report of an added dimension to crime: robbers had used a "getaway car" in carrying out a daring holdup.

With such happenings, one should not be surprised to learn that the birth of a baby to a couple eking out a hardscrabble existence as tenants in an area known as Jones Prairie, 13 miles north of Abilene, Texas, was of interest only to family members.

During the Civil War and thereafter, branches of Barrow families lived in parts of northern Florida and southern Alabama. Some were wealthy, and others lived on the poverty line. Henry Barrow's parents were among the latter, and when he was eleven years old, his parents drifted west, getting all the way into Texas.

In the vicinity of Nacogdoches, Henry met Cumie Walker, who pronounced her name "Keemie." Although only teenagers, the two fell in love and married in December, 1891. They both were on the young side—Henry eighteen and Cumie sixteen—but marrying at such ages was not at all uncommon among tenants. The newlyweds set themselves up by renting the farm next door to Cumie's parents. For Henry, leasing a farm which he himself could work was a big step up from being a day laborer. Yet the couple's living patterns did not change much; they still chopped cotton, cut firewood, and hauled water in buckets from nearby creeks. For the next decade and a half, what did change were the farms they worked and the number of mouths to feed.

Henry and Cumie Barrow had seven children—four boys and three girls. Each of the sons was given a nickname. Elden, the oldest, became "Jack." Next came Marvin, soon to be called "Buck." Next in line was Clyde, who as a youngster the family called "Bud" because he was so friendly with his brothers and chums. The fourth boy was named only by the initials "LC," but was given the nickname "Flop" because after a close haircut his ears seemed oversized.

In 1910, when the census was taken, in addition to their own children Henry and Cumie had a 17-year-old cousin living with them. For the couple, every year was a gamble. Would the price for their shares of cotton grown on their leased land be enough to cover costs of labor and tools? Would the landlord renew their lease or would he decide to put cattle on the land next year? Would their tenancy no longer be necessary? Would the next baby be a boy or girl?

In that year of 1910, Henry and Cumie's first boy, Elvin Wilson Barrow, was 16 and pulling his own weight. Their second son, Marvin Ivan Barrow, born March 12, 1903, was only seven and too small to do anything but eat, sleep, and get into mischief. It would be 1909 before his brother Clyde would enter this world.

At the age of eight or nine, Marvin quit going to school, hunted jack rabbits and cottontails, or hung around with boys his age or slightly older. By the time he was ten, everyone was calling him "Buck," and he was dodging whatever work or chores his dad tried to assign. Neither parent could discipline him. He was fast—could run like a deer—and would sneak off into the woods or meet chums in a nearby hamlet. Guns fascinated him, and he liked playing cops and robbers with his brother Clyde. There were always plenty of imaginary Indians or outlaws hiding in the hinterlands, and he didn't object to Clyde being in charge.

In 1925 or 1926, Henry and Cumie Barrow gave up the farm and with only two of their five children still at home, moved to Dallas. Buck had left the family and was running with a gang that helped make up the petty-criminal underworld in West Dallas. His parents thought he was working for his older brother in Dallas, repairing and repainting automobiles. In reality, he was living by thievery, minor gambling, and betting on boxing matches, dog or cockfights.

As a teen-ager, he had gotten addicted to cockfights; he liked nothing so much as watching two birds battle it out until one was killed. He was not alone in the addiction, for men of all ages would gather to watch the contestants and to bet on a winner. A Texas newspaper once reported a fight:

> The younger cock gained the ascendancy, several feet above the ground, and administered a lick that sent a thin trickle of blood down the side of the old cock's head, without, however, seriously wounding him. As they struck the ground they whirled almost simultaneously, the old cock going over the other this time, but in a lower flight. The young cock rushed the battle to close quarters and the two became a ball of rolling, kicking feathers and clicking, flashing steel. The old cock gave out a steady, dangerous shuffle when not fought off his feet, but the younger cock shuffled equally well on his feet or off, on his side or on his back; although his steel was flying, frequently cutting.[1]

Buck had a pit bulldog trained for fights, and the dog once tore off the back of his sister's dress. Marie, the sister, barely school age when her parents had moved to the Dallas campground, recalled watching Buck put spurs on gamecocks before a fight:

> Buck did fight them chickens, you know. . . Cockfighting. I remember him putting them spurs on them. And he had an old pit bulldog he used to fight. Mama made him get rid of it. It tore out the whole seat of my dress when I was playing ball. [2]

Cockfighting was illegal in Texas, but that merely added to its attraction. The word would spread that a match was going to be held, and ten, fifteen, perhaps twenty cars and a few horse-drawn wagons would show up on a farm. Birds from as far away as St. Louis or Mexico would be in cages in the back ends of pick-ups; their necks stretch out; beady eyes looking for a fight, while their owners were working the crowd for wagers.

There wasn't much else going on for the tenant farmers, and a jug or two of Texas moonshine was part of the show. And there was money involved, sometimes bets of a $100 with rumors of $1,000 on the really big matches.

Buck Barrow, a teen-ager, wasn't into that kind of money yet; for him a take of ten dollars was cause for celebration; more was a true bonanza. For a time he tried raising his own gamecocks, but that was too limited. Neighbors a few miles down the way had more promising birds in their coops, and he found it easy to steal chickens.

After Buck's parents had left their leased farm and moved to West Dallas, he met and married; his bride was Pearl Churchley. A daughter was born a year later, but the marriage didn't last. Buck and Pearl divorced, and Pearl dropped out of Buck's life.

Buck had begun working in different repair shops in the Dallas area, meanwhile stealing auto parts or tires before reselling them. He had a number of brushes with the law; in December 1925, he was arrested in Houston for stealing tires. He gave his name as "Elmer Toms." He was suspected of auto theft in several other Texas cities, including Dallas, Waco, Uvalde, and Waxahachie, but most of these charges were dropped. In late 1928, he was picked up for auto theft in San Antonio. Again, a generous judge gave him probation rather than a prison sentence. The next year, he met 19-year-old Blanche Caldwell, destined to play a large role in his life.

Blanche was born on New Year's Day, 1911, in Garvin, Oklahoma, a hamlet in the southeastern part of the state. Her parents, Hugo and Idabel Caldwell were a farming couple with Hugo also serving as a lay preacher. When her parents separated, Blanche was supported by Hugo, who she later said "spoiled her," but it was her mother who continued to rule her life.

Blanche's mother led her own speckled career, married four or five times and living with other men, merely adopting their last name. When Blanche was sixteen, the mother forced her to marry John Callaway, one of her own acquaintances. Most likely, the mother thought Callaway had considerable money, some of which would benefit her if she could offer her daughter in the deal.

Autumn of 1929 was a period of troubles for America. Industrial production fell; work forces were reduced, and unemployment rose. The stock market, which had reached dizzying heights in the mid-1920s, bounced up and down. Between the first of September, 1929, and Armistice Day the market plunged 48 per cent, and the worst was yet to come.

Blanche endured her marriage for more than a year and then ran away into West Dallas, at the time a poor, unincorporated neighborhood across the Trinity River from the main city. She lived with a friend, and one day, which she later testified was Armistice Day, November 11, 1929, she met a man who struck up a conversation. He introduced himself as Marvin Barrow and said his friends called him "Buck."

He was not a big man; at five feet four inches tall somewhat smaller than average, but there was nothing of the schoolboy about him. With his ruddy complexion, an engaging smile, and jaunty banter, Blanche was smitten. Their friendship was immediate and within days, it had swelled into affection.[3] A day or two after they first met, Buck had taken Blanche home to meet his mother Cumie. Cumie and the young girl liked each other, and not long after the marriage, Blanche moved into Cumie's household to stay there while she looked for a job.

In the late fall of 1929 following a burglary in Denton, Texas, Buck was arrested and sentenced to four years in the Texas State Penitentiary. He asked Blanche to write him often, which she did. He walked away from the Ferguson prison farm the following March and returned to Dallas, where he resumed his relationship with Blanche. A year later the divorce from her first husband was finalized, and she and Buck married on July 3, 1931.

Two weeks after meeting Blanche Caldwell, Buck Barrow together with his brother Clyde broke into a filling station in Denton, Texas. It was late October, 1929, and the New York Stock Market crashed, presaging a desperate period for the entire nation; over the next three weeks stocks representing more than $35 billion in shareholder equity—money enough to float a hemisphere of nations—lost 40% of their value.

At the end of November, 1929, Buck and Clyde stole a Buick and drove north to Dallas. Passing through the village of Henrietta, the two broke into a house to steal whatever they could find, but the haul was disappointing. They swiped a Ford and drove it back toward West Dallas but first went through Denton, a town larger than Henrietta. In Denton they saw the Motor Mark Garage, which looked undefended and promising. They broke into it and found a small safe which they were unable to open. So they carried it outside and stashed it in the stolen Ford, which Clyde smashed into a curb when the police gave chase. The cops came up shooting, and Buck was hit and captured. Clyde took off running and hid under the porch of a nearby house, remaining there until police gave up the hunt. The next day he hitch-hiked back to West Dallas, thinking his brother had been killed.[4]

In the encounter at Denton, Buck was wounded, shot through both legs. He was arrested, and by the end of the year was convicted of burglary and sentenced to prison. On January 14, 1930, he was transported to the main Texas State Penitentiary at Huntsville, Texas, to begin his five-year sentence.

From Huntsville, perhaps in a letter penned by someone else, Buck wrote his mother saying that he was in the hospital and that his wounded legs still hurt. According to Cumie, Buck was almost illiterate; he learned to write his name but could hardly read or write more.

He professed that he had learned his lesson and that he dreaded his prison term but would make it. Then he added, "Mother, try to get me a furlough and don't fail to write often. Don't forget to tell Blanche to write me and tell me all the news of the outside world."[5]

Blanche wrote often, telling him she was living with his mother, sharing daily experiences, and occasionally relating news events; each letter grew more intimate. Buck's prison behavior was good enough that in the spring of 1930 he was made a trusty and sent to the Ferguson prison farm near Midway, Texas about fifty miles southwest of Eastham.

Assigned to work in the kitchen at Ferguson, one day in March of 1930, he simply walked away. He went back to Dallas where he knew Blanche was with his mother, and aware that police would soon come there searching for him, he put Blanche in a stolen car and drove to an uncle's farm just outside Martinsville, Texas.

Buck and Blanche made Uncle Jim Muckleroy's farm their hideout for a few months until the heat wore off. At first they were happy just to be together. Blanche wanted a home of their own, where they could live a normal life, tend a little garden and raise a couple of children. She began to chafe as she thought more about their future—always on the lam one step ahead of the law and fearing police might at any time apprehend her husband. Buck already had served most of his sentence; if he would give himself up, he'd only serve a few more months and then he'd be let out and they'd be free afterwards.

She told Cumie of her dreams, and the two of them began pressuring Buck to surrender. He finally agreed, and on December 27, 1931, accompanied by Blanche, Cumie, and her little daughter Marie, he showed himself to the warden at the Huntsville prison. Buck served the remaining months of his term until March 1933, when he was given a pardon by Texas Governor Ma Ferguson. He and Blanche were re-united the night of the day he was released.

CHAPTER 7. CLYDE BARROW AND BONNIE PARKER

In 1909, the year in which Clyde Barrow was born, Henry Ford brought out his Model T Ford. The "new-fangled" contraption was a huge marketing success, with sales of more than 11,000 at a cost of $825 per car. Ford stepped up production and sales soared each year. With more cars available, auto thefts increased with many of them committed by young men.

In 1925, sixteen-year-old Clyde quit going to school, but that wasn't unusual. In the mid-twenties, across America only about 40% of all students ever went beyond the eighth grade. He found a dollar-a-day job with the Brown Cracker and Candy Company in Dallas. The wage was too low to provide him with the clothes and life style he wanted, and he switched first to a job with Procter and Gamble and then one with the United Glass Company. He was a dependable enough worker and never fired, but none of the jobs gave him enough income for things he had in mind.

Some of his pals held similar jobs but were living better because they were slipping a bit outside the law—distracting a shop clerk while an ally swiped some desirable merchandise or stealing a woman's purse usually enriching their own but sometimes doing it just for the hell of it. Clyde didn't give up his day job, but he started dipping his toe into shallow criminal waters. In his mid-twenty age, he would steal a car, drive it across into Oklahoma and sell it there to a fence who would paint it and market it as slightly used. A car in good condition might bring Clyde a profit as much as $100—more than he made in a month at his ordinary jobs. No wonder he started living higher.

His only problem was that Dallas police had become suspicious and were watching him. He thought it would be wiser to conduct his misdemeanors somewhere away from Dallas; Denton to the north and Waco to the south were prime locations.

In 1926 he rented a car and to save a few bucks didn't tell the agency he meant to drive it out of town. He drove from Dallas to East Texas to visit a girlfriend, and when the agency sent lawmen to recover their car, he hid in an attic. The agency got its car back but filed a complaint, so when Clyde returned to Dallas he was arrested. The rental agency chose not to press charges and Clyde was released, but his brush with the law was the start of his official criminal record.

Clyde Barrow met Bonnie Parker within a week or two after his brother Buck had been sentenced for the Denton escapade. The meeting occurred when Clyde went to the home of Clarence Day, who lived near the Barrow family.[1]

Clay had a daughter whom Clyde knew slightly. She had been injured in a traffic accident, and on the day Clyde made his visit one of her girlfriends also had come to see her. The visitor was about Clyde's age and very pretty, just under five feet tall. She had a stylish arrangement of reddish-blond hair accented by the deep blue of her eyes. She seemed to like Clyde's quips, swivelled her hips a bit in moving around the room, and thrilled Clyde when she rolled bedroom blue eyes at him.

The flirt Clyde met that day was Bonnie Parker, a pert, sassy, 20-year-old, born on October 1, 1910, the daughter of Charles and Emma Parker. Charles was a brick mason, and in the opinion of his wife his vocation placed the family at the top of the social ladder in Rowena, a little town in West Texas. Most men in the community were farmers—sodbusters whose yearly income depended upon whether enough rain fell to coax a cotton crop out of the dry soil.

Bonnie was the couple's second child, the first being a boy the parents named Hubert, and there would be a sister, Billie Jean, who arrived three years after Bonnie. Dutifully proud of her children, Emma gushed over Bonnie as "a beautiful baby, with cotton colored curls, the bluest eyes you ever saw, and an impudent little red mouth."

Bonnie had just passed her fourth birthday when her father died unexpectedly. There is no record of the cause of his death, but Emma suddenly was a widow with three small children. With almost no chance for her to support them in Rowena, she packed up the three and moved 240 miles east to live in Cement City, a settlement across the Trinity River from Dallas. Emma's parents, Frank and Mary Krause, lived there, and although as hard up as everyone around them, they didn't hesitate to take in their daughter and grandchildren.

Cement City was a dirty, boisterous place, twenty miles from the Trinity River and downtown Dallas; most adult residents in Cement City worked at a menial job either in Big D or in one of the nearby foundries. Emma Parker was able to find work sewing clothes, particularly overalls, and with considerable help from her parents managed to eke out an existence for herself and her three children.

When Emma was at work, Grandma Krause cared for the children along with another grandchild—Bess, a cousin to Bonnie and three years older. Bonnie was a mischievous little girl according to her mother and kept the household "generally in a stew from morning to night." The trait continued when she started school where she eagerly participated in play acting, usually being featured in dramas, readings, pageants, or other presentations. Undeniably she was cute and bright but also liable to do almost anything that might mark her apart and above others.

Everyone thought she had a temper; her mother said she was ready to slug it out with boys as well as other girls over stolen pencils or perceived snubs. Neat and pretty, Bonnie attracted boys and learned early to encourage their attention. She liked valentines or gifts of gum, candy or trinkets and always wanted to be some boy's girlfriend. It was not surprising that several young teens developed crushes on her.

As an early teenager, she was obsessed with clothes and cosmetics as she and her friends tried to look like the glamorous stars they saw on the screen. At about the age of fifteen, a heavily-made up Bonnie scraped enough money to pose for a "glamour shot," with her head tilted slightly and eyes gazing dreamily off-camera. If Bonnie had a problem, that was it; she lived in a dream world—one that would take her to Broadway, Hollywood, Europe, only God knew where, but wherever it was she would bask in plaudits from admirers.

She was a sophomore in high school when her fantasies changed. She met Roy Thornton, a big, good-looking athlete, with money to spend, and a lot of fun. Smitten by the idea of love as shown by Hollywood productions or described in *True Magazine*, Bonnie fell hard. She saw no faults in her lover and had two red hearts pierced by an arrow and the names "Bonnie" and "Roy" tattooed on her right hip. She overrode her mother's objections and couldn't wait for marriage. A wedding was not unusual for a girl of high school age, and on September 25, 1926, just a few weeks before her sixteenth birthday, Bonnie Parker became Mrs. Roy Thornton.

The marriage started slipping downhill almost immediately. As a husband, Roy was less attentive than he had been as a suitor, and Bonnie's temper, controlled during their courtship, flared with the slightest provocation. Nothing like that happened in movie versions! Also, Roy drank more heavily, and when Bonnie scolded him, he hit her. He left her for a couple of days but came back. In six months, he took off again, this time staying away for nearly three weeks. Bonnie had reasons to suspect he was shacking up with another girl.

Bonnie started looking for a job and in December found one waiting tables in a Dallas cafe. The salary was meager, but her looks and outgoing personality were assets that helped bring in larger tips. She dressed well and had plenty of male friends. If some of her wardrobe came from occasional prostitution, she wasn't doing anything out of the ordinary for working class women coming from the Dallas slums.

In 1929, Roy tried to rejoin her, but she told him they were through and meant it. She had freedom, her own income, and plenty of other men. They didn't divorce, and a month or two later, Roy was picked up for robbery and sentenced to five years in prison. She never saw him again, but neither did she divorce him, saying it wasn't right to kick a man when he was down.[2]

Bonnie must have liked what she saw upon meeting Clyde. He wasn't as tall or as good-looking as Roy, but he dressed well and his attention was obvious. When he asked for a date the next night, she agreed, and after that evening they began seeing each other regularly. Clyde found her bright and refreshing, making jokes about everything including herself, and she never asked where he got the money to spend on her, nor did she question his past. She might have suspected he stole it, but what the hell? He drove a fancy car and had plenty of money. She was on the loose, and there wasn't much in the life of a waitress anyway.

The attraction was mutual, for Clyde was small, and Bonnie fitted into his arms just right when they cuddled. In restaurants or bars she clung adoringly to him which bolstered his self image. It was clear to him, she was as determined as he to rise out of the poverty into which each had been born. By the end of the month Clyde and Bonnie were a duo, and friends rarely saw one without the other.

Their idyllic arrangement ended in the second week of February, 1930, when police knocked on the door of Bonnie's house and entered to arrest her lover. Although police got nothing from Buck concerning Clyde's participation in the Denton robbery, two other accomplices, Bill Turner and Pat Brewley, sang like canaries. The two of them confessed to more than thirty crimes, and in spilling such beans named Clyde as a frequent participant. Police arrested him and sent him to the McLennan County jail in Waco.

Bonnie wrote Clyde frequently while he was jailed at Waco, wording her letters in ways to assure him of her affection but also to whet his jealously by mentioning other young men paying her attention. Then she moved to Waco, and she and her cousin Mary visited Clyde often, bringing him cigarettes and other treats while promising him she would stick around until he got out.

William Turner also was a prisoner in the Waco jail, and he managed to tell Clyde that he had stashed a gun in his mother's Waco home. Clyde drew a map of the premises, gave it to Bonnie, and through her own cleverness she gained access to the Turner home.

The city's newspaper reported a burglary at the Turners:

> A burglary was committed Saturday night at the home of William Turner, while William was in jail waiting life sentences on burglary and theft charges. The intruder ransacked the Turner home, at 625 Turner Avenue in East Waco, while Mrs. L. Turner, William's mother and the rest of the household were at work. When they returned at 10:30 P.M., they found beds torn up, boxes emptied, and the house generally upset, but only a .38 cal. Colt revolver was missing. [3]

Bonnie found the gun, took it home, and schemed to get it to Clyde. Two days later, she donned extra clothes, strapped it inside her enlarged waistline, and early one evening after a guard permitted her to enter the jail slipped the .38 pistol to Clyde.

In planning for their break, Clyde and Turner decided they needed a third man, and they talked Emery Abernathy, also jailed on charges of burglary and bank robbing, into joining them. The trio was locked in adjacent cells on the jail's second floor, and in the evening chosen for their escapade, Turner called down to the guard below that he was sick. When the officer came up to investigate, Abernathy was waiting with the smuggled gun in his hand and immediately trained it on the guard, allowing Clyde to seize the gun from the belt of the helpless victim. Barrow, Turner, and Abernathy took the guard's gun, locked him in the cell, and rushed downstairs only to be confronted by another cop working at a desk.

Huse Jones, the desk cop, still had his weapon and came out the door in time to see the prisoners running down the street. He got off a couple of quick shots at them, but all of them missed. Within blocks of the jail, Barrow hot-wired a car, and the escaping trio hopped in. Driving only a short distance, they stopped to steal a better vehicle. They did this a couple of times, enabling them to get well west while police for the next twelve hours were on the lookout for three men driving the first car used in the escape. [4]

Barrow, Turner, and Abernathy sped west from Waco before driving out of the state north across the Panhandle of Oklahoma and into Kansas, stealing cars as they went. They wanted to get as far away from Texas as possible. By the third week in March, 1930, they were in Middletown, Ohio, a medium-sized city halfway between Dayton and Cincinnati.

Their funds were almost gone, so they had to find money somewhere. The local train depot looked like an easy pick, and on the afternoon of March 17, Barrow wandered into the station to case it. His actions aroused the ticket agent's suspicion, and as soon as Clyde left, the agent took down the license number of the car he got into with two other men already in it. That night the three bandits broke into the depot first, but their take from there was disappointingly low, a mere $60, so they burglarized a nearby dry cleaning shop.

The two robberies put local police hot on their trail, and in attempting to get out of town the next morning, the bandits got lost. The local police nabbed them. Barrow first tried to give his name as Robert Thomas, but the ruse was exposed when both Turner and Abernathy confessed to being Texas felons on the lam. That information was buzzed back to the Lone Star State, and very quickly telegrams from Waco identifying all three as the escapees. Four days later, authorities from Waco arrived in Middleton to take the captives back to Texas for trial.

Clyde and Turner were tried first, Abernathy a week later. All were convicted along with a lecture from the presiding judge, who admonished,

> I think it would be a good thing to save you boys from the electric chair eventually to send you up for long terms. You are liable to go around here shooting a peace officer—if you can shoot straight. You keep breaking into houses, and one of these days you're either going to get shot or shoot somebody else. With the records you've got, you'd probably get the chair when you were tried. [5]

Turner was extradited to Kansas where he would serve three-years before being shipped back to Texas to begin the forty-year sentence the Waco judge gave him. Abernathy in a subsequent trial was tried and also convicted. Clyde was sent to Huntsville, but during that spring and all of the summer of 1930 he was volleyed back and forth across the state to face various charges. One was a murder case in Houston, but the charge was specious and the grand jury there found the evidence insufficient for a conviction.

CHAPTER 8. CLYDE'S RAP SHEET

On the morning of September 18, 1930, Bud Russell was in Waco, Texas, to pick up two convicts. Russell was guard and driver of what Texans called the One-Way-Wagon—a transport used to take convicted felons from rural and city lock-ups to state prison facilities. Russell already had several prisoners in his Wagon and had orders to pick up two more in Waco, including Clyde Barrow, a convict who had escaped six months earlier from the jail at Huntsville after his girlfriend Bonnie Parker had smuggled a gun to him. Returned to Huntsville, Clyde first was put among prisoners ordered to work inside the main prison unit; assignment there was the usual practice for the first time offenders. The most callous, dangerous criminals were sent to the prison's Eastham cotton farm thirty-five miles northeast. On the 13,000 acres of swamp land there, they performed backbreaking labor under a broiling sun and heartless guards.

Short, scrawny Clyde Barrow had just turned twenty. His height was 5 ft. 5 and 1/2 inches, and he weighed 127 lbs. There is no record of misbehavior while imprisoned at Huntsville, and no one knows what happened, but in the middle of September 1930, Clyde got the bad news; he was to be transferred to Eastham.

Bud Russell had hardly driven the Wagon out of Huntsville before Clyde began quizzing fellow passengers about Eastham. They told him facilities there were terrible. The prison was overcrowded; the food inedible; the work relentless, and armed guards frequently tortured, maimed, or killed inmates.

In the Wagon, sitting next to Clyde was 19-year-old Ralph Fults, an escapee from Eastham just six months earlier, who recited distressing facts from his own experience. "The Eastham guards," he said, "are real bastards, and they kill their charges for two reasons—not working or running away. The Eastham graveyard is full of guys who thought otherwise."[1]

The two prisoners talked further as Fults shared more information about Eastham:

> Well, it sure ain't no damned picnic. There's two things they'll just flat out kill you for—not working, and running. You run once, they'll just rough you up a little. You run again, they take you over some hill and put a slug in the back of your head. "Attempted escape," they call it. [2]

Born in 1911, Fults was about the same age as Clyde and was also a native Texan. Fults had started his criminal career early, arrested first at the age of fourteen when police discovered he was carrying a suitcase full of stolen goods. Jailed, he managed to fashion a key out of a tobacco tin, and with that improvisation unlocked his own cell as well as others around it, thus precipitating a mass jailbreak.

Recaptured within weeks, he had been sent to the Boys' Reformatory at Gatesville, Texas, fleeing from there in April, 1927. Two years after that escapade he was nabbed for burglary of a grocery store in Greenville and sent to the main prison at Huntsville first, then assigned to work on the cotton farm at Eastham.

When Cumie, Clyde's mother, learned he was being sent to Eastham, she began badgering the Texas governor to grant him a pardon or parole because of his youth. Her appeals were unsuccessful, and Clyde was at Eastham when he learned that his brother Buck had walked away from the Ferguson Prison Farm. Scuttlebutt also let him know that his mother and Blanche, Buck's wife, were pressuring him to give himself up. If he did that, most likely he would be given light duty at Huntsville.

Clyde himself was very lonely at Eastham. He had few outside contacts, and he longed to see Buck, so he began plotting to get himself transferred back to Huntsville. The only way he could think of to do that was some sort of hospitalization.

Prisoners called the Eastham Farm the "Bloody Ham" because of the number of self mutilations. The best chance an inmate had of getting away from Eastham was to cut off a couple of fingers or toes. If a prisoner couldn't do it himself, he could ask a confidant to swing an axe or hoe. Amputations had to be complete; if the digits were only deeply cut, they were bandaged and the convict was sent back into the fields as an object lesson.

Clyde made his decision, and at the end of January, 1932, he was admitted to the main hospital at Huntsville because his left big toe and the one next to it had been cut off by an axe. Most accounts of Clyde Barrow's life allege that he arranged this injury in order to escape the drudgery and harshness at Eastham; however, he told Ralph Fults he did so in order to see his brother. [3]

The next month in Huntsville Prison and trying to learn to walk again, Clyde got the news that Texas Governor Ross Sterling had granted him parole. His mother's incessant pleading had brought results. He hobbled home on crutches, and told Cumie and the waiting Bonnie that Eastham had been a "burning hell." He vowed he'd die before letting himself be taken there again.

He also told his parents he wanted to go straight; perhaps open a small automotive parts and repair shop on the small lot next to the service station they were running. Neither he nor they had enough capital for such an enterprise, so he'd have to find work and save up his salary. He could hardly have chosen a worse time to be out of a job.

Federal, state, and local economies in 1932 were at their lowest point. Conditions were particularly bad in the South and Southwest. Cotton prices had dropped to four cents per pound; the wheat crop had set a record harvest, but each bushel sold for only twenty-five cents—about half of what it cost a farmer to grow it. Adding more misery to the failed economy, a series of dust storms—"black blizzards with an edge like steel wool"—swept across Kansas, Oklahoma, and Texas.

The land around Dallas was so flat, it was possible to see the storms coming from the west. Being caught outside was dangerous, and even inside it was not possible to escape the onslaught. Wind whistled dirt through seams around doors and windows, which Cumie wet down with blankets, but the floors were soon covered with grime.

Ralph Fults, Clyde's pal at Eastham, had been released earlier and had gone to McKinney in northwest Texas. Out of jail and in McKinney, he supported himself by gambling and small thefts, and when he read a newspaper article saying Clyde had been paroled, he hopped a train for Dallas. In the Eastham cotton fields, he and Clyde had swapped ideas about getting even someday on the brutal guards watching them; now both were free, and in Dallas they talked again about getting their revenge.

They were together in bitterness and determination to get back at Eastham officials who had allowed both to suffer physical abuse from guards or rape from other bigger and stronger prisoners, but they needed more help and money. The "Barrow Gang," destined to gain later notoriety, began forming.

Raymond Hamilton was one of the early additions. Details of his childhood are sketchy although it is known that he was born in Oklahoma and raised in Dallas. He was eighteen years old and in jail at McKinney when Ralph Fults helped him escape. Hamilton knew both Fults and Barrow casually, and in January, 1932, Fults posing as a visitor smuggled hacksaw blades concealed in magazines to Hamilton in the McKinney jail. Throughout much of the night, Hamilton played his cell radio as loud as possible to drown the sounds of sawing, and the next morning when the jailer made his rounds, a prisoner several cells down from Raymond's complained he was sick. While the jailer checked that inmate, Hamilton crawled through the small window in his own cell and walked down the hallway leading out of the jail.

Clyde had been out of Eastham less than a month when he got word Hamilton wanted to see him. Barrow and Fults got together with Hamilton, and a month later the trio attempted their first robbery—the Simms Oil Refinery just a few blocks from the service station run by Henry and Cumie Barrow. The escapade was an abject failure; guards were around, and the would-be thieves bolted. Clyde had encouraged and planned the scheme, and Hamilton, already more hardened, blamed Clyde for its failure. After the fiasco, Hamilton wanted to focus on auto thefts.

Clyde and Fults disagreed; they were anxious to get even for what both had suffered at Eastham, but to do that they would need a larger gang and more firepower. The only weapons they had were two or three cheap Saturday night specials and a couple of shotguns, but guns could be purchased easily if one had the money to pay for them. Even a Thompson machine gun—the Tommy gun—could be bought by mail and with no background checks. The three ruffians also wanted bullet proof vests and a supply of ammunition.

Following the failure at the Simms Refinery, Barrow and Fults decided to lay low until the heat wore off, and Hamilton went back to Bay City, Michigan, to live with his father. Bonnie Parker was in jail at Kaufmann having been arrested in February, 1932, when she was with Barrow and Fults in a shootout with local police. In that affray, Barrow was able to get away, but Fults was wounded and Bonnie was captured.

In West Dallas and without his brain trust, Clyde decided to undertake another caper. Without Fults and Bonnie, he wanted an easy heist. He learned of a jewelry and pawnshop business run by a man named C. N. Bucher. The store was in Hillsboro, a sleepy town in north central Texas, and Bucher was a 62-year-old man. It ought to be a piece of cake. Clyde teamed up with another thief named Bud Russell and plotted the robbery for April 30th.

Shortly before midnight, Barrow and Russell with a third accomplice came into Hillsboro and drove up to park in front of Bucher's pawnshop. Clyde remained in the car when the other two men got out and knocked on the door of the establishment, which also served as Bucher's home. Roused from within, Bucher came down the stairs, turned on the lights, and let the two men into the store.

The two said they wanted to buy guitar strings, and one of them pulled out a $10 bill and asked for change. Bucher said he'd have to call his wife to open the safe, but he had grown suspicious, and as she came down the stairs he tried to sneak out a gun from under his housecoat. One of the bandits was too quick, however, and shot him through the heart. As Mrs. Bucher crouched over her dying husband, Russell grabbed $40, and the two thieves raced out the door to climb in the car alongside Clyde. He floored the pedal, and the three sped away. The robbery and slaying of one of Hillsboro's prominent citizens made headlines, and after mug shots showed Barrow and Fults together, both were suspected. Clyde now was a wanted killer with blood on his hands.[4]

He retreated into the remote Mountain Creek bottoms south of Dallas where Raymond Hamilton joined him. The two lived a hand-to-mouth existence until Bonnie Parker released from the Kaufman jail with a no-bill record came to be reunited with her lover. Toward the end of June, 1932, the three of them were ready to leave. They went to Wichita Falls, where they rented a cottage and lived a normal life for about three weeks.

By that time, they had run out of money, and in the middle of July, Clyde and Raymond robbed a bookkeeper at the Ice Company in Palestine, Texas, and got away with nearly $1000. Flushed by success in that caper, two weeks later Clyde and Raymond, this time joined by Bonnie who drove and awaited them in the getaway car, strode into the First State Bank in Willis, Texas. Waving pistols into the faces of everyone inside, Clyde demanded that all moneys be placed in a sack. Then every employee and bystander was herded into the bank vault, which the robbers locked before rushing outside with their loot. Barrow, Hamilton, and Parker would be miles away before local citizens could free persons locked in the vault. The tactic would become the Barrow Gang's trademark.

For the next year, Clyde and Hamilton continued in their depredations mainly in Texas and Oklahoma. Bonnie was a regular accomplice, sitting in a car outside the bank or grocery while the two thieves now joined by a young boy named W. D. Jones committed the robbery.

William Daniel Jones, usually listed as W. D. Jones, was four or five years younger than Clyde and was a product of the same industrial slums in West Dallas as he. Jones was a friend of LC Barrow, the youngest son of Henry and Cumie. Cumie struck up a friendship with Tookie Jones, W. D.'s mother, and when Buck Barrow was on trial for auto theft in San Antonio, Tookie and her two young sons accompanied the Barrows and their two youngest children 300 miles to attend, traveling the miles by horse and wagon.

By the age of 15 or 16, W. D. was known to Dallas police. He hung around Henry Barrow's service station and swiped license plates that brothers of his pal LC Barrow could use on cars they stole.

During the Christmas season of 1932, Clyde and his girlfriend Bonnie came home to visit his parents, and when they left, W. D. went with them. Life around the slums of Dallas was too dull for 16-year-old Jones, and Clyde Barrow already was one of his outlaw idols.

Two weeks after Christmas, the trio of Barrow, Parker, and Jones stumbled into a Dallas trap set for another criminal. Barrow killed County Deputy Malcolm Davis by shooting him point-blank in the chest with a 16-gauge shotgun. Jones and Parker were sitting in the car when Clyde shot Davis, and they were identified as accessories to the crime.

After the murder of Davis, Barrow, Parker, and Jones lay low for a while. They traveled through the hills of Missouri and Arkansas, and may have gone as far east as Tennessee. Once during their travels, they dressed up as gangsters and photographed themselves. When the playful pictures were published—one showing Bonnie squinting at the camera, her foot on the bumper of the car, a pistol in her hand and a cigar in her mouth—notoriety for the Barrow Gang started its swell.

Mug shots of Clyde and Bonnie were posted in sheriffs' offices all over the Midwest as the two went joyriding, bank robbing, and killing their way through Texas, Arkansas, Oklahoma, and Missouri. An enforcement posse headed by a former Texas Ranger declared the Barrow Gang was Public Enemy Number One. Yet Clyde and Bonnie made fools of cops in dozens of counties, kidnapping a lawman once and ordering him to pilfer a car battery to replace the weak one in their stolen roadster. Bonnie must have sensed their imminent death, for she dabbled in sentimental poetry, writing verses which some newspapers would publish after she and her lover were slain. In her poetry, she said she and Clyde were friends to all but snitches and stoolies. The bravado helped push her and Clyde toward heroic stature among people in the hinterlands. Lawmen tried to dampen such reputations by pointing out that the two were killers and thieves, but many citizens remembered that banks, too, had plundered life savings of upright families.

Hundreds of people saw bankers as privileged persons ensconced in fine buildings and government as a cold relative unwilling to help families in need. Maybe outlaws who attacked the money-grabbing pirates were not bad characters after all; sure they robbed banks, but everybody knew what bastards ran those places.

W. D. Jones was in the back seat of a stolen V-8 and Clyde and was driving through the southern portion of the Texas Panhandle, when just outside of Wellington, the road suddenly disappeared. A bridge had been washed out; the V-8 overturned and landed in the dry wash of the Salt Fork River. Clyde was thrown clear, but Jones and Bonnie were trapped in the car. As Clyde was attempting to pull the dazed Bonnie from the front seat he heard the gurgle of leaking fuel. Jones already had started collecting their weapons intending to hide them in nearby weeds, when a spark ignited the gasoline collecting inside the car. Clyde and Jones worked frantically to get Bonnie out before the flames reached her, but it was too late. Fire engulfed her right leg and was licking at her face before the two men managed to get her out of the flaming vehicle.

Clyde with the help of Jones carried the stricken Bonnie to a nearby farmhouse, the home of Mr. and Mrs. Tom Pritchard, and forced Mrs. Pritchard to give Bonnie rudimentary medical treatment. Mrs. Pritchard insisted Bonnie needed an ambulance and more expert medical care if she were to survive, and while her husband started going out of the room to call for more help, Jones in panic fired his shotgun at him. His blast missed Pritchard, but pellets struck his Good Samaritan wife in the hand.

Before the bandit trio could get away, two lawmen drove into the Pritchard farmyard. Clyde and Jones by this time were hiding in the hedges surrounding the home and were able to capture the lawmen whose hands they tied before ordering both into the Pritchard family car. Then carefully placing the badly injured Bonnie on the lap of one of the captives in the car's back seat, while Jones kept a pistol aimed at the officer's head, Clyde got behind the wheel and drove away from the Pritchard farm.

He drove for nearly three hours with Bonnie in constant and excruciating pain before they reached Erick, Oklahoma, where Buck and Blanche were waiting. Upon arriving there, Clyde stopped and ordered the two officers, hands still tied, to get out of the car. Buck wanted to kill both immediately and get the hell away, but Clyde wouldn't permit it. "No," he said, "I've been with them so long I'm beginning to like them."

He added that they had treated Bonnie pretty well, so after tying the two to a tree he and Jones managed to get her back into Buck's car, and with them in it his brother drove away.[5]

Buck and Clyde alternated as they drove across most of Oklahoma before holing up at Ft. Smith, Arkansas. There Clyde hired first a doctor and then a full time nurse to care for the badly burnt Bonnie. At first her prognosis was very bleak, but after her younger sister Billie came to nurse her, she began a slow recovery although she would never walk again without a limp. To buy groceries and meet the medical costs for Bonnie, Clyde, Buck, and Jones staged a few robberies in the Ft. Smith area. On June 23rd, they had just robbed the Brown grocery in Fayetteville and were coming back to Ft. Smith when Buck who was driving ran into a stalled automobile. The driver of this stalled car was irate as he strode toward Buck's car with a wrench in his hand.

At that moment, Alma City Marshall H. D. Humphrey and Deputy A. M. Salyers happened to be driving by. They stopped their car, got out, and Humphrey took one step toward Buck's car before he was blown into the ditch by a shotgun blast. Salyers got off a shot of his own before he retreated for the shelter of a farmhouse 200 feet away. The trio of Clyde, Buck, and

Jones were able to scramble into the car the two officers had left parked on the road, and in it they raced north without pursuit toward Fayetteville.

Three days later, on Monday, June 26, newspaper headlines announced the death of H. D. Humphrey. In Ft. Smith, Clyde gave Billie Parker a stack of bills in payment for the care she gave Bonnie; then piling Bonnie into another car he had stolen, he drove to Great Bend, Kansas. There he rented rooms at a tourist court, where Buck and Blanche could join him, Jones, and Bonnie as she continued her recovery.

While in Kansas, Clyde took one of his Browning automatic rifles and had its barrel and stock cut so short he could drive with the weapon in his lap. He practiced with that sawed-off rifle often and paid a construction worker to weld three of its 20-shot clips together, thus making it almost a submachine gun.[6]

CHAPTER 9. IOWA MAYHEM

Buck Barrow, having gotten his release from jail, was back with Blanche, and he talked with her about wanting to see Clyde, saying he felt a sense of responsibility for the way his little brother was turning out. If he could see Clyde, he might be able to convince him to give himself up as he had done—to get straight with the law. From Joplin, Buck contacted Clyde, saying they ought to get together.

Clyde obliged and within days showed up, but he was not alone. With him were his young girlfriend, Bonnie Parker, and a kid named W. D. Jones. The trio was being sought in connection with a variety of crimes ranging from auto theft to murder.

Despite his promise to Blanche that he meant to go straight, Buck brushed that aside when Clyde asked him to go along on several robberies in Missouri or in the nearby corner of Oklahoma. Among the forays was one on the Neosho Milling Company in Newton County. After that heist had been made, someone tipped police that a roadster like the one used in the robbery was parked in the Joplin garage rented by Buck and Blanche.

On April 13, 1933, in the apartment on 34th Street all seemed quiet enough. Blanche was playing solitaire, and Bonnie sat at a table working on a poem she was trying to write, called "Suicide Sal." Clyde and W. D. were tinkering with something in the garage. Buck was behind the house washing the Marmon sedan; he and Blanche intended to leave the next morning and head for Dallas.

None of them was aware that Newton County Constable Wes Harrington had gathered a squad consisting of himself, State Troopers G. B. Kahler and W. E. Grammer along with City Detectives Tim DeGraff and Harry McGinnis. The officers were about to pounce. Buck saw them approaching and shouted, "It's the law!"

Clyde and W. D. grabbed shotguns and opened fire. Constable Harrington was hit immediately and fell to the ground, mortally wounded. McGinnis managed to poke his weapon through the garage door and squeeze off a couple of shots before he, too, was struck by shotgun blasts. He fell and lapsed into unconsciousness from the pain and shock of his serious wounds; he died within the hour.

One of the bullets from the gun of Detective McGinnis hit W. D. Jones in the side, and he was clutching at the wound as Buck rushed past him going upstairs to check on Blanche and Bonnie.

Blanche, Clyde, and W. D. were able to open the garage doors as Buck and Bonnie climbed into the Ford V8, already gassed up and ready. Bullets were slamming into the walls of the garage; Buck was grazed slightly, and a ricocheting bullet lodged just under Clyde's skin, but neither brother was seriously hurt.

Clyde got behind the wheel and raced the V8 past the parked police vehicles. Outside the city limits, he headed west and drove to Amarillo, Texas, 450 miles away, stopping only once for gas and oil.

Back in Joplin, police were trying to put together what had happened. The apartment on 34th Street gave them a lot of information about the identities of the men who had slain Officers Harryman and McGinnis. Buck's Marmon sedan was still there as was the roadster used at the Neosho robbery. The biggest finds were inside the house, where police discovered Blanche's purse containing Buck's prison release papers signed by Governor Ferguson and a marriage license issued to Marvin I. Barrow and Blanche Caldwell.[1]

The escapees didn't remain in Texas long. They made excursions into New Mexico, Kansas, Nebraska, Iowa, and Illinois, coming back through Missouri, Arkansas, Oklahoma, and Louisiana. When their funds ran low, another store, filling station, or bank was robbed.

In May 1933, the fugitives were in Indiana, staying at Winona Lake just outside Warsaw when they decided to hit a bank in Lucerne. That attempt failed, and investigators surmised that two men must have entered the bank the night before and rested on top of the vault until morning when the cashier arrived to begin setting up cash drawers in preparation for the day's business. One newspaper reported on the morning raid: "Two women, one of them a blond armed with an automatic rifle, fired several volleys from a moving car as they and their cohorts fled."[2]

A week after the Lucerne incident and now lower on cash, the gang zeroed in on the First State Bank at Okabena, Minnesota—a small town nestled in the southwestern part of the state just across from the Iowa line.

The robbery went off as planned, yet the take was a mere $100—not much when split four or five ways.

From Minnesota, Buck, Blanche, Clyde and Bonnie went back to Dallas to spend two weeks before leaving to drive east through Louisiana, southern Mississippi, and Alabama into northern Florida. In that state they loafed around in Tallahassee and Jacksonville before driving north along the Atlantic coastline. For the two couples—Buck and Blanche and Clyde and Bonnie—it was a time to celebrate, get so drunk as to pass out on several occasions, and talk about their next big caper.

Back in the west, the two couples separated for a time. In 1933, Buck and Blanche were at Erick, Oklahoma. Buck had contacted Clyde then in Dallas, and in consequence on the night of June 10th, Clyde with Bonnie in the seat beside him and W. D. Jones in the back seat of a stolen sedan was driving north for an intended rendezvous. As their car approached Wellington, Clyde lost control, and the vehicle plunged over an embankment. A fire exploded immediately, and Bonnie was seriously burned—so seriously that even a long period of nursing and recovery failed to prevent a permanent limp.

To finance the high cost of Bonnie's medical treatments, Buck and W. D. Jones undertook a series of robberies in the Ft. Smith, Arkansas, area. On June 23, the pair had robbed a grocery store and were driving en route to Fayetteville. They were not far from Alma, Arkansas, when Buck, the driver, was unable to stop before ramming into a slow-moving vehicle ahead of him.

W. D. was momentarily stunned by being smashed against the dashboard, but he looked up in time to see the driver of the hit vehicle walking toward them—anger in his face and a rock in his hand. Buck kicked open the car's door and leveled a 16-gauge shotgun in the face of the man approaching them.

At the same time, Alma City Marshall H. D. Humphrey and Deputy A. M. Salyers were driving by, hoping to spot the bandits who had robbed the town's grocery store. Humphrey and Salyers got out of their car and with pistols in hands came toward the two disabled vehicles.

Humphrey took one last step before a blast of buckshot struck him in the chest, knocking him into a ditch alongside the road. Salyers fired two or three shots from his own revolver as he retreated toward a farm house 200 feet away.

Giving up efforts to move his own car, Buck ran to the police vehicle, which he was able to start. In it he picked up W. D. and floored the gas pedal to make a successful getaway.

The following Monday, newspaper headlines announced the death of H. D. Humphrey. First reports were that he had been killed by machine gun volleys, but as more details were learned the truth came out; he had been slain by a shotgun blast. Buck would admit later that indeed he was the one who had killed the officer.[3]

After Bonnie had recovered enough to travel, the outlaws returned to the Midwest. On a balmy summer night in July, the five—Buck, Blanche, Clyde, Bonnie, and W. D. Jones—robbed a bank in Fort Dodge, Iowa, getting only about $150. Moving south, the five thieves reached Platte City, Missouri, on the outskirts of Kansas City. They registered for two cabins with a garage between them at the Red Crown Cabin Camp. The owner of the camp, filling station, and tavern, N. D. Houser, was suspicious and telephoned his concerns to Captain William Baxter of the Missouri Highway Patrol.

Baxter checked his messages and decided that the five must be the wanted Barrow Gang. He amassed reinforcements from sheriffs of both Platte County and nearby Jackson County containing Kansas City. Around midnight, this assemblage was in front of the garage door at the Red Crown establishment, and Baxter called, "Come out! We're police officers."

Blanche shouted back, "You'll have to wait 'til I get dressed."

Awakened by the commotion, Clyde grabbed his weapons, clamped his hand over Jones's mouth and whispered, "I'll carry Bonnie. You get behind the wheel."

He loaded Bonnie into the Ford sedan as Jones slid under the steering wheel, and then warned, "They've got us blocked with another car."

With an automatic rifle taken from a raid on a National Guard Armory at Enid, Oklahoma, Clyde started pouring lead into the armored car, wounding a deputy in it. From the other cabin, lit up by the spotlight, Buck also began shooting. The officers returned his fire with a volley from their own machine guns.

Inside the armored car, the wounded deputy decided to back up in order to be less exposed to fire coming from the cabin, but a stray shot must have hit a wire, causing the car's horn to start blaring. The other peace officers took that as a signal and stopped firing as Clyde replaced Jones at the steering wheel and ordered him to stand on the running board and keep his machine gun pointed at the officers.

Blanche, guiding the wounded Buck, came out of the other cabin, and Clyde slipped from under the wheel to help maneuver his brother into the car. Then returning to the driver's seat, he started the motor and floored the accelerator to dodge past the assembled lawmen while Jones, on the running board, held down the trigger on his machine gun.[4]

Clyde sped away from the motor court and got onto the highway at more than 70 mph, heading north while the befuddled officers hurried to telephones to set up road blocks ahead of his route. Clyde chose dirt roads, stopping once to pour hydrogen peroxide into Buck's open head wounds.

Others had been hit also but were less seriously hurt. Blanche was in agony from slivers of glass that had struck her eyes; Jones was slightly injured, and Bonnie was in pain from her damaged right leg. The gang made their escape but had paid a heavy price. Moreover, police succeeded in getting the license number on the fleeing Ford V8—Oklahoma plates numbered 75-872.

Clyde knew he had to get out of the area, so after giving his passengers minor treatments he kept driving north. Blanche cradling Buck in her arms cried constantly about him and her damaged eyes; Bonnie moaned a bit about her untreated burns, and Jones remained silent looking for roadblocks they might encounter.

At Mt. Ayr, Iowa, Clyde stopped long enough to change Bonnie's dressing, wash out Blanche's eyes, and with a cold compress bathe Buck's forehead. Then bundling them all back into the car, he continued driving north.

About 25 miles west of Des Moines, he came to Dexter, Iowa, and ten miles north of it was a recreational area called Dexter Park. The Park was abandoned and was exactly what he needed, with its thick woods and heavy underbrush for cover and a branch of the Middle Raccoon River nearby for fresh water to be used in treating his compatriots' wounds.

The Barrows were in a territory which had become a state in 1846. At that time there was a tract of land adjacent to Des Moines dubbed Dallas County. There, a village was platted and named Marshalltown before it was discovered that there was already a town with that name just north and east of them. The new community consequently chose another name, "Dexter," after a famous race horse.*

Dexter is a small community—a typical one-horse town. Its residents are so proud of that adjective that a prominent billboard on the east edge of town welcomes visitors by announcing:

The Original One-Horse Town

—DEXTER—

City Park—Walking Trail—Museum—Library—Fall Festival

The five thieves were momentarily safe but not without serious problems. The Ford V8—their getaway car from Platte City—was riddled with bullet holes, and Buck was near death from his head wound. Clyde had made up his mind to try to drive back to Texas, but a different car was needed, so he and

---

* The town has other reasons to be remembered. In 1910, President Taft made a whistle stop there and was presented with a silver spoon and cup marked, "To Our President, who smiles." Also, on Labor Day at the finals of the National Plowing Match, 1948, President Harry Truman spoke, touching off his campaign for election that year.

Jones drove to Perry and stole one belonging to Edward Stoner. With that vehicle they went back to pick up their three companions.

The fugitives camped at Dexfield hoped to regain their health and stamina. While there, Bonnie went to Perry and bought antiseptics, hydrogen-peroxide, Kotex pads, adhesive tape, and other over-the-counter supplies that Blanche could use on Buck's wounds.

One day a farm hand named Henry wandered into the Dexfield Park area to pick raspberries and noticed the remains of a campfire. There was no one around, but debris, including bloody bandages, lay on the ground nearby. As the hand went back to tell his employer what he had discovered, the car stolen from John Stoner, being driven by Clyde Barrow, passed him.

The farmer listened to his hired man and called the local sheriff. This officer had pictures from the shoot-out at Platte City, and he surmised the Barrow Gang must be the Dexfield campers.

Word spread quickly that criminals were at Dexfield, and Dallas County Sheriff C. A. Knee from Adel quickly organized federal agents and local authorities to move in on Dexfield Park. Rumors in Perry popped up like mushrooms, and from that town also came sightseers, teenagers, and bystanders, some of whom carried shotguns, rifles, BB guns, or whatever weapons they could lay hands on. This contingent was on the north and east when the lawmen circled the camp, came in from the west, and called, "Come out! With your hands up!"[5]

The yell set off the shooting. Crouched behind their stolen car, Clyde and W. D. Jones fired pistols and automatic rifles. Clyde tried to drive the car away but was met by more gunfire. Hit in the shoulder, he lost control of the car and impaled it on a stump he had tried to drive over. The lawmen continued blasting away at the car—shooting out all its windows, tires, and ruining the engine.

Bonnie was hit by shotgun pellets, and Buck had been shot again. The only thing for Clyde to do was get away. He put his arm around Bonnie and with W. D. Jones waded into the South Raccoon River, eluding the posse long enough to make it to the Vallie Feller farm.

Buck and Blanche were still at the Dexfield scene, now surrounded by officers and townspeople. At one time Blanche was yelling hysterically, "Daddy, don't die! Don't Die!" Then she was crying loudly as men placed her semi-conscious husband on a blanket and waited for an ambulance.

An ambulance showed up, and Buck on the blanket was placed in it. En route to Perry, the ambulance was followed by a police car in which two officers were sitting in the back seat with Blanche between them. When it arrived in Perry, more than a hundred people lined the street; they could see that Blanche had a huge bandage around her head. The temporary bandage had been placed there to stanch the flow of blood from the wound sustained at Platte City.

Marvelle Feller, son of the farmer on whose land Clyde had retreated, would recount later his remembrance of the happening:

> We were getting ready to milk our four cows, Dad, I, and the hired hand. I was nineteen and had a police dog named Rex. When the dog saw Clyde Barrow, he ran down into the lot and jumped over the fence. Clyde yelled, "Call off your dog or I'll shoot him!" He had a gun in his hand and blood all over his face. . . . He whistled and W. D. Jones came out of the corn carrying Bonnie. Clyde yelled again, "Help carry her to the car. We're not gonna hurt anyone, but we need a car because they're shooting the hell out of us. We have to have a car to get out of here." They made us back our Plymouth from the garage, and I had to get in to show Clyde how to shift it.[6]

The fracas at Dexfield was a heyday for local and regional newspapers. The day following it the *Des Moines Tribune* emblazoned its headline to read: "3 of Barrow Gang Escape Posse; Reported Fleeing in Kossuth County."[7]

From nearby Perry, the local daily kept citizens informed on the condition of the wounded Buck Barrow. Two days after the shootout, this paper reported,

> Marvin Barrow, Texas bandit near death at Kings Daughter Hospital from bullet wounds received in clashes with police, talked unconcernedly this afternoon of the killing of Marshall H. D. Humphrey in Alma, Arkansas, some weeks ago. . . . The Alma battle was the result of a grocery store robbery. . . . Officers caught up with the Barrow brothers at their hideout and in a gunfight Humphrey was killed. Barrow told questioners that none of his pals were wounded in the fight. Then Barrow said to the deputy standing by his bed, the officer who had identified him with the Alma incident, "It's a good thing you got out of the way or you might have gotten yours.[8]

Four days after the event, the paper offered readers more detail.

> Marvin Barrow, wounded bandit at the Kings Daughter Hospital, remains in a partial coma with little change in his condition since Wednesday morning. . . . A rumor spread in Perry last night was that the other three members of the gang had been captured in wounded conditions and had been brought to Perry. This was not substantiated, however, and later information was that Clyde and his wife as well as an unidentified man were still at large.[9]

At the Kings Daughter Hospital in Perry, Buck Barrow underwent immediate surgery. With a temperature of 105 degrees and a pulse rate fluctuating between 120 and 160, he was not expected to survive. One doctor examining him commented that it was amazing that the wounds had not become infected, given the dirt of the camp site. The doctor who performed the surgery on Buck said that in addition to the head wound, he had three bullets in his back, one of which had punctured a lung.[10]

Two doctors at the Hospital released a report to the *Perry Daily*:

Official Report on Barrow
Kings Daughter Hospital, 2 P.M.

> The condition of Marvin Barrow is growing steadily critical. The patient spent a quiet night but during the morning the pulse, temperature, and blood pressure became higher. The patient has a badly fractured skull and macerated brain tissue resulting from a bullet wound. . . . A virulent infection has set in making very doubtful recovery of the patient.

Keith M. Chaplet, M.D., Dexter, Iowa
Robert Osborne, M.D. Menlo, Iowa[11]

Blanche was taken to the Chapler-Osborn Clinic for treatment and for a short time was almost totally blind. Within days she was transferred to the Polk County jail in Des Moines and held there until being returned to Missouri to face trial for killing Sheriff Holt Coffee during the gun battle of July 19. At Platte City she pled guilty to the charge of intent to kill and was given a ten-year sentence in the Missouri State Prison.

Two years later, along with more than a dozen other defendants, she was brought to trial on charges of aiding and abetting Clyde Barrow and Bonnie Parker. Again, Blanche pled guilty and an additional one year was added to the sentence she was serving.

In the Perry hospital, hour by hour, Buck grew weaker. He was 30 years old. Another operation was performed to remove a piece of buckshot still in his chest. Pneumonia set in, and in mid-afternoon of July 29, 1933, Marvin "Buck" Barrow, if not the actual leader of the Barrow Gang, certainly its senior member, was pronounced dead.[12]

Chapter 10. Requiem for Bonnie and Clyde

In the aftermath of the Dexter affair, sightings of the three escapees were rife. Reports from all over the state came in that the fugitives had been seen in Des Moines, Dennison, Cedar Rapids, Waterloo, or other cities, but searches turned up nothing.

For a short time, Clyde, Bonnie, and Jones hid out near Sutherland, Iowa, in a ravine along the Little Sioux River north of Storm Lake. Cooking utensils, pheasant remains, and parts of a woman's dress were discovered at the campsite, setting off an intensive search of the area as well as throughout the adjoining three counties, but no further evidence was found.

W. D. Jones in testimony given when he was arraigned later for conspiracy in the murder of a Ft. Worth deputy said the three of them traveled all around Nebraska, Minnesota, and into Colorado. Jones eventually would desert Clyde and Bonnie and would be apprehended in Houston where he was sentenced for "murder without malice" to fifteen years in prison. Following his release from that servitude, he married and settled in Houston. He became addicted to an opium-based drug, which he mixed with Jack Daniels whisky and drank in a combination called "Black Jack." Jones lived until 1974 when he was gunned down in a Houston tavern.[1]

After the Dexter shootout, Clyde, Bonnie, and Jones remained in the northern half of Iowa, robbing banks in small towns whenever they needed cash. Rural banks at the time were easy pickings. Clyde would case the bank first, making certain security was lax, which it usually was in the small towns he selected, and he always made sure a good paved highway was close by so they could get on it quickly after the theft. Bonnie recovered enough that she could drive, and she would stay in the car with the motor idling while Clyde and Jones went inside to pilfer the cash. Their pickings might be small, but each holdup added to their record as public portrayals of them began shifting from one of cheap criminals to folk status heroes.

By September, Bonnie had recovered enough to help Clyde and Jones rob a grocery store in McKinney, Texas, a town both knew well through their association with Ralph Fults. Fults was the fellow thug to whom Bonnie had smuggled hacksaw blades, abetting his escape from the McKinney jail. The take from the grocery robbery wasn't much, and Clyde took the owner hostage for a short time before releasing him unharmed.

Fults was an accomplice of Clyde and Bonnie in several of their bank robberies. Two years younger than Clyde, he had been born in Anna, Texas, the son of a US postal worker. At the age of 14, young Fults was arrested after police found him carrying a suitcase full of stolen goods. Sentenced to jail, he managed to escape by making a key out of a Prince Albert Tobacco can. He was soon captured, however, and sent to the Gatesville Reform School, from which he escaped in 1927.

Within two years he was arrested again and convicted of selling stolen cigarettes to a grocer in Greenville, Texas. For this felony he was sent to the jail at Huntsville and eventually transferred to the prison at Eastham. During his prison terms, Fults became acquainted with numerous hardened criminals and on January 27, 1932, with aid from Bonnie Parker he helped smuggle hacksaw blades to imprisoned bank robber Ray Hamilton jailed in McKinney, Texas.

Fults then joined Hamilton to team up with Bonnie and Clyde Barrow for several felonies. On March 22, 1932, the four of them attempted to rob a hardware store in Kaufman, Texas, but a night watchman sounded an alarm and the four got away in their stolen car. They soon drove the vehicle into a bog, however, and although Barrow and Hamilton were able to escape on foot, Fults and Parker were arrested by arriving police.

Fults was imprisoned again until 1935 when he was granted parole by Texas Governor Miriam A. Ferguson shortly before she left office. He rejoined Hamilton, and the two continued their careers in car stealing and robberies. Fults' criminal spree came to an end with his capture after a bank robbery in Mississippi. For that crime he was sentenced to 50 years imprisonment during which time he was put in solitary confinement twice for instigating unsuccessful prison strikes.

Finally pardoned in 1944, Fults insisted he had learned his lessons. He landed a job as a security guard at an orphanage, ran a laundry facility, converted to Christianity, and spoke to children about the evils in a life of crime. As late as the 1960s, he helped create a television program called *Confession* which discussed criminals, cruelties and conditions in prisons, and the need to find legitimate jobs for reformed offenders. Fults passed away peacefully in Dallas on March 16, 1993 at the age of 82.[2]

For Bonnie and Clyde, the nine months between July 1933 and May 1934 must have been the most carefree period of their lives together. Accompanied by W. D. Jones, they drove in meandering patterns through Oklahoma, Arkansas, Missouri, and much of Texas. It was the nomadic, adventurous life they both craved. Gone were the squabbles between Bonnie and Blanche; there were no organized pursuits, and after pulling a heist they could easily outrun any small town cops. Usually they only had to show guns, not use them, and stealing a car or wielding a screwdriver to change license plates became routine. Their arsenal swelled to include more handguns, shotguns, BARs, and boxes of ammunition, some of which they used in practice at a remote lake or camping spot.

Clyde was the driver; Bonnie handled the road maps, and Jones was the photographer who snapped pictures during their camp outs. Clyde and Bonnie smoked cigarettes, and Jones smoked cigars, probably believing they made him look older than his teen years. One snapshot he took gained wide publicity. Bonnie was posing and just fooling around in the picture which showed her standing with a foot on the bumper of a car, a gun in her hand, and a cigarette dangling from her mouth.

The three outlaws were in the Dallas area when November 1933 began. Many citizens in the area knew of their presence, but a code of silence bred by hard times—times in which the establishment, with its police, was often blamed, kept residents from giving out any information about the bandits.

On November 21, Clyde's mother Cumie would be 59, and Clyde planned a family get-together to celebrate. Family members met in Sowers, a tiny settlement a dozen miles northwest of Dallas. There they spent the day together; Clyde was upset because he hadn't brought his mother a birthday present. Even though he didn't relish the idea of meeting two days in a row and in the same place, he agreed to return after dark the next day.

Darkness came early on November 22, and by that time an informant had told Dallas County Sheriff Smoot about the intended gathering. Smoot collected three deputies—Ted Hinton, Bob Alcorn, and Ed Caster. Most members of the Barrow family already had assembled, and the well-armed lawmen were hiding in the roadside outside Sowers before Clyde and Bonnie arrived. A few minutes before seven o'clock, Clyde driving a black Ford V8 sedan came in from the north. He either saw or sensed the lawmen's presence, so he sped past them without stopping.

As they were passed, the lawmen started shooting, their bullets striking not only Clyde's Ford but also the parked car in which Cumie and family members were sitting and waiting. Windows in Clyde's car were smashed, and either he or Jones returned the officers' fire.

Clyde managed to get his Ford off on a side road, and before the officers could mount an effective pursuit, he had driven his bullet-riddled car away. The trap had failed, but it was a near miss.[3]

By this time, Raymond Hamilton also was a participant in the Barrow Gang robberies. Following his escape from the Mckinney, Texas, jail in January, 1932—an escape made possible by hacksaw blades smuggled to him by Bonnie Parker and Ralph Fults—Hamilton teamed with Clyde Barrow on several depredations. Hamilton, like Barrow, was a diminutive Texas delinquent from the crime-ridden slums of West Dallas, and like Clyde his specialty was robbing banks. Together or apart, the two thieves used similar tactics, usually ordering a couple of bank employees to lie on the floor while others were locked in the bank's steel vaults.

In the middle of July, 1933, while the Barrow brothers were under fire at Dexter, Iowa, Hamilton was in the Dallas County Jail. Shortly thereafter, he was transferred to the notorious Eastham prison farm near Weldon. Again, the wily Hamilton planned to escape, but he would need accomplices. He found one in James Mullen, an eight-time loser, to whom he promised $1,000 if he would help. Mullen agreed, and with Floyd Hamilton, brother to the imprisoned Raymond, he planted two .45 caliber automatic pistols concealed in an old inner tube in a ditch near the cotton field where inmates were expected to work the next week. An Eastham trusty named Yost smuggled the weapons to Hamilton, who persuaded a cell chum to join in the scheme. The chum, Joe Palmer, an asthmatic, feigned sickness and was permitted to remain in bed enabling him to pass one of the pistols to Hamilton.

On the morning of January 16, 1934, Palmer and Hamilton were among the prisoners sent to work in the cotton field. Noticing that Hamilton was in the wrong work gang, one of the guards on horseback, Major Crowson, rode over, and as he approached the gang, both Hamilton and Palmer pulled their guns shouting, "Hands up!"[4]

Instead of obeying, Crowson yanked out his own weapon and fired, inflicting a scalp wound on Palmer. Palmer returned the fire with two shots, one striking Crowson in the abdomen and the other in the head. He slid to the ground, mortally wounded. Hamilton at the time was shooting another guard, hitting him in the hip. This victim clutched at his wound and fell over. Pandemonium reigned as other prisoners and guards scurried for cover.

Three other convicts, Henry Methvin, Hilton Bybee, and Joe French, taking advantage of an opportunity to flee, joined Hamilton and Palmer as they made a dash for freedom, and all five escapees reached the road where Clyde Barrow and James Mullen sat in a getaway car with its motor running.

The five fugitives piled into the car; Clyde floored its pedal, and the vehicle sped away. [5]

After the escapade at Eastham, the fugitives drove back to Joplin, Missouri, and stayed there only a couple of days before moving north into Iowa. In the Hawkeye State they occasionally robbed a filling station, but banks were more promising. Such institutions in rural communities were seldom well defended and lawmen were almost certain to be slow in reacting. Whenever their cash ran low, the bandits opted for a bank heist.

On January 23, 1934, two men entered the First National Bank at Rembrandt, Iowa, a town of 600 residents in northwest Iowa. One of the men asked cashier Lloyd Haroldson to change a large bill. As Haroldson did so, the other intruder ordered him "to stick 'em up and keep quiet." Haroldson and a customer found themselves facing guns as the two thieves gathered the money and hurried out the door to join other men still in the tan Ford with its engine running. Actually, there were three men in the car—one in the back seat and two in the front.

There would be differing reports of the amount of money taken in the robbery, but Joe Palmer, the man in the back seat of the Ford at the robbery scene, confessed just before his execution a year later (for another murder) said the take was $3800, and he identified Clyde Barrow, Raymond Hamilton, Henry Methvin, and Hilton Bybee as the other accomplices. [6]

Three days after the Rembrandt robbery, the Barrow Gang hit a small bank in Oklahoma; a week afterwards they returned to Iowa. Within a week they were casing a bank in Knierin, Iowa, 15 miles southwest of Fort Dodge and less than 50 miles from their earlier heist at Rembrandt. At Knierin, they made off with only $272 shoving the cashier and a customer into the vault but not harming them. One bystander was able to fire a shot as the bandits made their getaway, but his bullet missed its mark. [7]

Leonard Burmeister, a fifth-grade pupil in February 1934, and out of school that day, had been attracted by the black sporty Ford with shiny wheels. A woman driving it had parked in front of the bank next to his home. The woman remained in the car while two men wearing hats and long overcoats got out and went into the bank. The boy was still awed by the sporty car when a local farmer named George Nelson came up and also entered the bank. Years later, Burmeister remembered that George would recount numerous times what happened.

According to George Nelson's recitals, one of the men cradled a strange-looking weapon in his arms and pointing it at him said, "Don't move, Mister. Be quiet and you won't get hurt."

While Nelson obliged, the other bandit at the teller's window was waving a pistol in the cashier's face and ordering him to hand over the cash. The young boy outside saw the two men emerge from the bank and climb into the car. Then he watched it speed a quarter mile south to a larger highway.[8]

After the Knieren robbery, the gang went to Louisiana so that Henry Methvin, a small time crook and recent recruit into the corps, could visit his family. Staying only a few days, Clyde, Bonnie, W. D. Jones, and Henry Methvin headed back toward Joplin, Missouri. Police had been alerted, and there were several road encounters and shootouts en route, but the fugitives' stolen cars always managed to outpace pursuers. Clyde didn't have a road map and was wary about stopping to get one. As a consequence, he lost his way, and in the vicinity of Springfield, Missouri, the gang kidnapped a pedestrian hoping he could guide them out of the state. The pedestrian, Joe Gunn, was kept with them until they crossed the Arkansas border. Then he was released and given $10 for his guidance. He reported that he had been unharmed, and that besides his four male captors men there was a skinny, "cigar-smoking, gun girl."

As February 1934, moved toward its close, Clyde Barrow and Raymond Hamilton had settled their dispute over how loot from various robberies was to be distributed, but they were low on guns and ammunition. The two put their differences aside, and to restock their arsenal, the two of them accompanied by their molls, Bonnie and Mary O'Dare, they raided the National Guard Armory at Ranger, Texas. The bandits' two molls, Bonnie Parker and Mary O'Dare, waited in a stolen V8 while Clyde and Raymond went inside to collect more than half dozen Browning automatic rifles, Colt .45 pistols, and boxes of ammunition.

In Dallas, they ditched the Ford V-8 and joined Henry Methvin who had stolen a late model Chevrolet. In it, the five drove to Lancaster, 16 miles south of the city, and around noon on February 27, 1934, Bonnie drove the Chevy to park it near the side entrance of the R. P. Henry and Sons Bank. Mary O'Dare sat by her side. Clyde got out first with a sawed-off shotgun concealed under his brown-and-gray checked overcoat. Raymond with a blue-steeled .45 Colt automatic in the pocket of his own overcoat followed him into the bank. The women remained in the car.

A bank patron watched the teller take two tens, a five dollar bill, and two ones from the till before the customer in front of him, actually Clyde Barrow, reached through the window to take the bills from his hands. Then turning to face the other customers, Barrow waved his shotgun and said, "OK. This is a stick up. Get down on the floor; stay quiet, and you won't get hurt."

As patrons and other employees threatened by Barrow with his shotgun took positions on the floor, Raymond Hamilton went behind the cashier's cage and scooped up all available cash, stuffing it in a large paper sack. Then Hamilton ordered L. L. Henry, the bank's owner, to open the vault.

While Barrow kept his shotgun trained on captives lying on the floor, Hamilton prodded Henry into the vault. A minute later Hamilton emerged gun in one hand and the sack now bulging with currency in the other.

According to three sources, the theft at Lancaster netted Barrow and Hamilton $4,176.[9] Clyde wanted to divide the plunder into three equal shares distributed equally among himself, Raymond, and Bonnie, who had helped plan the raid and had driven their escape car. Hamilton insisted that his girlfriend, Mary O'Dare, also should get a share. Arguments and accusations arose between him and Clyde with the result that O'Dare got her share, but in a huff from the imbroglio, the gang broke up, and she and Hamilton went their separate ways thereafter. In March, 1934, the two of them robbed the State National Bank in West, Texas, of $1,862.[10]

Following the flare-up with Clyde over division of loot taken in the Lancaster bank robbery, Raymond Hamilton teamed up with several other criminals to continue robbing banks. Finally apprehended in the Ft. Worth rail yards in April, 1935, he was convicted in a jury trial and first sentenced to 300 years in prison; as more crimes surfaced and especially the slaying of the Eastham guard Major Crowson were added to his rap sheet, the sentence was changed to the death penalty, and he was electrocuted in Dallas on May 10, 1935.[11]

In getting away from the West Texas robbery, Raymond Hamilton crashed the car he was driving into an embankment; he and Mary were thrown against the dash and windshield; his nose was broken, and Mary was cut in the face. Hamilton hailed a passing motorist, and took its driver, Mrs. Cam Gunter, hostage. In Gunter's car, the trio drove around until Hamilton spotted a new Ford V8 parked in a driveway. He hotwired that Ford, released Mrs. Gunter unharmed, and Mary O'Dare climbed in beside him as he gunned the stolen vehicle away.

Mrs. Gunter reported her capture and told police she believed her captors were the infamous Clyde Barrow and Bonnie Parker. She was wrong, for Clyde, Bonnie, and Henry Methvin were basking in spring sunlight near Grapevine, Texas, two or three miles northwest of Dallas proper. Two Texas highway patrolmen on motorcycles came past the parked car, then made a wide circle to turn around intending to come back to Barrow's car.

When the two lawmen on their motorcycles got to about twenty-five feet from Barrow's sporty black V8 with its yellow wheels, it was obvious neither of them suspected their danger. Clyde with a sawed-off shotgun stepped from behind his car's open door, planning to take the lawmen captive. However, Methvin on the other side of the car immediately opened fire, striking one officer, E. B. Wheeler, in the chest with several steel-jacketed slugs.

Wheeler slipped from the seat of his bike and fell to the ground bloodied and lifeless. The other officer, H. D. Murphy dismounted, fished two shells from his pocket, and was attempting to get out a shotgun strapped behind him as Barrow squeezed off three rounds. When the smoke cleared, both lawmen were lying on the ground.

News of the slayings set off a flurry of public condemnations. Fingerprints from a whisky bottle found at the scene of the crime were identified as Barrow's, and newspaper headlines echoed one theme: "Get the killer, Clyde Barrow."

After the killing of Wheeler and Murphy, the trio of Barrow, Bonnie, and Methvin drove to Commerce City in the industrial mining district of northeastern Oklahoma. There City Marshall Percy Boyd received a complaint that a car with drunks in it was parked just outside the town's limits. He asked Constable Cal Campbell to accompany him, and the two drove out to investigate.

Clyde Barrow was still half-asleep when he saw the city car cross the railroad tracks and come toward him. He put his V8 in reverse before flooring its pedal to flee at high speed. He hadn't gone far before he lost control of the car, which veered off the road and sank into a ditch with mud up to the rims of the car's rear wheels.

Grabbing a BAR, Barrow jumped out and began firing at the lawmen who, in their own vehicle, were coming toward him. Both men responded by returning his fire. Boyd was grazed in the head and knocked down; Campbell continued shooting.

Methvin came over to where Campbell lay with a massive hole in his abdomen. He was not moving, and a thick puddle of blood was forming around him. Methvin poked the barrel of his BAR into the face of the other officer, Percy Boyd, and said, "Get moving; we're taking you with us."

In the vehicle in the ditch, Bonnie was still behind the wheel while Clyde, Methvin, and Boyd tried to push it out of the mud. Unable to do so, they flagged down another auto and ordered its driver to help them; even then the four couldn't get the car out. Finally, a passing truck driver was stopped; he had a chain, and fastening it to the bumper of the V8 in the mud was able to pull it out and onto the road.

With Bonnie in the front seat beside him and with Methvin in the back seat, a gun stuck into the ribs of the captured Marshall Percy Boyd, Clyde drove to Ft. Scott, Kansas, before pulling up to a country store. Methvin got out, went inside and ordered four hot dinners.

Eight miles north of town, Clyde stopped the car, gave Boyd one of the dinners, and pressed a ten dollar bill into his hands. With the bill in his hand,

Boyd asked, "What do you want me to tell the press?" Bonnie answered, "Tell them, I don't smoke cigars." [12]

Clyde's record embellished by newspaper accounts was enough to make him a minor celebrity. His dramatic raid on the Eastham Prison Farm along with numerous robberies were embarrassing to law officials in Oklahoma and more particularly in Texas. In the Lone Star State, Col. Lee Simmons, General Manager of Eastham, vowed to put an end to Barrow's depredations, and with approval from Texas Governor Miriam Ferguson, he called in Frank Hamer, a retired Texas Ranger. "I want you to track down Bonnie and Clyde," instructed Simmons, "and when you do, shoot everyone in sight." [13]

Hamer came to Iowa to interview Blanche Barrow just days after the Dexfield shootout; true to his reputation, he was a relentless pursuer when he got on a trail. Blanche gave him enough incriminating evidence to put away the fugitives for life if he could ever catch up with them. His chance came in May 1934, when informants told him Clyde and Bonnie were going to bring Henry Methvin to his father's home on a lonely country road between Arcadia and Gibsland, Louisiana.

Hamer recruited Manny Gault, another retired Ranger, along with Sheriff Henderson Jordan and his deputies Ted Hinton, Bob Alcorn, and Prentiss Oakley to join him in an ambush set up on the road leading to Methvin's farm.

The officers first took the protesting Methvin and handcuffed him to a chain wrapped around a nearby tree. Then they took a wheel off his truck to make it appear as if he had stopped to fix a flat. The officers hid themselves and were about to give up when around 9:15 A.M. a car with two persons in it approached. The car slowed to inspect Methvin's stalled truck and were close enough that the lawmen could identify Clyde and Bonnie.

Alcorn yelled, "Halt! You're covered!" Clyde jerked his head toward Alcorn, now exposed, and pressed the accelerator to the floor. Before his Ford could gain any speed, the six lawmen emptied their guns. First to fire was 29-year-old Bienville Parish Deputy Prentiss Oakley, whose shots from a lethal Remington Model 8 Rifle penetrated the V8's windshield and the driver's door. One of his deadly bullets struck Clyde in the temple just above his left ear plowing through his head before exiting out the right side of his skull. He died instantly.

Bonnie screamed—a high, shrill wail that would haunt some of the attackers the rest of their lives. Nevertheless, Clyde had died with his foot on the accelerator, and the tan Ford was still moving. All the surrounding lawmen kept firing, their heavy fusillade shattering the car's windows and penetrating it to strike the two bodies inside. There was no way to tell whose bullets killed Bonnie, but her corpse, like that of her lover, was riddled by the barrage from Hamer and his deputies. Frank Hamer had followed his instructions to the letter: "Track down Clyde and Bonnie; shoot them on sight."[14]

CHAPTER 11. JOHN HERBERT DILLINGER: EARLY YEARS

On September 26, 1933, ten convicts—with the aid of guns smuggled to them by a recent parolee—broke out of the state prison in Michigan City, Indiana, and escaped. The parolee was a 5 ft. 6 in. small-time thug, John Dillinger, whose crimes thereafter would make his name the epitome of 20th-century criminals.

On the eve of America's Civil War, Mathias Dillinger had left the Moselle Valley in France and come to America to settle, eventually, in Indiana. There he married, and from that union came John Wilson Dillinger.

To fellow townsmen, the hard-working John Wilson Dillinger was known as "Honest John." He married Molly Lancaster, daughter of a respected farmer living near Cumberland on the outskirts of Indianapolis, and before long in addition to farming the couple owned and ran a small grocery store. In 1889, a little red-haired baby whom they named Audrey arrived, and it would be fourteen years before they would have another child.

This second child—a baby boy—was born June 22, 1903, and was christened John Herbert Dillinger. His mother died when he was only three years old, and the infant fell under the care of his 17-year-old sister Audrey. While still a teenager, Audrey married Emmet Hancock from nearby Maywood, and young Johnnie Dillinger came to live with her and be raised as an older brother to two of her own sons.

There is nothing in young Dillinger's life to indicate that he was much different from the ordinary small town boy—no more mischievous than others around him—perhaps swiping candy bars from filling stations, tipping over outhouses on Halloween, and on nights in summer or fall stealing watermelons from a farmer's patch; otherwise unremarkable. When it came to formal education, the lad was no prodigy. To him, arithmetic was a drudgery, but he liked to read and would borrow books from neighbors or friends after he had gone through his school's scanty library.

He was not a big kid but strong for his age and not afraid to use his fists if forced into a fight. Two years after his first wife Molly died, John Wilson Dillinger married Elizabeth Fields, who had three children of her own—a boy Hubert, and two girls named Doris and Frances. Hubert, Doris, and Frances thought of young Johnnie Dillinger as an older brother when he left his sister's household and came to join them in his father's second family.

In early manhood, John Herbert Dillinger's life was typical of rural boys in central Indiana. He helped his stepmother with household tasks, worked during daylight hours on his dad's farm, and played baseball for recreation. In the sport, he was good enough to make the town's local team, the *Mooresville Giants*, first as a second baseman and then as the team's leading pitcher.

Not long after his father's second marriage, Dillinger became leader of a gang of boys in the neighborhood. He was only a sixth grader when he got pals to help him steal coal from the Pennsylvania Railroad. The boys would sell the coal to housewives, some of whom when arrested squealed on their suppliers. Dillinger was hauled out of bed by police to face a judge in Juvenile Court. The judge lectured the culprits, warned them against further misdemeanors, and released them without penalty.[1]

When not playing baseball or stealing coal, Johnnie Dillinger liked to spend time with a gun and his dog in the Hoosier woods. Proud of his marksmanship with a .22 rifle, he roamed the woods, sometimes shooting a cottontail but more often just banging away at a tin can or any other convenient target.

For a brief period he attended the Quaker school in Mooresville—not because of religious feelings but because he had become enamored with a girl who sang in its choir. The girl was Frances Thornton, and from statements Dillinger made years later, the two fell in love. According to him, her parents looked with scant favor on his courtship of their daughter, and it was their steely opposition that finally broke up the relationship.[2]

Like other swains in similar circumstances, the disappointed Dillinger wanted to get away from the scenes of his lost love affair. He left Mooresville to go to Indianapolis, where after a spell of carousing and dissipation he joined the navy in July, 1923. Orders and regimentation were hard for him to accept, and his naval career didn't last long. Assigned to the battleship *U.S.S. Utah*, he deserted after five months and made his way back to Mooresville where he told friends he had been discharged because of a weak heart.

At loose ends and still smarting from losing Frances Thornton, Dillinger began romancing Beryl Hovious. She was only sixteen years old, and he was 20, when she became his wife in April, 1924. As a young husband, he worked sporadically, but in 1925 naval authorities caught up with him. Arrested for desertion, he was given a dishonorable discharge and imprisoned at the Indiana State Reformatory in Pendleton.

Dillinger served his time and after being released from Pendleton returned to his wife and relatives around Mooresville. There he met a newcomer, Edgar Singleton. Singleton, an older man had served time in the Indiana State Prison and was a sawdust hero to Dillinger and his pals. Singleton liked to drink, and the boys would swill moonshine with him while he spun exaggerated accounts of what he had done.

On the night of September 6, 1924, the drinking had been heavy, and Singleton and Dillinger with minds befuddled by alcohol were sitting in the dark behind the Christian Church when Frank Morgan, proprietor of a Mooresville grocery store, came by. The two delinquents were hidden and prepared; they had heavy iron bolts wrapped in cloth, and with that weapon in the hands of each they set upon Morgan. The grocer had a pistol, though, which he pulled out and attempted to fire, but in the struggle the bullet intended for the assailants struck his own hand. By this time Morgan was yelling, and his calls brought out people to help. With their approach, the would-be robbers fled into the night.

On Monday morning, Dillinger was arrested on suspicion and when questioned claimed he had no recollection of his activities the previous Saturday night. Singleton had scooted out of town immediately and later put all of the blame on Dillinger, whose pleas of innocence were not believed.

Grocer Morgan was unable to make a positive identification, yet the evidence against Dillinger was overwhelming. He was advised that if he pled guilty he would get a lighter sentence. The advice was followed but the promise forgotten. Judge Joseph Williams handed him the maximum sentence—ten to twenty years with intent to rob. Ten years after this sentence was handed down, Indiana Governor Paul V. McNutt commented:

> The judge and the prosecutor took him out and assured him if he would tell certain things they would let him off with a lighter sentence. They didn't keep their word. They gave Dillinger ten to twenty years while his partner in crime, Edgar Singleton, got two to fourteen years, and was released at the end of two years. This made a criminal out of John Dillinger.[3]

Young Dillinger began his term in the State Reformatory at Pendleton on September 16, 1924. The Reformatory was close to Mooresville and for a while he received frequent visits from his wife and relatives. He was not considered a dangerous convict, yet three months after his arrival he failed in a clumsy attempt to escape, and in the following three years he was marked down seven times for disorderly conduct.

At Pendleton, Dillinger met 19-year-old Homer Van Meter, already hardened by thefts and physical assaults. Van Meter had been born in Indiana, had quit school after the sixth grade, and fled to Chicago where he found jobs as either bell boy or waiting tables in one of the city's moderate hotels. A slender young man standing five feet, ten inches tall with a tapering waist, he had no trouble finding women and contracted syphilis before he was eighteen.

Van Meter's first arrest was in 1923 when in Aurora, Illinois, he was picked up by two officers for larceny. When the charge was changed to "disorderly conduct and intoxication," he drew a sentence of forty-one days in jail and a fine of $200. Later in the same year, he stole a car, was caught, convicted and given a one-to-ten-year prison sentence.

Paroled after only one year in prison, Van Meter teamed up with another ex-con and robbed a *New York Central* train bound for Chicago. Fourteen miles east of Gary, Indiana, he and Con Livingston (alias Carl Hern), prodding a flagman and porter before them, entered the luxury train's sleeping car, locked the car's door, and robbed first the two crewmen and then Livingston, holding a pistol in one hand and a hat in other, collected money and jewelry from the passengers. Van Meter, armed with a shotgun, sat on a seat and waved the weapon toward anyone who moved.

As the train approached the Gary rail yard it slowed enough that Van Meter and Livingston could jump off and disappear. Railroad officials quickly notified police in Gary and Chicago as well as other law men in Indiana, but the two bandits could not be found.[4]

Van Meter and Livingston rode from Gary to Chicago on the South Shore—an electric train making frequent runs between South Bend and the Windy City. In Chicago, the two of them teamed up with a couple of other ex-cons: Michael Spicuzza and Frank Zelinski. This quartet hatched a plan to rob a bank in South Bend, Indiana, and on March 6, 1925, the four of them were in an auto and preparing to go into the bank when a passing patrolman, Officer Homer Ames, noticed the car and became suspicious. He came over to it and asked the occupants if he could talk to them. In answer, one of the four outlaws pulled a pistol, waved it in the patrolman's face, and said, "Stick 'em up, Copper!"

Ames ducked, pulled his own gun and got off a couple of shots. A cab driver passing by and a night mail truck driver doing the same saw what was happening and joined the gun battle. Spicuzza was hit in the right leg and captured immediately; Livingston was shot over the heart and died the next day. Van Meter and Zelinsky escaped only to be arrested three days later as they attempted to board a train headed west.

Van Meter was found guilty of this attempted bank robbery and sent to the Reformatory at Pendleton. The following January, he was taken handcuffed to Chicago where he was scheduled to testify in federal court against another accomplice. Somehow while in Union Station he managed to escape from his guard. Concealing the handcuffs in his coat sleeves and without a penny in his pockets until he panhandled thirty-five cents from a passerby, Van Meter evaded police on the streets for more than an hour. Caught and arrested at the corner of Wabash Avenue and Van Buren Street, Van Meter was returned to Pendleton, serving six months' time there before being transferred to the state prison in Michigan City where he would join a clique headed by Harry Pierpont.[5]

While at Pendleton, John Dillinger wrote honeyed letters to his wife Beryl, unaware that she was considering a legal separation. She waited four years before filing and being granted a divorce in 1929 on the grounds that her husband was an imprisoned felon. Dillinger didn't contest her action, and very soon after the divorce had been granted, his ego suffered another hit; despite his improved prison behavior his bid for a parole was turned down.

He next made an unusual request, asking to be transferred to the Indiana State Prison in Michigan City. Most biographers believe the prime reason for the request was his wish to play baseball, as the prison in northern Indiana was known to have a very good baseball nine. Regardless of its motivation, the move put him in touch with former friends already behind bars there: Harry Pierpont and Homer Van Meter.

Dillinger had met them both when all were at Pendleton. Harry "Pete" Pierpont, a strikingly handsome hard case with piercing gray eyes was there for helping rob a bank in Kokomo, Indiana. Van Meter, a tall, gangly runaway from Ft. Wayne, had been arrested for robbing passengers on a train to Toledo.

Van Meter was paroled from Pendleton in May, 1933, and a few months later when Dillinger was let out, the two were spark plugs of a gang that went on a one-year crime spree of robbing banks and having shootouts with law enforcement officers. Dillinger depended on Van Meter for advice and liked to hide out around St. Paul because of Van Meter's familiarity with the city and his contacts with the corrupt police department there.

Harry Pierpont was a slender, good-looking young man, who with his height of 6ft., 1 in. towered over the smaller Dillinger. Pierpont, a year older than Dillinger and already classed as incorrigible when the two first met, was smart and quick-triggered. Captain Matt Leach, Head of the Indiana State Police, considered him the brains of the hoodlums that gathered around Dillinger.

Born on October 13, 1902, in Muncie, Indiana, Harry Pierpont enjoyed a happy and uneventful childhood. Raised a Catholic, Pierpont attended a parochial school in Indianapolis where he was considered above average in intelligence and did well. As he grew older, he became more stubborn and irritable. He was hit on the head with a baseball bat when he was nineteen and lay unconscious for nearly five minutes, and this injury may have contributed to some of his subsequent idiosyncrasies. A relative once remarked, "He was never quite right since then." Not long after the incident he began suffering sleeplessness and showing signs of mental instability. He imagined he had bank accounts and wrote checks for money he did not have. He also developed a mania for firearms. His mother told doctors:

> He has been melancholy, nervous, walks the floor, and wants to carry a gun. He imagines he has money, wrote a check for $1401 when he had no money in the bank. He insists he has sums of money, which is untrue. This check was given to the Cleveland Auto Company. He refused to talk with anyone in the past two weeks. Harry was hurt in the past year with a baseball bat. He since said he did not feel good. He is dangerous to be at large and should be in a hospital.[6]

Pierpont and Van Meter were Dillinger's longest running associates, and his friendship with the two hardened him. Pierpont would be arrested in Tucson, extradited to Ohio, and imprisoned there for the October, 1933, murder of Lima Sheriff Jess Sarber. Together with another convict, Pierpont tried to escape from Ohio's death row in September, 1934, using fake guns carved from soap. Charles Makley, fellow inmate, was killed in the attempt; Pierpont was captured and executed at the state penitentiary in Columbus, Ohio the next month.

Van Meter, Dillinger's other partner, in July, 1934, was hiding out around St. Paul, Minnesota, with his girlfriend Mickey Conforti. An informant tipped off the FBI as well as Tom Brown, an easy-to-bribe St. Paul detective who had collaborated with the Barker gang on the Hamm and Bremer kidnappings.

One summer afternoon, Van Meter visited a car dealer in downtown St. Paul, and when he walked out of that office, four policemen with guns drawn and aimed at him yelled, "Stick 'em up!"

Instead of complying, Van Meter yanked out his own pistol and got off two shots at the officers before starting to sprint away. He dashed down the street and ducked into an alley, only to find it had a dead end. The officers followed him, and a blast from one of their shotguns knocked him two feet in the air, slamming his body into a brick wall. He tried to rise while the pursuing lawmen continued their firing, riddling his body with bullets. Van

Meter had told cronies he didn't want to die in some filthy alley, but he did just that on August 23, 1934.

Imprisoned at Michigan City, Dillinger rejoined his old friend Harry Pierpont, now the leader of a prison clique, and Homer Van Meter. These two introduced him to three other inmates who one day would become members of what was known as the Dillinger Gang: John "Red" Hamilton, Charles "Fat Charlie" Makley, and Russell Lee "Boobie" Clark.

Dillinger was assigned to work in the shirt factory. Outside, his friends and family tried hard to get him paroled. A retired pastor from the church in Mooresville went before the parole board to plead for his release, and the Judge who had sentenced him, Joseph Williams, expressed his belief that John was needed on the farm and had reformed enough to make a useful citizen. Even the grocer who had been assaulted added his signature to 183 fellow townsmen asking for Dillinger's release.[7]

Efforts to get him out finally paid off, and in May, 1933, John Dillinger was granted a parole. He listened to a lecture that crime does not pay, and then with $5.00 from the State of Indiana in his pocket he walked out beyond the prison's walls to where his step brother Hubert Dillinger was in a car waiting for him.

His release was bittersweet, for when he got back to Mooresville, he learned his stepmother, nee Elizabeth Fields, had died of a stroke just days earlier. "Mom" had been a devoted mother—a person for whom he felt great attachment. He had loved her truly and would miss her restraining guidance.

A lot happened in the world beyond Reformatory walls at Pendleton and prison bars at Michigan City during the eight and a half years of John Dillinger's confinement. In the year he was sent to Pendleton, Richard Loeb and Nathan Leopold, two privileged and well-educated young men, picked out a young boy in South Chicago at random and killed him just for the thrill of it. The two murderers were sentenced to life imprisonment after a sensational trial in which famed attorney Clarence Darrow pled for their lives.

Calvin Coolidge of Massachusetts in 1924 defeated John W. Davis of Illinois in the presidential election by an electoral college vote of 382–136, with 13 electoral votes going to Robert M. LaFollette. Gene Tunney knocked out Jack Dempsey for the heavy weight boxing title, and Gertrude Ederle swam the English Channel. Babe Ruth hit 60 home runs, and Charles Lindbergh flew solo across the Atlantic Ocean. In May, 1932, the famed flyer's infant son was kidnapped and killed after a $50,000 ransom had been paid, and in that same month a "bonus army" made up of about 1,000 ex-service men came to Washington, D.C. and camped out in open or unused buildings near the capital. The veterans announced they intended to stay until Congress authorized payment in full of soldiers' bonus certificates. The protesters stayed until federal troops commanded by General Douglas MacArthur arrived to drive them out.

Of greater import was the economic disaster which began sweeping the country. Twenty thousand businesses failed in 1930, and 29,000 more in 1931. By 1933, the year in which Dillinger was paroled, the Depression had hit rock bottom: banks had closed in 38 states; farmers and neighbors were preventing foreclosures; one-fourth of the nation's work force could not find jobs, and bread lines along with soup kitchens were found in every big city, which also was likely to have a Hooverville on its outskirts.

The only enterprise to prosper was crime. A rash of bank heists broke out in 1930. In the year before Dillinger was released, the U.S. suffered 631 bank robberies, 516 of them during daylight hours. In Illinois alone, more than 85 banks were robbed for a total of $300,000.

In the first month of 1919, the 18th amendment to the American Constitution, prohibiting liquor traffic in the U.S., was ratified. Prohibition when enacted gave rise to city mobs and gangsters; one of the most notorious was Al "Scarface" Capone in Chicago. There in 1929 his underlings carried out the St. Valentine Day's Massacre—the worst example of the Windy City's 500 murders during the decade. Capone in Chicago, Luciano and Diamond in New York, and Meyer Lansky in Florida were behind-the-scene operators, employing lesser thugs to do the dirty work.

John Dillinger committed the criminal acts himself. His prison pallor had hardly faded before he launched a fourteen-month career as Public Enemy Number One on the FBI's list of wanted felons. Eight weeks after being released from the Michigan City prison, he returned to Mooresville for a short stay before hitching a ride to Gary, Indiana. There he met up with Hilton Crouch and Harry Copeland. Crouch was a former dirt-track race car driver—supposedly a good man to have behind the wheel of a getaway car—and Copeland was a swarthy, heavy-lidded dimwit who would abet Dillinger on several jobs.

On June 10, 1933, Dillinger aided by two other men robbed the National Bank in New Carlisle, Ohio. It was his first bank heist, and the take was $10,600. He wasn't done, for later the same day, he and his two pals robbed a Haag Drug Store in Indianapolis as well as an adjoining supermarket. [8]

In the middle of July, 1933, Dillinger and Copeland joined William Shaw, his wife, and two ruffians named Noble "Sam" Clayton and Paul Parker to rob the Bide-a-Wee Tavern in Muncie, Indiana. That night they collected a mere $70, and Shaw, his wife, and the two thugs were arrested the very next morning. Shaw told police two other robbers had been accomplices but had escaped unnoticed: naming one "Dan" Dillinger and the other Harry Copeland.

Undeterred by Shaw's arrest, Dillinger the very next day went ahead with plans to rob a bank he had cased earlier—the Commercial Bank of Daleville, Indiana, a hamlet midway between Pendleton and Muncie. It would be a cakewalk, for there was not even a chief of police in the town.

On July 17, Dillinger, Copeland, and Crouch entered the bank to be confronted only by a nervous woman cashier in the teller's window. She opened the vault for them, and the three thieves got away with $3,500 in cash. Margaret Good, the woman teller, told investigators what she thought of Dillinger as he trained his gun on her: "I think he knew I was a kid and was sorry to scare me. He didn't want to scare me any worse than he had to."[9]

Indianapolis newspapers reported the crime briefly, identifying perhaps for the first time the robbers as a "Dillinger gang." The personnel of "the Dillinger Gang" often is presumed to have been constant during the months he pursued his nefarious career, but the make-up of the "gang" changed as members were killed, arrested, or drifted away. Dillinger himself kept rolling along—unrepentant, planning the crimes, and always in charge.

At the time of his parole from the prison in Michigan City, he told fellow convicts that after being released he would call upon their relatives or sweethearts to relay greetings or pass on whatever information the inmates wanted known. Among those to be informed was Mary Jenkins Longnacre, sister to Joseph Jenkins, a fellow prison inmate.

Mary, an attractive young divorcee and another girl about the same age, agreed to go with Dillinger to the World's Fair in Chicago, where the three took in not only sights at the Exhibition but enjoyed themselves in night clubs or watching the Cubs play baseball at Wrigley Field. After this Chicago interlude, Dillinger and Mary returned to her home in Dayton. Word of his whereabouts had been learned by Matt Leach of the Indiana State Police, who immediately notified Dayton authorities. On September 22, 1933, a team of lawmen raided the Longnacre residence, and Dillinger, although heavily armed, was taken by surprise; he surrendered without resistance.

A few days before his arrest in Dayton, Dillinger had managed to have three .38 caliber guns smuggled into pals still in prison at Michigan City. He had packed the guns in a box filled with spools from an East Coast Thread Company and somehow tipped off Harry Pierpont to be on the lookout for it. Then he had shipped the box to the shirt-making department where Pierpont worked in the prison.

On the afternoon of September 26, 1933, Pierpont with several fellow inmates used the smuggled guns to take the superintendent and an assistant warden by surprise. Using the two as hostages, the convicts, Harry Pierpont,

Charles Makley, John Hamilton, Walter Dietrich, and Russell Clark walked behind the two officials, past guards and beyond a series of checkpoints. The escapees were only steps away before anyone challenged them, and upon that challenge the convicts shot one guard, beat two others, and locked up several in an office. Then walking out of the prison, they stole a visiting sheriff's car to make a clean getaway. [10]

At the time of the break-out in Michigan City, John Dillinger was jailed in Lima, Ohio, awaiting trial for crimes committed in the Buckeye State. Meanwhile, a brouhaha had sprouted between Indiana officials and those holding him in Ohio. On October 12, a car drove up to stop just outside the red brick jail in Lima. Pals had come to rescue Dillinger as well as repay him for making the Michigan City escape possible.

In Lima, Harry Pierpont led the way into the office of Sheriff Jesse Sarber. Pierpont was followed by Charles Makley and John "Red" Hamilton. Staying in the car outside were Russell Clark and Harry Copeland.

Sheriff Sarber was reaching for a gun hanging in its holster on a wall rack next to his desk when a shot from one of the intruders rang out. A bullet tore through his abdomen, and he sank to the floor mortally wounded.

Down the hall in one of the cells, Dillinger was playing pinochle with another prisoner when Pierpont came to unlock his cell door, and within moments he was in the getaway car speeding out of Lima.

The wounded Sheriff Jess Sarber was taken to Memorial Hospital where he died a little more than an hour and a half after the shooting. His death sent police cars with sirens wailing racing up and down Lima's streets and neighborhoods searching for the killers. Officers from six counties blocked all the main roads throughout northwestern Ohio, but the efforts were to no avail. Dillinger, Makley, Hamilton, and cronies had fled to a Cincinnati hideout 140 miles south of Lima.

Having banded together, the outlaws were temporarily safe but they lacked guns or armaments. Deciding they'd have to get weapons from the police, they chose to raid the police station at Auburn, Indiana. There on October 14, Dillinger, Pierpont, and Mackley walked into the sheriff's office, aimed .45 automatics at the two officers inside, and forced one of them to unlock a metal gun case. Then taking all the automatic rifles and ammunition they could carry, the bandits fled before pursuers could mount an effective chase.

A week after getting the guns from the Auburn police station, Dillinger and Pierpont pulled a similar job at the police station in Peru, Indiana, 75 miles southwest. The haul there increased their arsenal by two more automatic rifles, riot shotguns, a teargas gun, and a half-dozen bullet-proof vests.

On the afternoon of October 23, 1933, two cars each containing four men drove into Greencastle, Indiana, home of DePauw University, slightly west of Indianapolis and Mooresville. For an hour, the cars cruised the town and then just before closing time parked in front of the Central National Bank and Trust Company. A driver remained in each car as the other six climbed out and with overcoat collars turned up to partially hide their faces entered the building. Once inside, the bandits pulled out their guns, herded bank employees along with twelve patrons over to one side, and ordered the cashier to open the vault. From it, the robbers scooped up $20,000 in cash and $56,000 in negotiable securities. While doing this, two more patrons came into the bank, and they, too, were quickly robbed.

Meanwhile, one of the bank's employees managed to step on a floor button alerting police, but by the time any of those arrived, the bandits had fled, and no immediate pursuit could be undertaken. This Greencastle episode as well as several others attributed to Dillinger and his associates touched off suspicions.

It should be remembered that the country was in the depths of its lowest Depression when banks and money lenders of all varieties were not highly respected. Insurance moneys usually covered whatever a bank lost through a robbery but not that of its depositors, who could be ruined by the crime.

After the Greencastle robbery, a frenzy swept over the Hoosier State. State Police Forces were put on twenty-four-hours duty, and the Indiana National Guard was called out to confront the menace. A special armed force of more than two thousand men was mobilized; major highways were blocked, and airplanes were gassed and readied at the state's several airfields. Along with such preparations, rewards for information leading to arrests skyrocketed. [11]

While Hoosier authorities were conducting an all-out search for them, Dillinger and Pierpont went to Chicago. There awaiting them in a hideout apartment were Billy Frechette and Mary Kinder. Dillinger and Frechette had met months earlier in a nightclub on the near North Side.

Evelyn Frechette, who in her adult years was called Billie, had been born on an Indian reservation in Wisconsin where her mother was a member of the Menominee Indian tribe. When she met Dillinger, Frechette was in her mid-twenties. She had married young and had yet to divorce George "Sparks" Frechette, then serving a fifteen-year term in Leavenworth for bank robbery.

Frechette was an alluring girl of average stature and weight, with innocent, good looks suggesting nothing of the "gun moll" character. Her Indian ancestry showed itself in raven-colored hair, creamy complexion, rather prominent cheek bones, and large, bedroom, brown eyes. Dillinger claimed she was the best bed partner he ever had. [12]

Dillinger and Frechette lived it up in North Chicago, going to night clubs, to Wrigley Field to watch a baseball game, downtown to the Loop, or rubbernecking at the newly-opened World's Fair which had opened in May, 1933. Occupying 427 acres in Burnham Park, the heralded celebration showed attendees multi-colored buildings chosen to contrast with the famous "White City" of the World's Columbian Exposition presented by the Windy City in 1893.

There was much to see at the Fair. In October, the German airship *Graf Zeppelin* arrived, first circling the nearby lakefront for more than an hour before mooring and refueling at the Curtiss-Wright Airport in Glenview. Sightseers at the Fair could gaze at exhibits from automobile manufacturers and other industries or visit night clubs where future Hollywood stars like Judy Garland danced. And visitors could see a so-called Midget City with its "sixty Lilliputians," or go watch Sally Rand and her erotic gyrations.

Hollywood magnate Cecil B. deMille had given Hattie Helen Beck the sobriquet *Sally Rand* when she appeared in silent films. After the introduction of sound, she became better known for fan dances, so enticing and popular that they financed the *Paramount Club* in Chicago. Her most widely-reported performances were at the World's Fair, where she had numerous arrests for indecent exposure—four times in one day alone for each of four shows. Sometimes she varied the fan routine by presenting a bubble dance, and on another occasion she was arrested while riding a white horse down Michigan Avenue.

Dillinger and Frechette in North Chicago enjoyed it all, and it wasn't long before Homer Van Meter joined them. Van Meter had known Dillinger when both were imprisoned at Michigan City. Van Meter had been paroled first, and upon being released had gone to St. Paul where he remained until coming to Chicago to link up with Dillinger.

Headlines were referring to the Dillinger desperadoes as the "Terror Gang," and as newspaper publicity soared, rewards for their capture likewise rose. The notoriety caught the attention of Matt Leach, a Serbian immigrant who had worked in Gary's steel mills before joining the U.S. Army in 1915. Active in the American Legion and related veterans' affairs, Leach was a strong supporter of Paul V. McNutt, and when McNutt became Indiana's Governor in 1932, he named Leach as first captain of the state's fledgling police force. Leach's relentless pursuit of John Dillinger would become a Hoosier legend, and in conducting the chase Leach elicited support from many others, including Forrest Huntington, a private detective hired by insurance companies. Reading about Leach's zeal for the chase, Dillinger quipped, "If they ever catch me, he's gonna want to pin me with Lincoln's assassination."

Huntington was the link who contacted Arthur McGinnis, once a minor operative with Dillinger. McGinnis, succumbing to offers of rewards along with guarantees of anonymity, started feeding information to Leach soon after the Greencastle robbery.

McGinnis told lawmen that Dillinger, Makley, Copeland, and Pierpont had pulled the Greencastle job and that they were now with their girlfriends in North Chicago. He gave police the license number and description of Dillinger's latest auto acquisition, an Essex Terraplane. The garrulous McGinnis also disclosed that Dillinger had barber's itch (an inflammation of the hair follicles) and had an appointment to see Dr. Charles Eye, a dermatologist with offices at 4175 Irving Park Boulevard in Chicago.

McGinnis convinced Matt Leach that it would be better if Dillinger not be picked up but would be followed, enabling lawmen to trail him and capture the entire gang. McGinnis said he was sure he could turn in the whole outfit if given a little more time.

Following instructions from Leach, four officers parked outside Dr. Eye's office early in the evening of November 15, 1933, and watched as Dillinger with Frechette in the seat beside him drove up. In the back seat of the Essex Terraplane sat another man and woman, most likely Harry Pierpont and Mary Kinder. Dillinger got out, went into the doctor's office, and came out about fifteen minutes later.

After emerging from the doctor's office, Dillinger, apparently unaware of the trap, got behind the wheel of the Terraplane and backed into Irving Boulevard before getting onto Foster Avenue and heading east. Huntington reported:

> We started after him at once, passed the two police squad cars, and caught up with Dillinger's car about two squares east. We pulled alongside his speeding machine, and Indiana State Police Officer Art Keller fired five loads of buckshot from a twelve-gauge riot gun into the left door of the Terraplane as well as the window and front tire. But Dillinger kept going. Officer Rooney and Artery also fired their revolvers into Dillinger's car but without effect. These guns were fired at a range of less than ten feet, traveling at a speed of about sixty miles per hour. [13]

Frechette testified much later that in this chase, no shots had been fired by either Dillinger or Van Meter, and that Dillinger had no idea police were watching him enter the doctor's office. Word soon drifted through the underworld grapevine that McGinnis had been the stool pigeon and now gang members were out to "get him."

For a month—an unusually long period during his violent years—Dillinger and his pals holed up, robbed no banks and raided no police stations. Then on November 20, 1933, they struck the American Bank and Trust Company in Racine, Wisconsin.

Dillinger, Makley, and Pierpont, aided by Russell Clark pulled the Racine job. The "Dillinger Gang" referred to so often in the press was not a single group always with the same members. On occasions others would join and some would drop out. Harry Pierpont, Homer Van Meter, and John "Red" Hamilton, were more or less regulars, but others like Charles Makley, Edward Shouse, Russell Clark, and Harry Copeland—all with known criminal records—were in for specific capers. Makley, a salesman, at 45, was older than the others. Clark, a tailor, had joined while in prison serving twenty years for a bank robbery, and Shouse had been imprisoned for auto theft and grand larceny.

Charles "Fat Charlie" Makley was one of six children born to a poor Catholic family in St. Marys, Ohio, in 1888. He left school after the seventh grade, and like a majority of others began his career in crime by petty thefts when he was in his teens. For a time during the Prohibition era, he dabbled as a bootlegger and con man. His first robbery of consequence occurred in 1921 when he and a companion held up two messengers employed by the National Bank in Kansas City of $97,000. Makley was arrested for the crime and convicted two years later but was released on a hefty bond.

Then he began collecting fellow outlaws forming a gang that robbed banks throughout the Midwest. Leader of the horde, the portly Makley looked like a prosperous businessman, was usually accepted in that guise, and was able to talk his way out of trouble. One estimate was that the Makley bunch in less than two years stole more than $500,000 from banks in Indiana, Ohio, and Missouri. [14]

Makley's demise came in 1926 after he and three associates held up and robbed a messenger and guard taking $79,000 to a bank in Kansas City. When arrested, Makley broke down and confessed to bank robberies at Linn Grove, Indiana, Ansonia, Chickasaw, and St. Henry in Ohio, as well as banks in Festus and Ferguson, Missouri.

Behind bars in the death house of the Ohio State Penitentiary, Makley in 1934 joined Harry Pierpont in an attempted jail break. The attempt failed, and when the prison riot squad arrived and fired a volley of shots at the two convicts, Makley was wounded fatally. He died within the hour in the prison hospital.

Pierpont was shot twice, one bullet striking him near the base of his spine, the other creasing his scalp. Neither was fatal, and he recovered enough for his sentenced execution to take place slightly more than a month later. At midnight on October 17, 1934, Harry "Red" Hamilton dressed in a blue serge suit, no necktie and with coat unbuttoned, seated himself in the electric chair. A current of 2,000 volts passed through his body, and he was pronounced dead at 12:14 A.M. [15]

Russell "Boobie" Clark was eight years younger than Makley. After finishing the sixth grade, he had left home. In 1919 at the close of WW I, Clark enlisted in the army but was given a dishonorable discharge four months later for reasons now unknown.

"Boobie" Clark had a long rap sheet by the time he was arrested and arraigned for the murder of Sheriff Jesse Sarber. In February, 1934, Clark along with Harry Pierpont and Charles Makley were tried in a state court sitting at Lima, Ohio, for first degree murder charges. Pierpont and Makley were found guilty and with no recommendation for mercy faced the death penalty. Clark was the last to be tried, and although judged guilty there were enough extenuating circumstances to win him a recommendation for mercy, which meant that he was given life imprisonment rather than the electric chair.

Clark served his time in the state prison at Columbus, Ohio, until 1968. In August of that year, dying of cancer he was released and passed away on Christmas Eve, 1968, in Hazel Park, Michigan. [16]

John Hamilton, called "Red" by fellow hoodlums, had been imprisoned at the penitentiary in Michigan City since March, 1927. Twenty-nine years old, he had been born in Ontario, Canada, and had worked briefly as a lumberjack, a deck hand on cargo ships crossing the Great Lakes, and as a freight hustler for the Oakland Motor Company.

His first brush with the law was in 1923 when for bootlegging he was forced out of the town where he and his wife were living. Some friends said that his wife's desire for high living was what put him on his criminal path.

The first major crime in which he was known to have participated was a $33,000 heist of the Lakey Foundry in Muskegon, Michigan, in July, 1925. The next year he and an accomplice tried to burglarize a coal company in Grand Rapids but were scared off by police. A week and a half later, Hamilton accompanied by four or five companions stole $25,000 from the Fulton Street Branch of the Kent State Bank in Grand Rapids. [17]

A woman's tip led to the arrest of Curtis Turner, one of the thieves committing the State Bank robbery in Grand Rapids, and he squealed like a stuck hog. Turner also disclosed that the cadre of thugs was planning to hit a bank in South Bend, Indiana. Alerted, police staked out the banks and went to the house where Hamilton and Raymond Lawrence, a former rumrunner, were staying. Arrested and tried, the two bandits were sentenced to 25 years in the Indiana State Prison after pleading guilty to the charges against them in order to avoid possible life sentences if tried in a Michigan court. As the court pronounced the verdict, sentence, Hamilton's wife sitting in the courtroom with her four-year-old son wept. Her grief was not long lasting, however, for she divorced Red soon thereafter and remarried, dying in childbirth three years after Red's incarceration.

A few days before Hamilton's trial, Pierpont, Makley, and Mary Kinder had cased the bank in Racine, Wisconsin, checking out cages, position of the vaults, personnel, and getaway routes. Two other associates, Ed Shouse and Harry Copeland were in on the planning, but Shouse fancied himself a ladies' man, and Mary heard him talk of ditching Dillinger. She relayed that information to Dillinger who threw a roll of bills on the table and told Shouse to get the hell out while he was still alive. Shouse didn't need to be persuaded; he grabbed the money and headed for California.

On the morning of the proposed robbery, the four gang members were eating breakfast in a Milwaukee restaurant when they saw Dillinger's name in a newspaper story from Chicago. Harry Copeland, a "Dillinger gangster," had gotten drunk in a tavern, started a fight in an alley with a woman, and gotten picked up by police. Dillinger spoke for all when he said, "We don't need Cope or Shouse anyway."

In mid-afternoon of the 20th, Harry Pierpont, tall, good-looking with light blue eyes walked into the Racine bank carrying a roll of paper under his arms. A bookkeeper thought he must be a salesman as she watched him go over to a window on the left side and paste up a large Red Cross poster almost blocking out any view from the street. Three other men then entered the bank: the first was middle-aged and stout—Makley. Both the second and third were short and stocky—Dillinger and John "Red" Hamilton.

Makley pointed a revolver at a cashier, Harold Graham, and said, "Stick 'em up." Graham busy with a customer and hardly noticing, muttered, "Next window, please." With that, Makley fired a shot striking Graham in the right elbow, who stepped on an alarm button as he clutched his arm. The button was connected to the police station but did not sound inside the bank.

Responding to Dillinger's commands, employees and patrons dropped to the floor while he prodded Bank President Grover Weyland and two cashiers into the vault. The alarm tripped by the wounded teller brought Sergeant Wilbur Hansen and Patrolman Cyril Boyard to the bank. Without drawing their weapons, they rushed indoors where Boyard was confronted by Pierpont who tried to yank the patrolman's revolver from hits holster. The attempt was unsuccessful because the weapon was fitted too closely, and just then in came Sergeant Wilbur Hansen with a machine gun pointed downward. "Get that punk with the Tommy gun!" yelled Pierpont.

Makley obliged by firing and hitting Hansen twice but not wounding him seriously. By this time, Dillinger had cleaned out the vault, and Hamilton had scooped up the money from the tellers' cages. Their sacks loaded with twenty-eight thousand dollars in bills, the bandits moved toward the front door while prodding President Weyland and three female employees in front of them.

Outside, a small crowd had gathered and watched as Dillinger climbed behind the wheel of a large black Buick. With his pointed pistol, he motioned for President Weyland and a cashier, Mrs. Henry Platzke, to stand on the running board beside him. On the other side of the car, Harry Pierpont had gotten in and ordered Patrolman Boyard to do likewise by standing on the right side running board.

Dillinger backed the car out of the parking lot and started toward the lake just as a police car appeared from the opposite direction. Weyland frantically waved it away, fearing any shots from it might hit the hostages.

Dillinger turned right and headed south along the lake shore, but after three or four blocks he turned again and started driving west. Reaching heavier traffic, he stopped and ordered Boyard to get off, and under the menacing guns of Hamilton and Pierpont, Weyland and Platzke were waved into the back seats.

Dillinger kept on small country roads, and as evening approached, he stopped to refill with gasoline. Then on more dirt roads he came to a clump of woods, where he stopped. He and his companions ordered Mrs. Platzke and Grover Weyland out of the car, tied their hands loosely with shoe laces, and warned them not to summon help too quickly—twenty minutes would be about right.

Then the gang drove away. The two hostages managed to free themselves and were able to walk to a nearby farm. Another crime was chalked up on the Dillinger Gang's rap sheet.

Gang members enjoyed spending their Racine loot for nearly a month before any of them got into further trouble. On December 14th, John Hamilton, the older ex-con easily identified because of two missing fingers on his right hand, went to a North Side Auto Shop to pick up his repaired car. With him was a girlfriend named Elaine DeKant Dent. Hamilton's car had been identified from a previous heist, and police were watching to see who came to get it.

Among the watchers was Sergeant William Shanley, decorated WW I veteran, father of four daughters, and winner of the *Chicago Tribune's* "Hero of the Year" award. Shanley approached Hamilton and Dent and asked Hamilton if the repaired car was his. When Hamilton answered yes, Shanley told him to keep his hands visible and then started to search him. Hamilton was too quick and pulled a gun from his own shoulder holster, shooting Shanley twice, fatally. Hamilton got away on foot, leaving his companion Elaine Dent behind, and was able to get back to Dillinger's apartment.

The slaying of a policeman, particularly one the newspapers had honored, touched off a barrage of publicity. *Chicago's Tribune* emblazoned, "Escaped Convict Slays Police Hero," and papers from Illinois, Indiana, Ohio, and as far away as New York echoed the charge. [18]

Despite the fact that he had nothing to do with the death of Officer Shanley, Dillinger was tarred by it. Hamilton was known to be a Dillinger gang member, and readers assumed the leader had orchestrated the policeman's death. Wire service stories penetrated even small towns, and in Chicago the city's Crime Commission named John Dillinger Public Enemy Number One, laying crime after crime upon him and his cohorts. The city's police organized a group of forty men designated the "Dillinger Squad" and put out hints that the outlaws were hooked up with Jewish and Italian syndicates in New York or Chicago run by such titans as Dutch Schultz, Lucky Luciano, and Al Capone.

The pot was stirred more when on December 20, 1933, an Indiana state policeman was killed during the capture of Ed Shouse, another known member of Dillinger's gang. With the heat on them, Dillinger, pals, and molls fled southeast to Florida's Daytona Beach. They were lolling in the Sunshine State when police in the Windy City acting on a faulty tip raided an apartment in Rogers Park and killed three men. The men in truth were bank robbers but had no connection with Dillinger. [19]

Nevertheless, another crime in Chicago was attributed to Dillinger even though he was in Florida. By the second week in January, 1934, he was running low on funds and decided to leave his Florida sanctuary and return to more familiar haunts. On January 15, almost as soon as he got back up north, he, Hamilton, and an unidentified third man robbed the First National Bank in East Chicago, Indiana, of $20,376.

As was their practice, the robbers entered the bank a bit before three o'clock in the afternoon, just shy of closing time when deposits were at their height. Dillinger opened his overcoat to expose a machine gun cradled in his arms and yelled, "This is a stick-up! Put up your hands, everybody!"

A dozen employees and more than fifteen customers obeyed instantly as Hamilton stepped behind the counter and began scooping up money from the cages. The robbers were unaware that a vice president had stepped on an alarm button notifying police in the station a block and a half away.

Patrolman Hobart Wilgus was the first cop to arrive, and he burst into the bank with his pistol drawn. However, Dillinger's machine gun was trained on Wilgus as he entered, and he was forced to drop his weapon and to line up with the other captives.

Seeing other police approaching, Dillinger called to Hamilton: "There's been an alarm, and the cops are coming. But take your time; get all the dough, and we'll make out all right."

The two bandits collected more than twenty thousand dollars before they moved to the door, shoving bank president Walter Spencer and police officer Wilgus before them as human shields, the same as they had done with hostages in the Racine hold-up.

As the four emerged from the bank, a policeman on the street, William O'Malley, thought he had a clear shot. He got off shots all right, but at the same time so did Dillinger with his machine gun. Officer Wilgus later described what he saw.

> There were about thirty of us lined up before Dillinger's machine gun. When we got outside the door, O'Malley, who had put himself in front of a five-and-ten-cent store across from the bank, yelled, "Wilgus, Wilgus!" I knew he wanted me to jump to one side so that he could get a shot at Dillinger. I jumped, and O'Malley opened fire. He and Dillinger shot at about the same time. O'Malley shot Dillinger four times in the chest, but Dillinger was wearing a bullet-proof vest, and the bullets just splashed off. When they picked up O'Malley afterward he had eight bullet holes in him. The bullets went right on through—not a bullet in his body.[20]

Dillinger and Hamilton freed their two hostages and raced to the Plymouth they had stolen for the caper. Officers on the street let off a fusillade at them as they sped away, wounding Hamilton, whose blood-stained pistol was later found on the street.

In addition to bank robberies, Dillinger now had murder—a capital crime—on his record. He headed back into Chicago proper where he could find medical care for Hamilton. In the city were doctors on the skids for one reason or another—alcoholism, drug addiction, performing illegal abortions, or other malpractices. Underworld pals passed the name of Dr. Joseph Moran to Dillinger. Joseph P. Moran, 39 years old, had an office on Irving Park Boulevard and was clinging to the last shreds of respectability. An alcoholic, he had stooped to specializing in illegal abortions and gunshot wounds—the last retreats of an M.D. on his way further down. He had been convicted of performing a botched abortion and sentenced to ten years in prison, but after serving only two years of that sentence a lenient judge had granted him a parole, allowing him to return to medical practice. He quickly linked up with high level criminals including felons from the notorious Barker gang.

In 1934, when Dillinger and Pat Cherrington brought the wounded Hamilton to Moran's office, Dr. Moran determined that Hamilton had taken six shots in the shoulder and left arm and one just above the pelvic bone. He callously told Dillinger and Cherrington that he doubted if their friend would make it. Dillinger told him to try anyway. Moran removed the slugs, dressed the wounds, and then hit Dillinger with a $5,000 bill—a whopping amount for those Depression years.[21]

Billie Frechette had come down from Wisconsin, and she joined Dillinger in finding a house to rent where Hamilton could rest up and recover. Hamilton would remain in Chicago until his wounds healed enough to permit traveling. When they had done so, he moved to Ft. Wayne, Indiana and stayed there in relative safety under the care of his half sister.

In the meantime, Dillinger by telephone contacted former pals for help in finding a safer haven for himself. Charles Makley told him of a woman friend in Arizona. She would provide shelter, and the western desert would be an excellent place in which to disappear for a while. Makley said he and Russell Clark would come out and rendezvous with him, so with a brand new car and plenty of cash still in his pocket, Dillinger along with Frechette headed west.

Makley, Clark, and Clark's girlfriend Opal Long arrived first and registered at the Congress, a three-story hotel. A day later Dillinger accompanied by Frechette drove into town and registered at a motor court as Mr. and Mrs. Frank Sullivan. They hardly had time to settle in before Harry Pierpont and Mary Kinder came to the same motor court and were given adjoining cabins. Together with Clark and Makley, both of whom picked up local dates, Dillinger, Frechette, Pierpont, and Kinder spent the days sightseeing; in the evenings they explored the town's night life. They were a flashy crowd with their big cars and plenty of money.

On January 23rd. a fire broke out in the Congress Hotel, and while firemen were trying to put out the blaze, an engineer named William Benedict saw Makley and Clark trying to hoist a ladder up to the third floor. He asked them what the hell they were doing and got a reply that they wanted to save valuable documents in a strong box in their room. Benedict was persuaded to help them get the box out of Room 329, and Benedict was handing it to another fireman when Makley yelled, "Be careful of that box! Don't drop it!"

Benedict didn't know the box in his hands contained machine guns and ammunition, but he had been warned and realized whatever was in the box must indeed be valuable. His belief was boosted when Makley gave him $2.00—a generous tip in those times.

At the fire station next morning Benedict was leafing through a detective magazine and happened to come across a picture of a wanted criminal: Russell Clark. Resemblance between the picture and one of the two strangers who had warned him about the strong box at the Congress fire was unmistakable. Benedict alerted Tucson police who in turn learned the hotel fire had forced Clark and Makley to find new living quarters. They had chosen to rent a one-story house a few blocks from the University of Arizona, and Makley had introduced himself to the owner, Mrs. Hattie Strauss, as George Davis, a successful shoe salesman from Indiana.

Police quickly staked out the Strauss home hoping to catch either Clark or Makley, and the next afternoon they followed Clark when he came out, climbed into a Studebaker and drove to an appliance store. There he was arrested but claimed his name was George Davis and that he should be taken back to the Strauss house to get identification papers. Instead, police took him to the city jail.

More police were recruited, and Sergeant Frank Eyman was put in charge. He along with three others—all in civilian clothes—went in an unmarked car to the Strauss home. The plan for capturing Clark was for Chet Sherman, a small man of about 5'4", to don a Western Union cap and pretend he had a telegram for Clark. A fourth man, Dallas Ford, would wait across the street to back up Sherman.

When Clark came forward to accept the expected telegram, Sherman drew out his pistol. Clark, a much bigger man, grabbed him, knocked the weapon out of his hands, and wrestled him toward the bedroom just as Ford from across the street came running up the front steps. Opal Long was standing alongside Clark and the struggling Sherman; she tried to slam the front door on Ford's hand, but he was too fast. The door caught him, breaking two fingers although he managed to force himself inside the house.

By this time, Sergeant Eyman and his partner had broken in the rear door. In the bedroom, the wiry, determined Sherman had been able to yank the gun from Clark's grip, and with it he slugged Clark twice who crumbled to the floor. The four policemen cuffed the prostrate Clark and took both him and Opal to the station. If the police had waited a half-hour longer, they might also have captured Harry Pierpont and Mary Kinder.

Pierpont and Kinder returned to the Strauss house expecting to find Clark and Makley there, but the messed up furniture and blood on the front door made Pierpont suspicious. He got back in the car with Mary and drove to their own cabin. From it he phoned a lawyer friend and told him two friends, Mr. George Davis and Opal Long, had been picked up by police. Pierpont urged the lawyer to hurry to the police station and try to get them out on bail.

Earlier in the week, Pierpont had driven through a boulevard stop sign, and Earl Nolan and Milo "Swede" Walker, two motorcycle cops, had stopped him. Pierpont told them he had been driving fast because he thought he was being followed by another car. Both policemen believed him, let him off with a warning, and invited him to report any further fears to the police station. In their friendly exchange, Pierpont disclosed he was staying at the motor court on Sixth Avenue.

The arrest of Clark and Makley touched off a lot of discussion at police headquarters, and some of it referred to other gang members. When Patrolman Earl Nolan heard fellow cops describe Pierpont, he suddenly remembered the timid driver he had stopped a few days earlier. He shared that information with Sergeant Eyman who quickly organized a squad to surround the motor court on Sixth Avenue.

While Eyman and Nolan were en route to the motor court, they passed Pierpont and Mary Kinder going in the other direction. Nolan recognized the Buick and ordered the squad car's driver to turn around and give chase. The police car caught up with Pierpont after only a few blocks.

Eyman knowing he now was confronting a desperate criminal adopted a ploy; after stopping the Buick he pointed out to its driver that the car had been stopped because it did not show an inspection license. "You'll have to get one; otherwise, you'll be stopped by every traffic cop in Arizona," he assured the unsuspecting Pierpont.

Eyman said he'd guide Pierpont to the police station and help him get a sticker. Then he got into the back seat of the Buick. As soon as they walked into the station, a waiting policeman stuck a gun in Pierpont's ribs; Eyman also pulled his own, and Pierpont found himself under arrest.

In frisking him, police found two valuable leads: 1304 East 5th St., the Tucson house Dillinger and Frechette had rented, and an Indiana driver's license made out to John Donovan, one of Dillinger's aliases.

A force was mobilized and sent to the Strauss home just after dusk on January 25, 1934, and when Dillinger and Frechette returned from a sightseeing trip, they had no idea their companions had been arrested. Dillinger attempted an excuse, saying he must have come to the wrong house, but the cops didn't buy it. Tucson police were elated; they had captured most of the Dillinger gang, and the event was a bonanza for radio and newspaper reports across the country.

With so many of the gang's members in custody, a media mania began. A caption for the lead story in the prestigious *New York Times* read "Bandits Fare Poorly," and the story following it implied it was a mistake for criminals to abandon security in big city hiding places because enterprising, capable police were everywhere and always on the lookout. [22]

The *Chicago Daily News* reported Dillinger's arrest along with photos of cops in big Stetson hats leading the manacled prisoner to his cell. In another story two days later the same paper quoted him:

My God! How did you know I was in town? I'll be the laughing stock of the country. How could a hick town police force ever suspect me? [23]

The *Chicago Tribune* headlined "Catch Dillinger and Three Aides," in its story about the "desperate Indiana outlaw" who for months had been committing robberies and murders, evading police and militia along the way.[24]

The *Tribune* story included the fact that Dillinger's sweetheart, a woman identified as Anne Martin, had been seized with him. That was the name Billie Frechette gave, and it was not until Dillinger's death while she was in a Michigan jail for harboring him that she admitted to posing as Anne Martin, the woman with John Dillinger when he was arrested in Tucson.

Chapter 12. Crown Point Melodrama

The captured criminals were given a preliminary hearing in the Pima County Courthouse where sightseers overflowed into corridors and onto the lawn. The hearings were brief, and the four men were held in bonds of $100,000 for each. The three women—Opal Long, Mary Kinder, and Anne Martin (Billie Frechette)—were held on bonds of $5,000 each for obstructing justice.

When the name "Anne Martin" was called, Harry Pierpont laughed and said, "There ain't no such animal." Miss Martin was not further identified, and Dillinger added a romantic touch to the proceedings when, being led past her at an adjoining table, he stopped long enough to kiss her.

Hundreds of newsmen and photographers from all over the country poured into Tucson with the result that Dillinger's name, formerly known mainly in the Middle West, was spread nationwide. As newspapers throughout the country printed their stories, authorities from Indiana, Ohio, and Wisconsin came to the Tucson jail with warrants seeking custody of the prisoners. The Indiana delegation was first to arrive and wanted Dillinger for the slaying of Officer O'Malley in East Chicago.

The Wisconsin delegation came a day later and claimed it ought to get Dillinger because it had solid evidence of his participation in the Racine hold up.

Lawyers from Ohio came with announcement that Indiana authorities had assured them their only interest was John Dillinger and that his partners Pierpont, Makley, and Clark could be handed over to Ohio for prosecution in the murder of Sheriff Jess Sarber. There was a great deal of legal wrangling before the custody issue was settled. While attorneys and authorities vied for such control, reporters were permitted to interview the prisoners, and each stereotyped thug began to show his personality. Harry Pierpont raged and swore, vowing to get even with the "God damned cops who had captured him." Charles Makley, told he was being investigated for the kidnapping of Edward Bremer in St. Paul, joked that he was too good a gunman to stoop so low as kidnapping, adding that he "had broken out of better Bastilles than this one." [1]

At times, Dillinger was sullen and refused to talk, but more often he was light-hearted and affable, conversing with reporters freely and politely. He had a trickster streak and liked to banter, making him very quotable. Hassles over custody finally were settled, and with approval from the Arizona governor, it was agreed that Dillinger would be returned to Indiana to face charges for the murder of Officer O'Malley; Pierpont, Makley, and Clark would be sent to Ohio for robbery and murder charges in that state.

East Chicago, where O'Malley had been slain, was in northern Indiana lying on the southern shore of Lake Michigan. The community also was in Lake County, the second largest county in Indiana. The county's seat was Crown Point, a town four miles northeast of Cedar Lake and equidistant south from the heavily traveled U. S. Route 30.

The Lake County Sheriff holding office in Crown Point was Mrs. Lillian Holley, a middle-aged widow who had inherited the position after her husband had been fatally shot just months earlier. Mrs. Holley and a nephew named Carroll Holley were among the Hoosiers who came to Tucson to pick up Dillinger. The two Holleys along with other authorities decided it would be best to try to get the culprit back to Indiana with a minimum of publicity; consequently, plans were adopted to move him east by aircraft.

On January 29, five men escorted Dillinger, handcuffed to Deputy Sheriff Carroll Holley, out of the Tucson jail. The prisoner and the five officials guarding him were flown in a chartered plane to Douglas, Arizona, where they transferred to an American Airlines plane that carried them to Dallas, Little Rock, Memphis, and St. Louis before landing in Chicago. Reporters had gotten wind of the flight, and they along with ever larger crowds gathered at each stop along the way. In Chicago, more than three dozen policemen brandishing rifles and shotguns met the plane as it taxied in. A number of Indiana troopers joined them, and a thirteen-car convoy took the notorious captive to Crown Point. Meanwhile, back in Arizona, authorities put Pierpont, Makley, Clark, and Mary Kinder on a Southern Pacific train for shipment back to Ohio. [2]

About 7:40 in the evening of January 30, the Dillinger cavalcade arrived at the Lake County jail in Crown Point—a jail widely hyped as escape proof. A crowd of four hundred curious onlookers had assembled to see the noted criminal. Sheriff Lillian Holley, 38 years old, 5'5" tall and weighing 110 pounds, was in charge. Her husband, Dr. Roy F. Holley, a Gary dentist, had been elected sheriff, but just two weeks after beginning his second term he had been fatally shot by a crazed gunman. Lillian Holley had been quickly appointed her husband's successor.

Dillinger's arraignment was set for Friday, February 9, 1934, and before that date he hired white-haired, 49-year-old Louis Piquett as his chief attorney. Piquett had been a bartender who put himself through law school before slithering his way upward through Democratic bigwigs in Chicago to become Cook County Prosecutor. He abandoned that office to take up the more lucrative career as a gangland mouthpiece, and among his clients were abortionists, bootleggers, killers, and the scum of Chicago's crime syndicate.

After agreeing to defend Dillinger, Piquett went back to Chicago to prepare his case—a case he never got to argue in court. Nevertheless, he became a vital cog in the machinery which kept the bandit's name in the public view and contributed to the folklore built around him.

The bank robber was in a good-natured mood when he and his escorts arrived at the Lake County jail. He bantered with reporters and got off a couple of one-liners while pausing on steps of the jail. Newspaper cameramen were taking movies, and Dillinger clad in a white shirt and an unbuttoned vest with a lead pencil stuck in one vest pocket and a black comb sticking out from another was standing next to Indiana prosecuting attorney Robert Estill. On Estill's right was the motherly looking Sheriff Lillian Holley and behind these three a gaggle of men crowded around. A newsman called out asking Estill to put his arm around Dillinger. Estill obliged, and Dillinger, giving a sardonic smile, draped his own arm on the shoulder of the man scheduled to prosecute him. What a scoop! Piquett made certain that photo was flashed to newspapers from east to west, and many readers interpreted the photo as one showing Dillinger just a hometown boy caught in a minor escapade.

At Dillinger's arraignment, Piquett and Lake County Prosecutor Robert Estill got into a shouting match until Judge William Murray warned both to calm down. Dillinger at the defense table wore a trademark grin and sat throughout the exchange with no other expression. When it ended and a trial date was set for March 12, he leaned over to whisper to Piquett, "Atta boy, counsel."[3]

Despite Piquett's efforts to ballyhoo the name of his infamous client, there was other news to report. Food, housing, clothing, and jobs were still uppermost in the minds of most citizens, and an energetic federal administration was taking remarkable steps to meet those needs. Before the year ended, there would be 33 new government agencies created, 24,303 new federal employees, and an increase of 20% in the national debt.

In California, Dr. Francis Townsend advocated an appealing "Old Age Revolving Pensions Plan" whereby each person over the age of 60 would receive $200 each month, providing he would spend it within thirty days. From cameras in the tinsel town of Hollywood emerged Shirley Temple, a dimpled darling who captured the hearts of every movie-goer. William Ashley "Billy" Sunday, American revivalist began a bonanza two-week revival run in New York City, and auto mogul Henry Ford made a confident gesture by establishing $5.00 per day as a minimum wage for more than half his 75,000 workers.

And there were other crimes and criminals. Clyde Barrow and his companion Bonnie Parker were named as the robbers of the State Savings Bank at Knierim, Iowa, and two and a half weeks later the pair with help from others broke into the National Guard Armory at Ranger, Texas. On February 22, Clyde Barrow and Raymond Hamilton robbed the R. P. Henry & Sons Bank at Lancaster, Texas, of $4,138. The Bremer kidnapping case in St. Paul had not been solved, but newspapers were trumpeting that Arthur "Doc" Barker and Alvin Karpis were suspects. Barker was identified through fingerprints on a gasoline can, and a sales clerk picked out Karpis as the purchaser of an incriminating flashlight.

There was an hiatus of news from the prisoner at Crown Point, but a story was building there which would make his former deeds pale by comparison. The story would match any scripts Hollywood screenwriters could produce and began with his hiring of a lawyer.

Dillinger had boasted that no jail could hold him, yet Sheriff Holley and her deputies were confident that theirs—a guardhouse touted as being escape-proof—was up to the job. What really happened when he escaped from there on March 3, 1934, is still murky, for there have been wild, fanciful, and conflicting versions. The extent to which bribes and abettors played their parts is uncertain, but it is incontrovertible that the breakout was one of the most audacious jailbreaks in history.

An early version of the event claimed Dillinger himself used razor blades to whittle a piece of washboard into something resembling a small automatic pistol with which he disarmed guards before getting his hands on their weapons. Then with help from another inmate, Herbert Youngblood, behind bars for murdering, he locked up more than twenty-six guards or jail employees, took two hostages, and marched out of the escape-proof jail to climb aboard a waiting automobile. The Crown Point jail was shown as escape proof as the Titanic was unsinkable!

Louis Piquett had been a university athlete, prize fighter, and bar tender before he managed to secure a license to practice law. Through a circle of bigwig Chicago politicians he became city prosecutor and yielded that position only when he realized representing criminals rather than prosecuting them was far more lucrative. His reputation took on darker shades as the money rolled in.

One of Piquett's first acts as Dillinger's attorney was to take Billie Frechette to the jail and introduce her as Mrs. John Dillinger. Billie told her sweetheart that "Red" Hamilton, the pal Dillinger hoped might lead a jail raid or dynamite enterprise was still recovering from wounds received at the East Chicago confrontation. Moreover, he had been contacted and said he did not favor either idea.

Among Piquett's contacts was Arthur O'Leary, a suave, bon vivant, and wealthy bond salesman. O'Leary is the person who conceived the idea of a fake weapon. He had read that a prisoner in a Wisconsin jail had made a good imitation out of soap, dyed it with black ink, and would have made a successful escape if it had not been for an alert guard. Perhaps a guard or two at Crown Point could be persuaded to join in the scheme.

O'Leary broached his idea to Piquett and went with him to visit the jailed Dillinger, who still wanted gangster pals to either dynamite the jail or raid it. Piquett pointed out drawbacks: the jail was well guarded; in the outer lobby were heavy, tripod-mounted machine guns, and a sizeable contingent of state police had been collected and put on full alert.

Dillinger, reluctant to give up the idea of using gangster muscle, finally agreed with Piquett's stratagem when the lawyer said Deputy Sheriff Ernest Blunk had turned down every effort to smuggle in a real gun.

The break began on Saturday, March 3, when Sam Cahoon, the jail's turnkey and handyman, was bringing an armload of soap to 14 prisoners doing exercises in the corridor outside their individual cells. Among those prisoners was Dillinger, and when Cahoon attempted to pass him, suddenly there was a gun stuck in his ribs, and he heard Dillinger warn, "Do exactly as I tell you or I'll blow you apart."

Cahoon was ordered to call Deputy Ernest Blunk, and when the deputy with a holstered pistol on his hip arrived, Dillinger quickly grabbed this real gun. Watching was a trustee who carried a full set of keys. Dillinger waved him over and took his keys to unlock a cell holding Herbert Youngblood, a black inmate awaiting trial for murdering a Gary fruit peddler. Dillinger knew Youngblood was desperate, ready to do anything to escape.

Blunk was told to call Warden Lou Baker, and when Baker came onto the scene, he, too, was ordered to put up his hands. Youngblood and Dillinger, now armed with Blunk's gun with a bullet in its chamber, prodding Cahoon, Blunk, and Baker before them, moved through the jail to pass and enter a small room where a guard was sitting half asleep with a machine gun in his lap. Dillinger pointed his pistol at the head of the guard, who offered no resistance when Youngblood seized the machine gun. Now both prisoners were fully armed, and when Warden Hiles of the Indiana National Guard happened along, he, too, had to give up his .45 pistol.

Dillinger and Youngblood roamed the jail, taking more guards or attendants; before they were done the two had seized more than two dozen guards, trustees, or employees. Knowing he would need money, Dillinger robbed several of them but got only $15. Then he and Youngblood, pushing Deputy Ernest Blunk in front of them, emerged from the jail and went to the nearby Main Street Garage where mechanic Edwin J. Saager told them Sheriff Holley's new Ford V-8 was gassed up and available. Saager would be indicted later for abetting in the escape, but the charge was dismissed for lack of evidence.

By stealing Sheriff Holley's car and driving it across the Indiana state line, Dillinger violated interstate commerce laws, specifically the Dyer Act. Now he was wanted for another crime as well as for murders and bank robberies in several states; moreover, this transgression permitted FBI Director J. Edgar Hoover legitimately to put men on his trail.

Blunk and Saager were ordered to get into the Ford, and Blunk was told to drive. He did that while Youngblood sat in the front seat alongside him with a machine gun cradled in his arms. Dillinger sat in back with Saager and kept his loaded pistol out and ready.

Blunk was instructed to head west, and the car soon crossed the Indiana state line before stopping at a crossroads a few miles northeast of Peotone, Illinois. Blunk and Saager were released and given four dollars to get home, and the two remained standing by the roadside as Youngblood drove the V-8 north toward the friendly confines of Chicago. [4]

CHAPTER 13. DILLINGER RAIDS

After the jailbreak, investigators theorized Dillinger must have had help; somehow accomplices had smuggled a real weapon into his hands. Deputy Blunk was reported as having been paid $5,000 and garage mechanic Ed Saager $2,500 to grease the scheme. Both were charged with abetting the escape, but each was acquitted for lack of evidence.[1]

Upon arrival in Chicago, Dillinger phoned lawyer Piquett and arranged to meet him that afternoon. When Piquett got to the designated location on Belmont Street, he found Dillinger lolling in the driver's seat of a late model Ford V-8 and Herbert Youngblood asleep in its back. Dillinger said he needed money, and Piquett gave him all the cash he had with him—three hundred dollars.

The next move was for Dillinger to separate himself from Youngblood, who because of his color made the two a conspicuous pair. He gave Youngblood a hundred dollars and two of the pistols taken from Crown Point before directing him to get on a southbound street car and disappear.

Youngblood did not really disappear, for on March 16th, he was trapped by three deputy sheriffs in a small tobacco and candy shop in Port Huron, Michigan. In the ensuing confrontation, one lawman was killed, the other two wounded. Youngblood, fatally hit by six bullets, claimed just before dying that Dillinger had been with him a day earlier.[2]

Two hundred dollars wouldn't last very long, and Dillinger quickly called pals to help carry out another heist. While working in the shirt division at the Indiana State Prison, he had struck up friendship with Homer Van Meter, a fellow inmate. Van Meter's criminal career had started in his mid-teens. After the sixth grade, he had run away from his home in Ft. Wayne, Indiana, to Chicago, where he worked for short periods as a bellhop, waiter, or salesman. He joined accomplices in a few petty crimes before with one of them he boarded a Pullman observation train passing through Gary, Indiana, and held up the passengers. Police nabbed him almost at once, and he was sentenced to ten to twenty years for highway robbery. While serving his sentence, one official described him: *"This fellow is a criminal of the most dangerous type... He is a murderer at heart, and if society is to be safe-guarded, his type must be confined throughout their natural lives."*[3]

Dillinger in Chicago needed money and lots of it; no small time bank yielding a couple of hundred dollars would do the trick. He'd need a bigger haul, and for that he'd have to have more men. With Van Meter's help, he summoned Lester Gillis (Baby Face Nelson), Tommy Carroll, Eddie Green, and the recovering Red Hamilton. All agreed with Dillinger's scheme for a heist at a bank in Sioux Falls, South Dakota, cased months earlier.

On March 6, 1934, three days after his sensational escape from Crown Point, Dillinger and five fellow thugs were five hundred miles from Chicago in Sioux Falls, and ready to enter the Security National Bank. The weather that morning was freezing as Tommy Carroll waited on the sidewalk; Eddie Green and Red Hamilton took positions near the front door, and the other three men, Van Meter, Nelson, and Dillinger, entered the bank. Once inside, they opened their overcoats and pulled out Thompson machine guns to train on patrons and employees.

Nelson shouted, "It's a stick-up! Everybody on the floor!"

With that, someone tripped an alarm, which started to ring loudly. The alarm didn't stop either Dillinger or Van Meter from raiding the tellers' cages and stuffing money into sacks. Then at gunpoint the two forced the bank president into the vault, where they helped themselves to more cash.

Meanwhile, a crowd attracted by the alarm, had formed outside the bank, and seeing a motorcycle cop among them, Nelson fired a shot through the plate glass window. His bullet struck the policeman, but luckily the wound was not fatal.

Then as had been their pattern in other robberies, the bandits grabbed a half dozen hostages, mostly women, and ordered them to stand on the running boards of their Packard sedan as in it they sped away.

The hostages were released unharmed just outside the city limits, and late that night in St. Paul, Dillinger and his companions divided more than forty-six thousand dollars.[4]

At the time of the robbery in Sioux Falls, Harry Pierpont's trial for murder was taking place in Lima, Ohio. Evidence against him was overwhelming, and the jury deliberated less than fifty-five minutes before returning with a verdict of guilty—with no recommendation for mercy—for murdering Sheriff Jess Sarber. The judge sentenced Pierpont to die in the electric chair on Friday, July 13th.

In the trial, Dillinger's name came up often as an accomplice in the crime. He was still on the loose, but police learned he was in Chicago. There were wild speculations about his next moves: he intended to kidnap either the governor or his daughter and demand Pierpont's freedom as a ransom; he and his gang were making plans to storm the Lima jail and free Pierpont. All police in northwestern Ohio were alerted to be on the lookout for an Illinois car with three men heavily armed, one of whom would be John Dillinger.

Dillinger, in fact, was planning another bank robbery. Three or four days after splitting the loot from Sioux Falls, he sent Eddie Green and Homer Van Meter to Mason City, Iowa, where they registered for a room at the YMCA and spent a day or two wandering around the town, paying particular attention to the neighborhood of the First National Bank.

Mason City was a typical Midwestern community in appearance and manner with a population of 25,000 citizens. The town was reasonably prosperous for the Depression era; indeed, in its vaults that day were more than $240,000—a sizeable sum for such a small city.

March 13, 1934, was cold and snowy when Green and Van Meter checked out of the Y and drove to the southeast of town where they parked across from a rural school and waited for a half-hour. Then from the north came a large black Buick; in it were Dillinger, Red Hamilton, Tommy Carroll, and Baby Face Nelson. Green and Van Meter got into the Buick with the newcomers, and the big auto now loaded with six armed men headed into town.

At 2:20 P.M., Harry Fisher, a bank teller, was in his cage serving a customer when he heard yelling. He looked through his teller's window and saw three well-dressed men waving guns and shouting, "Stick 'em up! This is a hold up!"

The gunmen were Green, Hamilton, and Van Meter. Van Meter said he was looking for bank president Willis Bagley, and almost at the moment he said it, he saw Bagley sitting at a desk facing the other direction. When Bagley swung his swivel chair around to face him, there was a machine gun in Van Meter's arms pointed right at him. Bagley, who later said his first thought was that a "crazy man" had gotten loose, jumped out of his chair and tried to make it to his private office. He reached it in time to slam the door in Van Meter's face, but that didn't keep the gunman from firing. Van Meter's bullets went through the door, most of them missing Bagley, only one wounding him slightly.

Swearing in frustration, Van Meter went back to help Green and Nelson who were rounding up people in the bank's lobby. The three bandits prodded the hostages outside to the sidewalk in front of the bank where John Dillinger, dressed in a gray overcoat with a striped muffler and topped by a gray Fedora, was lining up other persons who could serve as living shields.

A crowd had gathered across the street, apparently coming to watch what they thought was a film being made of a bank robbery. A few onlookers pushed forward hoping to get a glimpse of movie stars. When some persons began to realize what they were witnessing was not a movie take, pandemonium broke out. A reporter coming onto the scene saw Baby Face Nelson holding a machine gun and across the street from him Tommy Carroll holding another. As the reporter ducked for cover, Nelson fired a wild spray at him, hitting only store windows, and another longer misdirected burst at an auto speeding by.

At the same time, R. L. James, School Board Secretary, was approaching. James was nearly stone deaf and completely unaware of what was happening. As he casually walked into the scene, Nelson shot at him, hitting him in the leg, and James slumped to the cement walk.

The action was complicated further when John C. Shipley, an elderly police judge peering out from his window on the third floor of the bank building, looked down and saw Dillinger holding hostages at gunpoint. The judge had a pistol in his office confiscated from an earlier case; he grabbed that weapon, took careful aim, and pulled its stiff trigger. Dillinger clutched his right shoulder, looked up, and let loose a quick burst from his own machine gun at the window, but the judge already had ducked back in.

Inside the bank, Hamilton had collected $23,000 from tellers and patrons, but the big money was still stacked in the vault. Pressing a gun into Harry Fisher's back, Hamilton forced the teller to open the vault's massive door. Fisher knew there was more than $200,000 in the vault, but he gave Hamilton a heavy bag of pennies used as a doorstop and through ruses and deception began doling out packages of one dollar bills—one package at a time—through the narrow bars of cages in the vault.

There was confusion inside the bank; plans the bandits had rehearsed were not working out. Making everything worse, a guard stationed in the balcony across the lobby witnessed what was going on below him, and picking up an available tear-gas gun fired it through a horizontal slit in the cage. The eight-inch-long pellet hit Eddie Green in the back before releasing 25,000 cubic feet of gas. Nearly blinded, Green could only swear in pain and disgust.

Van Meter ran back inside the bank to urge Hamilton and Green to make it snappy; Dillinger and Nelson couldn't hold the crowd outside much longer. Above them, Judge Shipley returned to his window and seeing Hamilton now carrying bags from out of the bank got off another hasty shot. This bullet struck Hamilton in the shoulder, but the bandit didn't go down.

Lydia Crosby, a young stenographer, was one of the first captives, and as Hamilton emerged from the bank tears streaming down his face, Dillinger ordered them all to move around the corner.

Dillinger, Hamilton, Green, Van Meter, and Carroll piled into the big black Buick parked nearby while Nelson swore at assistant cashier Ralph Wiley before ordering him to stand on the running boards of the crowded auto. Several others, either employees or patrons, were forced into the car where they wedged themselves between robbers or sat on a bandit's lap. Lydia Crosby would say later that she thought at least twenty-one persons were either inside the car or perched on its running boards; whatever the number, it looked like a circus comedy vehicle as it proceeded north at less than ten miles per hour.

Chief of Police E. J. Patton entered the fray in another car and pursued the Buick but told cops accompanying him not to fire at it for fear of hitting the hostages. Glass had been removed from the Buick's back window, and from this vantage Baby Face Nelson with a high powered rifle fired away at pursuers.

The overloaded auto worked its way south, but after three-quarters of an hour it was a mere three miles from Mason City. Hostages were still inside or clinging on the running boards, but the weather was very cold and the air was spitting flurries of snow. The Buick stopped; hostages on running boards were let off, and the ones inside, too, were set free.

Then the Buick with its six robbers headed for the sand pit, where Van Meter and Green had parked the slightly smaller car they had driven from the YMCA. Toting guns, ammo, and parts of the loot, three of the bandits got into the smaller car and followed the larger one to St. Paul, getting there around midnight.

First aid bandages and ordinary antiseptics were put on Dillinger's and Hamilton's wounds, and early the next morning Dillinger called Pat Reilly, a confederate, who took Dillinger and Hamilton to the city health inspector for treatment of their wounds. The doctor did treat the wounds but said they were not serious, and dismissed the two fugitives without informing the police.[5]

After the heist at Mason City, Tommy Carroll with his moll Jean Crompton spent some time with Baby Face Nelson and his wife at Lake Como in Wisconsin. Jean was pregnant and when Carroll left for a week she stayed with Nelson's wife Helen. During that time there was either a miscarriage or an abortion, and when Carroll came back, the two of them retreated to Chicago.

In the first week of June, Carroll and Jean started a motor trip west and got as far as Waterloo, Iowa. Carroll thought their car needed an oil change and grease job, so while that was being done he and Jean went to a movie. At the garage, a mechanic had noticed three different license plates on the car and had notified the police.

When Carroll and Crompton came out of the movie, two detectives were waiting for them. The officers approached Carroll, and placing his hand on the shoulder of the outlaw one of them said, "We're police officers and want to have a little talk with you."

"The hell with that," snapped Carroll as he reached for a .38 pistol in his shoulder holster. With that the brawny officer struck him in the jaw, knocking him to the ground. As Carroll tried to rise and aim the pistol still in his hand, the other officer fired his weapon, and a bullet tore through the bandit's body just below the left armpit. Carroll slumped to the ground, mortally wounded, and was rushed to St. Francis Hospital where he died at 6:55 that evening.[6]

* * *

Dillinger had reached St. Paul, and from there he phoned Billie Frechette inviting her to join him. He also instructed Eddie Green to find a hideout where he and Frechette could live apart from persistent and pestiferous police. Green and his wife Beth, a comely woman with red hair, rented a furnished apartment on Lexington Avenue in St. Paul, telling the owner that it would be occupied by a Mr. & Mrs. Carl Hellman, one of the aliases Dillinger had used. When Dillinger and Frechette showed up, they were accompanied by Red Hamilton and his girlfriend Pat Cherrington along with Cherrington's sister Opal Long.

Federal agents, however, had received tips about suspicious goings-on in the Lexington apartment and decided to raid it. One policeman knocked on the apartment's door. Billie opened it a crack and heard the cop's query: "Is your husband Carl at home?"

She answered that he was not there but would be home that evening. When the police asked if they might come in and talk with her for a few moments, she replied, "I'm sorry, but I'm not dressed. You'll have to wait a minute."

Closing the door, she rushed back into the bedroom to find Dillinger dressed and ready to make his break. He had called Homer Van Meter living only a block away to come quickly for reinforcement in just such an emergency.

The police meanwhile encircled the building to make certain no outlaw could escape. Inside the apartment, Dillinger finished his packing and then raked the door with a volley from his specially adapted machine pistol. Van Meter showed up driving a green coupe, and an agent, hoping to forestall any help for the outlaws they were trying to capture, flattened the tires of the car by firing bullets into them.

Confronted by cops, Van Meter immediately opened fired and made a successful dash out of the developing melee. Hearing the shots, Dillinger clearing the way further with another burst from his own machine pistol together with Frechette ran out of the now unguarded back stairs of the apartment to a garage in its back. He kept the safety off his gun and his hand on its trigger while he watched for any cop who might have followed. Frechette backed the new black-and-yellow Hudson bought three days earlier out of the garage. Then she scooted over to make room for Dillinger who slid in under the wheel. Then laying his machine pistol between them, he sped away without pursuit.

Federal agents showed up to help local police probe the Lexington apartment for more evidence on the man FBI Director J. Edgar Hoover now was designating as Public Enemy Number One. As that search was being conducted, Dillinger and Frechette were in an apartment on Fremont Avenue where Eddie Green and a woman were living under the name of Stephens.

Green took the wounded and bleeding Dillinger to Dr. Clayton E. May's office, who dressed the wounds before escorting him to the home of a nurse, Mrs. Augusta Salt. Dillinger was recuperating at this residence in Minneapolis when police acting on further clues, surrounded Green's apartment. When Green appeared there, he tried to get away but was shot several times and taken into custody.

Green would die within the week, but in that interval he gasped out valuable data about Dillinger: accomplices, addresses, weapons, doctors who treated the bandits, and names of those who robbed the banks at Sioux Falls and Mason City.

After learning Green had confessed, Dillinger decided to visit his family and the old homestead in Mooresville, Indiana. Early in April with Frechette beside him he drove to Mooresville. The day after his arrival, he and his brother Hubert made a quick drive to Leipsic, Ohio, to drop off money for Harry Pierpont's defense. About 3:00 A.M. on the way back to Mooresville, Hubert was driving the Hudson Terraplane when near Noblesville, he lost control of the car and struck an oncoming one before plunging into a nearby ditch. No one in either car was hurt, and the next day Evelyn Frechette bought a new black sedan from a dealer in Indianapolis, paying $730 in cash taken from a purse bulging with ten dollar bills.[7]

The Dillingers had a grand reunion with the father, John Dillinger, Sr., and his notorious son mingling with family members who upon hearing that young John was in town had hurried to make him welcome. On Sunday noon after most had attended church services, thirteen adults sat around the dining table. On the table were dishes of fried chicken, mashed potatoes, thick gravy, garden peas, lettuce, celery, hot biscuits and jellies, along with coconut cream pie, which Audrey Hancock, Johnnie's sister, remembered was his favorite.

Dillinger and Frechette left Mooresville the next day and drove their new black sedan to Chicago. Federal agents would raid homes of Dillinger family members, and consider arresting John Dillinger Sr. for harboring and abetting a known criminal until it was pointed out that his son, John Dillinger, already was becoming somewhat of a Robin Hood figure, robbing the rich to help the poor. No bad man since Jesse James had won such widespread sympathy. Journalists suspected that Hoosiers around Mooresville operated as a big family, and even persons who had nothing to gain protected him and refused to cooperate with authorities trying to nab him. The *Chicago Tribune* ran a banner declaring, "Dillinger Given Warm Welcome in Home Town." The newspaper in Coshocton, Ohio, went even further: "Dillinger Regarded as Hero in Old Home Town." [8]

Indeed, so sympathetic were feelings for Dillinger that when the state paved the dirt road leading into Mooresville, Hoosier wags said the paving was done so that he could enter more easily and make a quick getaway if necessary.

From Mooresville, Dillinger and Frechette drove back to Chicago. On the night of April 9, 1934, Billie, who if not a lush was ever near its edge, sat at a small table in a tavern with Lawrence Strong, an underworld figure and boyfriend of Opal Long across from her. It is not clear who tipped off the police, maybe it was the heavy-drinking Strong; Billie gave conflicting versions.

At any rate, someone called the feds, and several agents arrived to arrest both Strong and Frechette. She was held incommunicado and would claim she had been treated harshly: interrogated over blinding white lights, deprived of food and sleep, and handcuffed constantly.

The FBI did not release news of her arrest for fear of alerting Dillinger, and when finally given a chance to speak to the press, Frechette added more color to his public persona:

> John Dillinger and I sat in the tavern quite a long time eating and drinking. . . . Suddenly these agents came bursting in—from the front, the rear, and all sides, it seemed. They had all kinds of shotguns and rifles. There were more agents than I knew existed. John saw the agents come in. He got up and walked up to the front where he mingled with the people and agents. Then he walked outside and sat in his automobile. I sat still, and soon the agents came along and they started questioning me. Then they took me away; John was sitting

in his car when the agents brought me out, but when he saw I was pinched, he drove away.[9]

No matter the actual circumstances of Frechette's arrest, the important fact was that again John Dillinger had gotten away unscathed. Angered over reports of Frechette's arrest and her alleged mistreatment, he vowed to get even with those dirty feds, but he was powerless. Police were holding her in the Bankers Building in downtown Chicago—a place too fortified for any rescue attempt, but it was rumored that she would soon be transferred to St. Paul. Something there might be worked out, but he would need help and lots of guns.[10]

In preparation for just such an escapade, Dillinger and Van Meter raided the jail at Warsaw, Indiana, a town of 12,000 in the north central part of the state. The two desperadoes, each brandishing a machine gun, grabbed 54-year-old veteran policeman Judd Pittenger on the street and ordered him to lead them to the jail. Pittenger reached for Dillinger's machine gun, but the outlaw growled, *"Don't be a fool, old man. Just do as you're told. We don't want to kill anyone."*[11]

Pittenger led Dillinger and Van Meter to the jail where they were disappointed to find no machine guns; the two could take only a couple of .38 cal. pistols and four bullet-proof vests. Then holding their loot, they withdrew while the disarmed Pittenger watched them climb into a black sedan and roar out of sight.

The Warsaw raid raised hysteria over Dillinger an octave higher. By mid-morning, 5,000 Indiana lawmen were blocking roads and searching the hundreds of empty cottages in the lake district. Investigators surmised that he would try to get back to friends around his home town of Mooresville. Acting on that hunch, police and vigilante road blocks were set up all over northern Indiana.[12]

Dillinger didn't follow the expected route. Instead, he and Van Meter executed a U-turn and went back to Chicago. After Frechette was transferred to St. Paul, Dillinger was itching for action again and called Red Hamilton to come to his hideout above a barbecue stand at the intersection of North and Harlem Avenues. Hamilton brought along his girlfriend Pat Cherrington, and within days Dillinger had amassed a squad consisting of Hamilton and Cherrington, Van Meter and his girlfriend Marie Conforti, Tommy Carroll with Jean Crompton, and Baby Face Nelson with his wife Helen Gillis. Tension arose between Dillinger and Nelson when Dillinger told compatriots he thought Nelson was out of control in violence.

Although not a member of the inside group, Pat Reilly, once a mascot of the St. Paul baseball team and a hanger-on with underworld figures, was present at times when the fugitives talked about getting away from the constant surveillance police were keeping on them because of recent crimes.

The gang wanted a secluded spot, and the place chosen was Little Bohemia Lodge, so named by its proprietor Emil Wanatka in tribute to his native land.

Chapter 14. Little Bohemia

To neighbors and friends in the hunting and fishing country of northern Wisconsin, Emil Wanatka seemed a legitimate small businessman, yet his record was not spotless. Before buying the Wisconsin lodge, he had owned and run a bootleg joint in Chicago and had faced charges of auto theft and murder but had beaten both raps.[1]

The Dillinger gang started arriving at Little Bohemia Lodge in the afternoon of Friday, April 19, 1934. A party of ten staying for a few days during the off-season seemed like a bonanza to proprietor Wanatka and his wife. The guests were friendly enough and profligate with money, yet he noticed that the men wore hats with turned down brims and sometimes their coats flapped open enough to show holsters with a revolver butt protruding.

Wanatka, no fool, began to suspect his guests could be the Dillinger gang on the run. He confided that concern to his wife, who told her brother, and he in turn drove to Rhinelander, 50 miles away, to relay the suspicion to agents of the FBI.

The tip eventually reached Melvin Purvis in Chicago, and after making certain it was not just another hoax, by telephone he rounded up fellow agents. Within hours, dozens of G-men in autos or chartered airplanes were heading toward Mercer, Wisconsin, the nearest town of any size to Little Bohemia Lodge. The agents rendezvoused in Rhinelander and while there heard rumors that the gang planned to leave that very night; time was short, so in five cars commandeered from a local dealer, the agents set out for the lodge. It was dark, cold, and the roads were muddy; one car slipped into a ditch and rather than trying to pull it out, the occupants, holding loaded machine guns, simply climbed on running boards of the remaining four autos driving to the lodge.

The lodge fronted on Star Lake, so lawmen were able to surround the establishment on the remaining three sides, but plans for the arrest were far from being well-made. First, it was not clear as to who was in charge. J. Edgar Hoover's well-known reluctance to share information or authority with local officials had left Wisconsin police unaware that federal agents were operating within the area. As a result, no roadblocks of any kind had been set up.

Secondly, the lawmen lost any chance of surprise when as soon as they got out of their cars, several dogs began barking. Through a megaphone Purvis shouted that the lodge was surrounded by lawmen and that occupants from the lodge ought to come out, unarmed with hands raised in peaceful surrender. He and Special Agent Hugh Clegg from the St. Paul Office saw three men on the lodge's front porch get into a Chevrolet sedan and move slowly toward them. Both officers assumed the men were surrendering and that their captives were about to be taken without bloodshed. Purvis, Clegg, and G-men would be heroes like ones who had netted Dillinger in Tucson.

Purvis again yelled for the car to stop, but it did not, and as the oncoming car crept closer he and Clegg ordered their crouching confederates to open fire. A fusillade of machine gun and small arms bullets flattened tires and shattered windows. Two men jumped out of the car and dashed back into the lodge while one federal agent, 29-year-old Carter Baum, with his machine gun raked the vehicle as it rolled to a stop.

Purvis and Clegg discussed what to do. They had fired at several cars without knowing who the occupants really were. Now a man could be seen slumped over the wheel of the stopped Chevrolet with its flattened tires and its motor still running and its radio blaring. An agent was asked to reconnoiter the car, and as others covered him he dropped to his hands and knees to crawl toward it. In its front seat behind the wheel, was slumped a young man, his head drooped forward and his shoulder covered with blood. The agent felt for a pulse, found none. He turned off the radio and motor before finding a wallet in the dead man's coat pocket. Taking the wallet, he crawled back to Purvis and reported that a young man in the car was dead.

Purvis and Clegg opened the wallet, found a driver's license, and learned that the man just killed was Eugene Boisneau—a 35-year-old worker at the CCC camp near Mercer.[2]

When fellow agents informed Carter Baum there was a dead man in the Chevrolet, the young agent was filled with remorse and replied, "Certainly there is. I killed him with this machine gun. I'll never fire it again."[3]

Horrified by knowing he had killed an innocent man, Baum was so distraught that Purvis wanted to get him away from the scene. He sent Baum along with another agent, Jay Newman, to find a phone in another lodge nearby and call the Rhinelander airport to see if the ordered tear gas had arrived.

Newman made his call and during it, the switchboard operator told him a mysterious car had driven up and was parked nearby. Newman decided to investigate, but first picked up Carl Christianson, a local police officer. Newman, Baum, and Christianson pulled up alongside a Ford auto with two or three persons inside.

Newman asked them to identify themselves, and a small man stepped out, pulled a gun from his shoulder holster, and before they could reach for their own weapons fired point blank into the heads or bodies of Newman, Baum, and Christianson. Newman received a head wound; Christianson was more seriously hit, and Baum died instantly. The murderer was Baby Face Nelson, who had departed from Little Bohemia long enough to kidnap a couple of local residents and hijack their late model Ford.

The crazed Nelson was shooting at everyone or anything in sight. Running out of moving targets, he jumped into the car the three agents had driven up, slammed it into reverse and stomped the accelerator so violently bits of gravel from the driveway ricocheted against the adjoining home. Shifting gears, he then drove away rapidly as Agent Newman, slightly revived, emptied his own revolver in frustration toward the fleeing gunman.

Dawn was breaking when word of this happening got back to Purvis where his posse of lawmen was still keeping vigil around little Bohemia Lodge. The tear gas finally arrived, and the agents prepared to attack. A canister of tear gas was tossed into the lodge, flooding it with poisonous air, but only three people emerged: Helen Gillis, wife of Baby Face Nelson, Jean Crompton, Tommy Carroll's moll, and Marie Conforti, Homer Van Meter's lover. The three were arrested and taken to Madison to be held incommunicado for a month while federal agents questioned them.

Dillinger and his gang had escaped again. When the shooting first started at Little Bohemia, he had returned the fire with his machine gun. Then as agents sought cover, he along with Hamilton and Van Meter leapt from a second story window into a deep snow bank behind the building. Out of the lodge, they descended stairs leading to the lake, and ran along the strand a short distance before entering the woods.

The fugitives then stole a car from a cabin, and the fact that no road blocks had been set up made it easy for them to get away. Hours later with Van Meter at the wheel, they came toward St. Paul from the south, assuming that police had been alerted and that all northern approaches would be heavily guarded. They were wrong in assuming an easy entrance from the south.

A few miles south of St. Paul, a local sheriff and his deputies recognized the car's license number from an FBI bulletin and gave chase. Van Meter stepped on the gas, and as the two vehicles hurtled toward the city, Dillinger broke out the back window and blasted away with his machine gun. The pursuing police returned his fire, and from it Red Hamilton received a mortal wound in his lower back. The three criminals had to abandon the FBI car they were in, but they flagged down another and in it turned around to head for Chicago.

First accounts of the events at Little Bohemia were in praise of agents who had carried out the achievement, but as details of what really happened began leaking out, reporters had a larger treasure trove. The *Associated Press* dramatized the happenings by first declaring that the Dillinger gang, not federal officers, had left two dead and wounded four others. The *AP* added a patently false report that the gang had mounted machine guns on the roof of the lodge in order to do battle with lawmen.

The *Chicago Tribune* echoed such sentiment but also reported there had been "confusion on the ground." FBI Director Hoover in Washington declared that Dillinger was trapped in the lodge, but simultaneously came reports of the dead and wounded. The *Chicago Tribune* was forced to run another story asking outright: "*Had Dillinger Been Caught?*" A day later the same paper headlined: "*Hunt Dillinger, 2 Die, 4 Shot.*"[4]

The *Chicago Daily News* was equally confused. On the Monday after the shoot-out, the paper's lead story announced, "*2 Die, 4 shot, as Killer Escapes Wisconsin Trap.*" The next day, however, one of the paper's staff writers, Robert J. Casey, posed questions about police claims that Dillinger would be in custody within a few hours. Casey taunted that in the future federal agents should be less distracted by such decoys as CCC workers.[5]

The search for Dillinger mounted, and as more days went by, the ineptitude of agents conducting the raid overshadowed the manhunt. Reporters kept titillating readers by giving such details as the women arrested and Director Hoover's braggadocio.

At Little Bohemia, Purvis and Clegg weren't sure of their next move. They still had the lodge surrounded and believed Dillinger and his gang remained trapped inside; eventually they would have to try to make a break. The two officers decided it would be better to wait for that happening rather than to try storming the place; they had no tear gas or bullet proof vests although both had been ordered from St. Paul. Minutes ticked by and hours passed while lawmen huddled behind trees and blew on their hands for warmth.

An ambulance from the CCC camp showed up, and from it stepped Dr. S. X. Roberts. Purvis was surprised, for as far as he knew, no one had phoned for an ambulance. Then Dr. Roberts explained that he had received a call from John Morris, a CCC worker who said he had been wounded.

Three days after first reporting the tragedy of brave federal agents shot by bloodthirsty felons, the *Chicago Tribune* led with the headline: *"Charge U. S. Men with Bungling Dillinger Hunt."* Other newspaper picked up the scent, and by mid-week newspapers throughout the nation were questioning the competency of the FBI.[5] Questions turned to criticism and then to ridicule. A columnist for Hearst newspapers proclaimed that Dillinger blasting his way out of a so-called police trap was not news: "If officers should meet him and *not* have their revolvers and weapons taken from him, that would be news!" The most pointed quip came from Will Rogers, humorist, actor, and syndicated columnist, who penned,

> Well, they had Dillinger surrounded and were all ready to shoot him when he come out, but another bunch of folk come out ahead, so they just shot them instead. . . . Dillinger is going to get in accidentally with some innocent bystanders sometime; then he'll be shot. [6]

Red Hamilton had been wounded in the East Chicago robbery, and at Little Bohemia another bullet from a federal gun pierced his intestines. After leaving St. Paul to head for Chicago, Dillinger and Van Meter managed to get him, bleeding and in great pain, into the car with them. On April 23, as they approached the Spiral Bridge over the Mississippi at Hastings, Minnesota, twenty miles from St. Paul, they were spotted by lawmen. Van Meter was driving with Hamilton on the passenger side and Dillinger in the middle.

Ten miles from the Bridge, the lawmen caught up with them and began shooting. Dillinger climbed into the back seat and with the butt of his automatic smashed out the rear window. Then he returned the fire as Van Meter floored the gas pedal until their vehicle reached its maximum speed but not before one of the bullets from the pursuing lawmen struck the nearly comatose Hamilton in the back.

Van Meter got far enough ahead of the police car to turn off onto a dirt road, park, and wait until the pursuers had passed. With cops in such hot pursuit, it was too dangerous to keep going toward St. Paul, so Dillinger and Van Meter with the seriously wounded Hamilton headed for Chicago. Reaching that city, they deposited the wounded Hamilton in a friendly saloon and searched for a doctor. Unable to find a licensed doctor for their emergency, a woman they knew told them about Volney Davis, a man who had been with them in a couple of earlier escapades. Davis was living in nearby Aurora, not far from Chicago, and might be able to help.

The trio of outlaws made it to Aurora, found Davis, and his girlfriend who did what she could to ease the pain of the dying Hamilton, cleaning his wounds and giving him aspirin, but gangrene already had set in. It was too late, and Hamilton died on the night of April 26, 1934. His gangster friends took his body for burial in a gravel pit nearby. Dillinger poured lye on the face of the corpse hoping to forestall identification, and remarked, "I hate to do this, Red, but I know you'd do the same for me."[7]

By the end of April, newspaper readers in America knew federal agents had bungled at Little Bohemia. The public image of Dillinger, the escapee, swelled to impossible proportions. He was a throwback to bad men of the old West—a combination of Jesse James, Billy the Kid, and Wild Bill Hickok—a modern Robin Hood who robbed the rich and gave to the poor.

Hard economic times encouraged the theme of rich men stealing from the poor. Authorities received an untold number of letters echoing that Dillinger robbed banks from the outside while bankers and money lenders did even worse from the inside. The mania spread, and along with idolatry came letters from ordinary citizens offering advice on how to catch the wily fugitive. One man wrote President Franklin Roosevelt suggesting he call out the marines to comb the Midwest countryside like they had done recently in Nicaragua. Another proclaimed that God had revealed to him a plan which would bring in Dillinger within a month—officers would be told the plan if they paid the writer $5000. An entrepreneur from Dallas wanted to arm law enforcers with autogyros, i.e., helicopters, which his company just happened to sell. Another man advised authorities to seize John Dillinger Sr., slap him in jail, and when his son and gang came to break them out, arrest them all. A housewife advised, "*Cherchez la femme!* Let Billie Frechette escape." The feds could then trail her as she rejoined her lover.

In truth, after Little Bohemia, life for John Dillinger turned pretty grubby. The heat was on him; he was ill with bad colds or other ailments, and he needed money. Although robberies everywhere were attributed to him, in May, 1934, he and Van Meter robbed only one bank, the First National Bank of Fostoria, Ohio, just south of Toledo. The take was seventeen thousand dollars, just enough to tide them over for a while.

Chapter 15. Movie Night

In mid-summer, 1934, a heat wave covered most of the Southwest and large parts of the Midwest. Oklahoma experienced a ravaging drought with temperatures reaching 117 degrees. Two years of near drought conditions caused further crop failure, and numerous farms were going bankrupt with more land turning from fertile soil to dust bowls.

The Depression was at a very low ebb. Average cost of a new home was $5,970, but no one had money or sufficient collateral to buy. Average wages per year were $1600; a gallon of gasoline cost 10 cents, a loaf of bread 8 cents, a pound of hamburger 12 cents. and for those with money to spend there were men's shirts by Arrow for $2.50 or a Studebaker truck for $625.00.

On Sunday, July 22, 1934, Chicago sweltered in degrees over 100, but that temperature was not high enough to keep more than 15,000 fans from attending a baseball game in Comiskey Park, where the visiting New York Yankees swamped the White Sox 15 to 2.

In addition to weather reports, newspapers were reporting details on what was happening in the lives of five babies—the Dionne Quintuplets, the only ones known to survive infancy—born a month earlier to Elzire Dionne and her husband Oliva Edoard in an isolated farm house just outside Callender, Ontario.

Interspersed with weather reports, sports, and stories about the Dionnes were accounts of Dillinger and other nefarious criminals such as Baby Face Nelson, Pretty Boy Floyd, along with grimy details of how FBI men had ambushed Bonnie Parker and Clyde Barrow in Louisiana killing them both.

The Little Bohemia affair had happened near the end of April, and for two months there was not much hard news about John Dillinger. There were the usual rumors about his sightings: he had bummed cigarettes from an outlaw in Minnesota; a retired private investigator claimed to have seen him in a restaurant and sought permission from the attorney-general to make a citizen's arrest if he saw him again; a woman in Chicago followed a man she thought was Dillinger, but he turned out to be a traveling salesman. There were no bank robberies, shoot-outs, or jailbreaks, and speculation spread that Dillinger must have died while fleeing from the Bohemia shoot out.

In fact he was holed up in south Chicago keeping a low profile. He read newspapers avidly with special interest in crimes and criminals. Also, from magazines and buddies he learned of advances that had been made in plastic surgery following the carnage of WW I, so he started toying with the idea of changing his own appearance in order to be more free from ever present threats of exposure.

His guardian lawyer Louis Piquett introduced him to William Loeser, a middle-aged German émigré in and out of trouble with the law because of drug abuse. Trained in American universities, Loeser practiced medicine illegally under the alias Dr. Ralph Robeind and agreed to do plastic surgery on Dillinger with assistance from a younger doctor named Dr. Harold Cassidy, who had legal troubles of his own.

The operation was a bloody mess, and during it Dillinger came out of the anesthesia several times, vomiting and needing further anesthetics. The operation was not entirely successful, but Loeser cut away three moles, tightened the skin on his patient's face, and filled in his chin dimple. Dillinger revived, and a day or two later when the bandages were removed, he paid Loeser $5000 and said he was satisfied.

There were more alterations. Van Meter declined any facial surgery but along with Dillinger let Loeser cut away epidermis on their finger tips before dousing them with hydrochloric acid mixed with strong alkali solutions. That was painful, and neither man could use his hands for several days.[1]

While recuperating from their surgeries, Dillinger and Van Meter debated over their next target. They considered several banks in Illinois and Indiana before deciding on the Merchant's National Bank in South Bend, Indiana.

By this time, rumors and myths about John Dillinger and his gang had swollen into gigantic proportions; it was hard to separate them from facts. First reports of the robbery at South Bend were contradictory. Most newspapers reported that Dillinger and his gang had pulled off the raid, but a few papers denied he was even there and claimed that it was Pretty Boy Floyd, the Oklahoma outlaw who had never met Dillinger, who led the caper.

The facts were that Dillinger, Van Meter, Nelson, and probably one or two others unidentified pulled the job. A little before noon on Saturday, June 30, 1934, a brown Hudson with Ohio license plates drove into South Bend and parked near the bank. The street was filled with passing cars as Van Meter and Nelson took up positions outside the bank building.

Dillinger leading the others strode inside, flourished his machine gun, and announced, "This is a stick up!"

Then ordering tellers to hand over the cash from their respective cages, he waved his weapon at patrons as he commanded them to keep their hands aloft. Most did so, but several dropped to the floor. In the confusion, one of the robbers pumped a burst from his machine gun into the ceiling, and the noise alerted a traffic cop outside, Howard Wagner, who left his post to rush toward the bank. Seeing him approach, Nelson drew a bead on him and fired. Bullets struck Wagner in the chest and he fell immediately, mortally wounded.

Citizens on the street screamed and ran for cover, but one, Harry Berg, a local jeweler, pulled a pistol and got off a shot at Nelson, hitting him in the chest. The shot only jarred Nelson because he was wearing a bullet-proof vest, and Berg scampered back into his own store as Nelson raked the street with machine gun fire, badly wounding two bystanders.[2]

Van Meter had come out from the bank and with his own machine gun had forced a half-dozen people from the sidewalk to stand together making human shields. Dillinger and an unidentified partner came out of the bank carrying more than $28,000 in cash, herding before them three hostages, including Delos Cohen, the bank's president. From the streets' intersection, one of the patrolmen fired a shot or two, hitting Cohen in the ankle and a cashier in the leg, neither wound serious.

As Dillinger, Van Meter, and the unidentified companion prodded their hostages toward the getaway car a gun battle ensued. The patrolmen fired again and again while Nelson swung his machine gun, shooting wildly, breaking windows and shattering the State Theatre's marquee.

Suddenly Van Meter fell, blood gushing from a head wound. Dillinger, abandoning the hostages, grabbed Van Meter beneath the arm pits and managed to hoist him into the Hudson. More police bullets struck it as Dillinger tore his way out of town.

He was able to get the bleeding Van Meter back to Chicago, and that night Jimmy Probasco, a grimy little figure who worked the fringes of Chicago's underworld fencing stolen goods and illicit liquor, poured antiseptic on Van Meter's wound and bandaged it. A day later the borderline physician, Dr. Cassidy, showed up to treat the wounds more properly.

In contrast with Clyde Barrow, who showed no interest in women other than Bonnie Parker, John Dillinger was a ladies' man. He missed Billie Frechette, but in her absence he often wined, dined, and sported with several others. He stayed hidden in Probasco's apartment on the west side of Chicago, well away from Lake Michigan for almost a month before he met Anna Sage, a Romanian immigrant known as Ana Kumpanis prior to her marriage to Alexander Sage. Anna was a prostitute turned brothel keeper who offered Dillinger an apartment in her North Side apartment complex. Anxious and with cabin fever, he moved to 2420 Halstead Street on July 4th. There Sage provided him with a locked closet to store his machine guns, bullet proof vests, and other tools of his trade.

Sage, an entrepreneur, had worked her way up as a single mother waiting tables in night clubs while being an occasional prostitute and eventually becoming a brothel owner first in East Chicago and then on the more prosperous north side of Chicago. Payoffs were routine in her line of work. She had numerous arrests in Indiana and Illinois but had been able to escape prosecutions until her case was turned over to federal authorities. A week after Dillinger moved into one of her apartments, she received notice from immigration officials that her appeals had been turned down and a warrant for her deportation back to Romania had been issued.

Among Sage's male friends was Martin Zarkovich, an East Chicago patrolman, who had begun availing himself of her robust charms in the early 1920s. Sergeant Zarkovich had maneuvered himself until he was in charge of graft payments from Lake County speakeasy owners, and by 1934 he was a suspect in numerous shady deals—even being considered a person of interest but with no substantive proof of having been an accomplice in Dillinger's celebrated jail break from Crown Point.

Zarkovich had fixed many of Sage's problems with the law—fixings which resulted in "not guilty" verdicts, small fines, or very short prison terms. Facing imminent deportation in the late spring of 1934, she dumped in Zarkovich's lap her proposal for capturing America's Public Enemy Number One if the feds would rescind the emigration edict.

At Jimmy Probasco's house in the 2500 block on Crawford Avenue in north Chicago, Dr. Cassidy had cleaned Van Meter's head wound with antiseptic, dabbed it with iodine, and given him a tetanus shot. The following Monday, Van Meter was well enough to meet with Nelson, John Chase, Joseph "Fatso" Negri, and Dillinger when the five gathered in a cottage at a small lake northwest of Chicago proper.

The fugitives talked over an intended train robbery but decided to sit tight until the heat cooled off. Actually, the world was closing in on John Dillinger. Federal officials had raised the reward for capturing him to $25,000. He had few friends or relatives left who could help, and an assortment of former associates was itching to collect that $25,000 reward.

Meanwhile, Melvin Purvis, the agent FBI Director Hoover had installed in Chicago with specific instructions to capture Dillinger dead or alive, believed he was moving closer to the outlaw. FBI men had slain two of Dillinger's former gang members, Eddie Green and Tommy Carroll, and maybe John "Red" Hamilton. The stooge Pat Reilly was in jail as were four of the gang's molls—Billie Frechette, Pat Cherrington, Bernice Clark, and Jean Delaney. Moreover, Purvis believed the increased reward would be incentive enough to bring further informants out of the woodwork.

The immediate supervisor of Melvin Purvis was Sam Cowley, a man Hoover had put in charge of all FBI operations in the Midwest. Cowley updated Hoover in Washington on the offer Zarkovich had transmitted. Delighted with such a potential break, Hoover gave Cowley a full go ahead and asked to be kept apprised.

There was a series of phone calls between Zarkovich and Purvis before a meeting with Anna Sage could be arranged. Purvis and Zarkovich met her in a room Cowley had rented at the Great Northern Hotel. Cowley and Captain Tim O'Neill, head of the Indiana cops pursuing Dillinger, sat in an unmarked car a half block away where they could watch Sage enter and leave the hotel.

At the meeting, Purvis was cagey. He avoided giving Sage a definite promise for what she really wanted, that is, assurance that she would be permitted to stay in the U.S. Instead he danced around the question, saying he didn't have such authority, but he would see what he could do. He was equally indirect in saying that if Sage helped deliver Dillinger she would get "a substantial part" of the $25,000 reward.[3]

In a poor bargaining position, Sage disclosed that Dillinger often asked her to go with him and Polly Hamilton, one of her tenants, when they went out. In fact, Sage said, he and Polly were going to a movie the very next night and had invited her to accompany them. Melvin Purvis relayed the information to Sam Cowley, who immediately called Hoover in Washington to advise him of Dillinger's intention and to ask for further instructions. Hoover, wanting no repeat of the Bohemia fiasco, told Cowley to have his agents armed only with pistols, not machine guns, and to use the utmost precaution in avoiding injuries to witnesses. If possible, Dillinger should be taken alive, but in no case should he be allowed to escape.

Early on Sunday morning, Cowley assembled the nineteen hand-picked agents Hoover had assigned to him as members of a "Dillinger Squad," and parceled out their respective duties. The blistering heat in Chicago that day made weather the top news story.

Around 5 o'clock in the evening, Anna Sage was fixing dinner for Dillinger, Polly Hamilton, and herself. She said she was out of butter and would run downstairs and to the delicatessen next door. Under that ruse, she phoned Purvis and confirmed the plans for a movie; she believed it would be either the Marbro or the Biograph.

In checking movie programs, FBI men learned that the Marbro was showing a Shirley Temple film; at the Biograph was a gangster film entitled "Manhattan Melodrama" starring Clark Gable and William Powell. It didn't take a genius to convince agents which film Dillinger would choose.

The Biograph was at the end of the block which held Sage's apartment complex. One of the city's earliest movie houses, the Biograph was sandwiched within a row of two-story commercial buildings that stood shoulder to shoulder on the east side of Lincoln Avenue. In the same block but nearer the other end were Sage's apartments.

Late that afternoon an army of more than thirty lawmen gathered in an office of the Bankers' Building where Melvin Purvis unfolded the strategy. He also introduced Sgt. Martin Zarkovich who updated them on Dillinger's changed appearance—fuller face, missing a previous mole from an eyebrow, a less prominent cleft on his chin, and now black hair, and a pencil-thin mustache. Purvis added that the fugitive would be accompanied by two women, one of whom would be dressed in red.

Zarkovich and two or three FBI agents were sent to watch the Marbro in case agents were wrong in surmising which theater their quarry would choose. Just before eight o'clock, Sage was able to phone Purvis again and tell him it was going to be the Biograph.

Within half an hour, Purvis and Cowley had men deployed in pairs along the sidewalk in front of the Biograph, across the street, in the alley a few doors south, and at emergency exits along the back and sides of the building. Together, Purvis and Cowley watched a man and two women come up the street and go into the theater. One woman was heavier and appeared slightly older than the other who had hung on the arm of the man. He wasn't wearing a coat, so he must not be too heavily armed. The older woman was wearing a white hat and an orange skirt—just what Sage had promised.

Purvis and Cowley talked hurriedly and decided it would be better to take Dillinger on the street rather than trying to capture him inside where risk to other patrons would be high. The agents watching for their prey spent two hours pacing, chatting, and smoking, trying to ease their tensions.

The film ended just before ten-thirty, and patrons started coming out. Purvis stood by the ticket booth, an unlit cigar in his mouth. Lighting that fag would be his signal to confederates that the identification was positive. Suddenly, striding toward him was Dillinger, Polly Hamilton clinging to his left arm, and Anna Sage a step behind them in a white hat and an orange skirt that appeared red under the glaring neon lights.

Purvis lit his cigar, and at the same time Dillinger turned to see three men in suits standing by a parked car. He must have sensed immediately that a trap had been set. As Purvis was lighting his cigar, Dillinger walked past an agent in the next vestibule, who stepped aside to let him pass. Behind them, Purvis and fellow Agent Ed Hollis closed in with guns drawn. Dillinger saw them coming and sprinted toward the alley while pulling a Colt automatic from his right trouser pocket.

Purvis would claim later that he called out, "Halt?" If he did call, Dillinger paid no attention to his command. Hollis and two other agents fired at the fleeing figure. Two bullets grazed Dillinger; another struck him on the left side, tearing into his stooped back. This was a fatal shot that rose to pass through his neck, pulverizing vertebrae at the top of the spinal cord before crashing into his brain and exiting just above his right eye. Dillinger pitched forward a couple of steps, fell face down on the pavement in front of the alley, and died. Purvis with gun still in hand approached the body and attempted to speak to it, there was no answer.[4]

There was a long moment of silence as Dillinger's blood oozed out onto the cement. Then pandemonium broke out. Autos and street cars stopped as passengers emerged to gather round the sprawled corpse. Voices shouted, "Dillinger—Dillinger!" and above the din voices of two women could be heard, screaming they'd been hit. That was true; each had been struck by an errant shot or perhaps one of the bullets that hit Dillinger, yet neither woman was seriously wounded.

Anna Sage and Polly Hamilton melted into the crowd and got away untouched. Polly later testified,

> I looked to see what had happened, and there was Jimmy lying there shot. . . . I ran to the grocery next door and bumped right into a gun in the hands of one of the officers, a government man I suppose. He didn't pay any attention to me, so I ran on to the corner. There in all that crowd I bumped into a woman who turned out to be Anna, who was running away, too. Then a policeman stopped me. I guess he lost his head or something, for he let me go.[5]

Anna Sage also slipped away from the scene unnoticed. She haggled with the FBI for a share of the reward money and eventually was paid $5,000, but her request to wipe out deportation proceedings was denied. Ruled an undesirable alien for her criminal past running brothels in Gary, Indiana, federal authorities arrested her in April, 1936, put her on a train to New York City, then on a boat to cross the Atlantic where on European shores she would entrain back to Romania.[6]

The mysterious "woman in red" died in her native land twelve years after having ratted on the nation's number one fugitive.

Curious onlookers and souvenir hunters, some police among the latter, swarmed around the fallen corpse in Chicago before authorities could establish order and before an ambulance arrived to take the body to the Cook

County Morgue on Polk Street. There despite considerable scarring on the fingers, authorities were able to get a set of prints which they immediately sent to Washington. In FBI labs there, a match clear enough for positive identification was made; so much for Dr. Loeser's acid treatment!

Grapevine reports of Dillinger's death spread throughout Chicago before newspaper extras hit the streets. By 2:00 A.M. Monday, throngs of spectators were milling in front of the Biograph hoping to catch a glimpse of whatever was left. Onlookers were not timid about seizing any remaining tidbit of history. The body had been removed, but several women dipped handkerchiefs into the blood still on the street, and one wild report was that another woman had used the hem of her skirt.

At the morgue, a full autopsy was performed and all the known physical markings of John Herbert Dillinger were accounted for: plastic surgery cuts and finger burns, leg wound from the St. Paul shooting, neck and shoulder scars from the Mason City heist, and old scars left from various childhood injuries. After the autopsy, the body was put on public display, and a line of rubberneckers two blocks long, mostly women, came for a look at the infamous gangster.

Dillinger's death dominated the news. For days, the Hoosier outlaw was the lead story as newspaper editors yielded entire front pages to details: eyewitness accounts, chronologies of bank robberies, persons killed, and speculations over whereabouts of remaining gang members.

The prestigious *New York Times* headlined, "Dillinger Slain in Ambush." The *San Francisco Chronicle* echoed, " Dillinger Killed by Federal Officers." The *Los Angeles Times* blazed, "Kill Dillinger Here." With city pride, the *Chicago Tribune* boasted the event. Smaller towns picked up the theme. In Butte, Montana, the *Standard* bannered "Federal Men Kill Dillinger." In Mansfield, Ohio, citizens sipping morning coffee could read, "Dillinger Dies in Trap After Woman 'Tips Off' U. S. Agents," and in Reno, Nevada, morning readers of the *Journal* saw in bold caption: "U.S. Agents Kill Dillinger."[7]

John Wilson Dillinger, father of the slain bank robber, came with the hearse from Mooresville to the Chicago mortuary to claim his son's body, which was taken back to the home town in Indiana. Virtually the entire population of the community came for the public viewing at the Harvey Funeral Parlor.

John Dillinger had requested that in the event of his death he wished to be buried next to his mother in the family plot at the Crown Hill Cemetery in Indianapolis. His father and other family members did their best to give him a decent burial there despite the throng of morbid spectators who crowded into the graveyard, along with a heavy police guard, and the roar of airplanes flying overhead on the lookout for possible interruptions.

A summer rainstorm burst just as family and friends under a temporary awning gathered round the grave. A local minister who had known him as a boy intoned a brief sermon, and a small bouquet was laid on the coffin by Audrey (Dillinger) Hancock, the bandit's older sister. John Herbert Dillinger, villain in life and hero in folklore, was laid to rest destined to return to dust.

Acknowledgements

"Writing is an adventure," remarked one of the greatest statesmen of the 20th century. "To begin with," continued Winston Churchill, "it is a toy and amusement. Then it becomes a mistress; then a master, and next it becomes a tyrant. The last phase is that just as you about to be reconciled to your servitude, you kill the monster and fling it to the public."

Although the author of the present book is the person who must stand in the dock awaiting a verdict, others have encouraged and abetted the deed's perpetration. A bevy of accomplices includes parents, friends, students, and teacher colleagues. The last named group warrant special tribute.

Ask an adult to list persons most influential in his or her life, and a teacher's s name will pop out. In my case, I'd say Miss Donnelly, the short, dumpy, proverbial old maid with a rough voice and manner to match, my teacher in the second grade. About half the kids in the class were raised in families which spoke a language other than English and were prone to say something like "My parents *they* took me to the park last week" or "My mother *she* baked a cherry pie." Miss Donnelly taught English, and such transgressions would send her up the wall. Her habitual shout was "Your parents are *they*" or "Your mother is a *she*."

After decades and countless grammatical errors, thanks to Miss Donnelly those are mistakes I rarely make.

Like other professions, teaching has good and bad practitioners. Much of my adult life has been spent in schools of one sort or another, and throughout the years I've been privileged to know from elementary through universities many outstanding teachers. They were persons who would have achieved distinction in whatever profession undertaken, but for reasons inexplicable they chose to be educators in the finest sense of the term. Ranked with Miss Donnelly would be Lew Sarett and Ernest Wrage of Northwestern University, William Brigance of Wabash College, and Keith Huntress and Clarence Matterson of Iowa State University. There were others, but these are the half-dozen I would always name.

Today, producing a book involves far more than just the ideas it presents. A modern book rests on the skills and technologies of numerous persons who help author and manufacturer. I'd be remiss if I failed to mention Professor Herb Harmison, the computer genius who always comes to my desk to correct troubles I make on this infernal word processor.

Members of a small book club to which I belong, Chuck and Carolyn Jons, Pat Severson, Mary Watkins, Colleen Nutty, and Roy and Carol Zingg, have thrown into the pot words, phrases, or ideas which spice or dilute my scribblings. These comrades as well as long time friends such as Fred and Terry Schlunz and Bob and Lois Vohs listen to my rantings and thoughts before I ever put them on paper.

I've drawn from books, magazines, and journals in putting together these stories. Also, newspaper morgues are treasure chests filled with accounts of events and persons involved. Archivists at the William Parks Library at Iowa State, the Mason City Public Library, the Ames Public Library, and historians at the National Archives in Washington, D. C. have been quick and accurate in honoring my every request.

Finally, my greatest debt is to my daughter Sue and her husband Dr. Kenneth Mills. Sue consistently offered suggestions on organization and was ever on the lookout for tidbits concerning my principals. Ken was invaluable when I got into difficulties of formatting and end notes.

There are shortcomings in every book, and whatever ones a scrutinizing reader may find in this production are faults of the author alone. He stands before the court asking for mercy.

Robert Underhill
August 2015

NOTES

Chapter 1

[1]R. D. Morgan. *The Tri-State Terror: Life and Crimes of Wilbur Underhill*. Stillwater, OK: New Forums Press, 2005. Pp. 11-12.

[2] Reports of this crime can be found in every Chicago newspaper then publishing. My summary rests chiefly on Douglas O. Linder, *The Leopold and Loeb Trial: A Brief Account, 1997*. Retrieved April 11, 2007. Also, see *Chicago Daily News*, June 2, 1024 and *Chicago Tribune* of the same date.

[3]Morgan, *op. cit.*, pp. 21-22.

[4] *Okmulgee Daily Times*, December 28, 1926.

[5]*Ibid.*,February 12, 1927.

[6]*Ibid.*, February 15, 1927.

[7]Morgan, *op. cit.*, pp. 55-56.

[8]*Ibid.*, pp. 78-80.

[9]*Ibid.*, pp. 96-102.

[10]*Ibid.*, pp. 101-08,

[11] William J. Helmer and Rick Mattix. *The Complete Public Enemy Almanac*. Nashville, TN: Cumberland House Publishing, 2007. P. 67.

[12]Robert Unger. *The Union Station Massacre*. Kansas City, MO; Kansas City Star Books, 2005, *passim*, especially pp. 4-7, and 53-60.

[13]As quoted by R. D. Morgan, *op. cit.*, pp. 272-73.

[14]Letter written by Agent R. H. Colvin to Division of Investigation, Department of Justice, dated December 31, 1933.

Chapter 2

[1]Alvin Karpis with Kent Bell, *The Alvin Karpis Story*. New York: Coward McCann and Goheegan, 1971.

[2]Bryan Burrough. *Public Enemies*. New York: Penguin Books, 2004, pp. 508-09.

Chapter 3

[1] William J. Helmer and Rick Mattix. *The Complete Public Enemy Almanac*. Cumberland, TN: Cumberland House Publishing, Inc., 2007, pp. 480-81.

[2] *St. Paul Pioneer Press*, June 17, 1933.

[3] *New York Times*, June 19, 1933.

[4] Bryan Burrough. *Public Enemies*. New York: Penguin Group, 2004, p. 109, n#2.

[5] *Ibid.*, pp. 184-75.

[6] Curt Gentry. *J. Edgar Hoover: The Man and His Secrets*. New York: W. W. Norton, 1991.

[7]Alvin Karpis with Kent Bell, *op. cit.*

[8]Burroughs, *op. cit.*, p. 522.

[9]Burrough, *op. cit.*, pp. 533-41.

Chapter 4

[1] Michael Wallis. *Pretty Boy: The Life and Times of Charles Arthur Floyd*. New York: SW. W. Norton & Co., 1992, pp. 134-35.

[2]*Ibid.*, p. 198.

[3] *Ibid.*, p. 248.

[4]*Ibid.*, p. 209.

[5]*Ibid.*, pp. 268-69.

[6] Jeffrey S. King. *The Life and Death of Pretty Boy Floyd*. Kent, Ohio: Kent State University Press, 1998, pp. 36-37.

[7]Wallis, *op. cit.*, pp. 280-86.

[8]Heyton Preston. *They Shoot to Kill: Secrets of the G-Men*. London: Readers Library, 1938, pp. 92-93.

[9]King, *op. cit.* pp. 117-18.

[10]Report of R. E. Verletti, Kansas City, June 26, 1933,FBI File 62-28915-92.

[11]Robert Unger. *Union Station Massacre*. Kansas City, MO: Kansas City Star Books, 2005, p.53.

[12] Wallis, *op. cit.*, pp. 406-11.

[13]King, *op. cit.*, p. 126.

[14] *Ibid.*, p. 129.

[15]*Ibid.*, pp. 182-85.

Chapter 5

[1] Steven Nickel and William J. Helmer. *Baby Face Nelson: Portrait of a Public Enemy*. Nashville, TN: Cumberland House Publishing, Inc., 202, pp. 19-20.

[2]*Ibid.*, pp. 29 and 34-35.

[3]*Ibid.*, p. 31.

[4]*Ibid.*, p. 43.

[5]*Ibid.*, p. 47.

[6] Bryan Burrough. *Public Enemies*. New York: Penguin Group, 2004, p. 103. Also see, Nickel and Helmer, *op. cit.*, pp. 46-52.

[7] Nickel and Helmer, *op. cit.*,357.

[8]Nickel and Helmer. op. cit., pp. 155-56.

[9]*Ibid.*, pp. 164-66.

[10]*Ibid.*, p. 179.

[11] Burrough, op. cit., pp. 315-22. Also see Nickel and Helmer, *op. cit.*, pp. 242-43.

[12] Burrough, op. cit., pp. 474-77. Also see Nickel and Helmer, *op. cit.*, 342-46.

[13]*Ibid.*, p. 74.

Chapter 6

[1]"The Younger Cock," *Dallas Morning News*, May 9, 1926.

[2]*Paul Schneider, Bonnie and Clyde: The Lives Behind the Legend.* New York: Henry Holt and Company, 2009. P. 47.

[3]Blanche Caldwell Barrow. *My Life With Bonnie and Clyde*. John Neal Phillips, ed. Norman, Oklahoma: University of Oklahoma Press, 2004, P. editor's introduction, xxix-xxx.

[4]Guinn, *op. cit.*, pp. 41-42.

[5]Blanche Caldwell Barrow. *My Life With Bonnie and Clyde*. John Neal Phillips, ed. Norman, Oklahoma: University of Oklahoma Press, 2004, Appendix C. pp. 204-05.

Chapter 7

[1]Guinn, *op. cit.*, pp. 41-42.

[2]*Ibid.*, 51-52.

[3]"If William Turner," *Waco Sunday Herald-Tribune*, March 9, 1930.

[4]Guinn, *op. cit.*, p. 65. or pp. 61-62.

Chapter 8

[1]Phillips, *op. cit.*, p. 8.

[2]*Ibid.*

[3]*Ibid.*, pp.54-55, and p. 331, n. *Ibid* 57.

[4]Underwood, *op. cit.*, pp. 8-10.

[5]Blanche Caldwell Barrow. *My Life With Bonnie and Clyde*. Norman, Oklahoma: University of Oklahoma Press, 2004, p. 263, n. 5.

[6]Phillips, *op. cit.*, p. 140.

Chapter 9

[1]Phillips, *op. cit.*, pp. 129-30.

[2]Blanche Caldwell Barrow, *op. cit.*, p. 64.

[3]Guinn, *op. cit.*, p. 229.

[4]"Shootout with Bonnie and Clyde," *St. Louis Post-Dispatch*, July 20, 1933. Also, Jan Fortune, *Fugitives: The Story of Bonnie and Clyde*. Dallas, Texas: Ranger Press, 1934, pp. 191-93.

[5]Phillips, *op. cit.*, pp. 145-58. Also, see *Des Moines Register*, January 22, 1968.

[6]"Reflections About the Barrow Gang," Marvelle Feller. Courtesy of the Dexter Historical Museum.

[7]*Des Moines Tribune*, July 24, 1933.

[8]*Perry Daily*, July 25, 1933.

[9]*Perry Daily*, July 27, 1933.

[10] Notes from the Video—Eye Witness Account of the Dexfield Shootout. Obtained through courtesy of the Dexter Public Library. Video produced by Pegasus TV—Doug Wood.

[11]*Perry Daily*, July 27, 1933.

[12]Phillips, *Running With Bonnie and Clyde*, p. 157.

Chapter 10

[1]*Houston Post*, August 20, 1974.

[2]This brief biography is taken from Michael Newton, *Encyclopedia of Robbers, Heists, and Capers*. New York: Facts on File, Inc., 2002.

[3] Guinn, *op. cit.*, pp. 238-40.

[4]Lee Simmons. *Assignment Huntsville: Memoirs of a Texas Prison Officer*. Austin, Texas: University of Texas Press, 1957. P. 167.

[5]This account of the escape from Eastham Prison is taken from Sid Underwood. *Depression Desperado: Chronicle of Raymond Hamilton*. Eakin Press: Austin, Texas, 1995, pp. 41-45.

[6]Rick Mattix. *The "Bloody Barrows" Come to Iowa*. Dexter Museum, Dexter, Iowa.

[7]Winston G. Ramsey. *On the Trail of Bonnie and Clyde: Then and Now*. London: Battle of Britain Prints, 2003.

[8]The incident as related to this author on September 23, 2013, by 91-year-old Leonard Burmeister in his home next door to the robbed bank.

[9]*Dallas Evening Journal*, February 28, 1934; *Dallas Daily Times Herald*, February 28, 1934, and *Dallas Dispatch*, February 28, 1934.

[10]Helmer and Mattix., *op. cit.*, p. 380.

[11]Underwood, *op. cit.*, pp. 96-113.

[12]Phillips, *op.*, cit., 184-88.

[13]Lee Simmons, *Assignment Huntsville*, p. 132 and p. 170.

[14] *Ibid.*

Chapter 11

[1]John Toland. *The Dillinger Days*. New York: Da Capo Press, 1995. P. 17.

[2]G. Russell Girardin and William J. Helmer. *Dillinger: The Untold Story*. Bloomington, Indiana: Indiana University Press, 1994, p. 13.

[3]*Ibid.*, p. 17.

[4]Jefferey S. King. *The Rise and Fall of the Dillinger Gang*. Nashville, TN: Cumberland House Publishing, 2005. Pp. 14-15.

[5]*Ibid.*, pp. 15-16.

[6]*Ibid.*, pp. 18-19.

[7]Girardin and Helmer, *op. cit.*, p. 21.

[8]Helmer and Mattix, *op. cit.*, p. 350.

[9]Cromie and Pinkston, *op. cit.*, p. 37.

[10]Elliott J. Gorn. *Dillinger's Wild Ride*. New York: Oxford University Press, 2011. Pp. 38-41.

[11]Girardin and Helmer, *op. cit.*, pp. 36-38.

[12]G. Russell Girardin and William J. Helmer. *Dillinger: The Untold Story.* Bloomington, Indiana: Indiana University Press, 1994, p. 39.

[13]Cromie and Pinkston, *op. cit.*, pp. 101-02.

[14]King, *op. cit.*, pp. 34-36.

[15]*Washington Star*, Oct. 17, 1934; *New York Times*, Oct. 17, 1934.

[16]Helmer and Mattix, *op. cit.*, p. 446.

[17]King, *Dillinger*, pp. 30-31.

[18]*Chicago Tribune*, December 15, 1933, pp. 1, 12; *Van Wert (Ohio) Daily Bulletin*, December 15, 1933, p. 1; *Salamanca (N.Y.) Republican-Press*, December 15, 1933, p. 1.

[19]Helmer and Mattix, *op. cit., p. 371.*

[20]Gorn, *op. cit., p. 57.* Also see, Girardin and Helmer, *op. cit.*, pp. 54-55.

[21]Dary Matera. *John Dillinger.* New York: Da Capo Press, 2004, pp. 168-69.

[22]*New York Times*, January 27, 1934, p. 1.

[23]*Chicago Daily News*, January 27, 1934, p. 1, and January 29, 1934, p. 1.

[24]*Chicago Tribune*, January 26, 1934, p. 1.

Chapter 12

[1]Gorn, *op. cit.*, pp. 61-63.

[2]"Tucson Sighs as Gangsters Leave Arizona." *Arizona Star*, January 31. 1934, p. 1; "Three Dillinger Bandits and Woman Companion are Sent East by Train," *Arizona Citizen*, January 30, 1934, p.1. [3]Burrough, op. cit., pp. 216-17.

[4]Every biographer of Dillinger pays attention to this sensational jailbreak. My account is condensed from the following: Elliott J. Dorn, *Dillinger's Wild Ride*, pp. 75-80; Robert Cromie and Joseph Pinkston, *Dillinger: A Short and Violent Life*, pp. 159-56; John Toland, *Dillinger Days*, pp. 210-16; Bryan Burrough, *Public Enemies*, pp. 234-42; G. Russell Girardin and William J. Helmer, *Dillinger, the Untold Story*, pp. 70-88.

Chapter 13

[1]Burrough, *op. cit.*, footnote on pp. 242-43.

[2]Toland, *op. cit.*, p. 243.

[3]As quoted, Gorn, op. cit., p. 37.

[4]"Thugs Get $46,000, Kidnap 5 in Bank," *New York Times*, March 7, 1934, p. 2; "Bandits Raid Bank, Take Police Guns," *Gary Post-Tribune*, March 6, 1934, p. 1; "Machine Gunmen Rob Sioux Falls Bank of $46,000," *Chicago Tribune*, March 6, 1934, p. 8.

[5]This account of the Mason City robbery is condensed from reports in several biographies. See, Toland, *op. cit.*, pp. 228-39; Gorn, *op. cit.*, pp. 86-87; Girardin and Helmer, *op. cit.*, pp. 117-20.

[6]King, *Dillinger Gang*, pp. 192-94.

[7]Cromie and Pinkston, *op. cit.*, pp 191-92.

[8]As quoted by Gorn, *op. cit.*, p. 101.

[9]"Taunts Police on Dillinger's Escape Here," *Chicago Herald Examiner*, April 19, 1934. Also, "Woman Friend Brags," *Chicago Tribune*, April 19, 1934, p. 3.

[10]Frechette was taken to St. Paul where she was tried on a charge of conspiracy to harbor a fugitive. Convicted, she was fined $1,000 and sentenced to two years in prison.

[11]Related by Pittenger to this author when he was a 15-year-old boy at Silver Lake.

[12]The author, thirteen years old at the time, remembers being shown a machine gun placed above a funeral parlor in the hamlet of Silver Lake, Indiana, twelve miles south of Warsaw. Across the street from this parlor, another machine gun was installed on the second floor above a drug store. Both guns were trained on the center of town, where State Routes 15 and 14 intersected. That was the key intersection, and every car was supposed to stop for the sign. If Dillinger did intend to go to Mooresville, authorities figured he most likely would take Rte. 15, a major state highway which led from Warsaw to Indianapolis.

Chapter 14

[1]Matera, *John Dillinger*, p. 264.

[2]Burrough, *op. cit.*, pp. 306-12.

[3]FBI John Dillinger File 1561: Statement of Agent Virgil Peterson, May 9, 1934; also, quoted by Burrough, *op. cit.*, p. 313.

[4]*Chicago Tribune*, April 23, 1934, p. 1.

[5]*Chicago Daily News*, April 24, 1934, p. 1.

[6] "Will Rogers Says," Newark, Ohio, *Advocate*, April 24, 1934, p. 1. Also, Frederick, Maryland, *Post*, April 26, 1934, p, 4.

Chapter 15

[1]Girardin, *Dillinger*, pp. 171-77; Burrough, *Public Enemies*, pp. 365-67.

[2]"Dillinger Gang Kills Officer," *South Bend Tribune*, June 30, 1934, p. 1. Also, *Chicago Tribune*, July 1, 1934, p. 1.

[3]Matera, *op. cit.*, pp. 339-41.

[4]Matera, *op. cit.*, pp. 350-54; also, Gorn, *op. cit.*, pp. 144-45; Toland, *op. cit.*, pp. 324-25.

[5]As quoted in Matera, *op. cit.*, p. 355.

[6]"Dillinger's Betrayer to Sail Monday," *Syracuse Herald* (NY), April 15, 1936, p. 1.

[7]Each of the cited newspapers carried the story on July 23, 1934, page 1.

BIBLIOGRAPHY

Books

Barrow, Blanche Caldwell. *My Life With Bonnie and Clyde.* Norman, Oklahoma: University of Oklahoma Press, 2005.

Block, Lawrence, ed. *Gangsters, Swindlers, Killers, and Thieves.* New York: Oxford University Press, 2004.

Burrough, Bryan. *Public Enemies.* New York: Penguin Books, 2004.

Clayton, Merle. *Union Station Massacre: The Shootout that Started the FBI's War on Crime.* New York: Leisure Books, 1975.

Cromie, Robert and Joseph Pinkston. *Dillinger: A Short and Violent Life.* Chicago: Chicago Historical Bookworks, 1962.

Fortune, Jan I. *Fugitives: The Story of Clyde Barrow and Bonnie Parker, as Told by Bonnie's Mother (Emma Krause Parker) and Clyde's Sister (Nell Barrow Cowan).* Dallas, Texas: Ranger Press, 1934.

Gentry, Curt. *J. Edgar Hoover: The Man and His Secrets.* New York: W. W. Norton, 1991.

Girardin, G. Russell and William J. Helmer. *Dillinger: The Untold Story.* Bloomington, Indiana: Indiana University Press, 1994.

Gorn, Elliott J. *Dillinger's Wild Ride: The Year that Made America's Public Enemy Number One.* OUP: USA, 2009.

Guinn, Jeff. *Go Down Together.* New York: Simon and Schuster, Inc., 2009.

Girardin, G. Russell and William J. Helmer. *Dillinger: The Untold Story.* Bloomington, Indiana: Indiana University Press, 1994.

Gorn, Elliott J. *Dillinger's Wild Ride.* New York: Oxford University Press, 2009.

Hamilton, Stanley. *Machine Gun Kelly's Last Stand.* Lawrence, Kansas: University of Kansas Press, 2003.

Helmer, William J. and Rick Mattix. *The Complete Public Enemy Almanac.* Nashville, TN: Cumberland House Publishing, Inc., 2007.

Hoover, J. Edgar. *The Alvin Karpis Story.* New York: Coward McCann and Goheegan, 1971.

King, Jeffrey S. *The Life and Death of Pretty Boy Floyd.* Kent, Ohio: Kent State University Press, 1998.

_____. *The Rise and Fall of the Dillinger Gang.* Nashville, TN: Cumberland House Publishing, Inc., 2008.

Louderback, Lew. *The Bad Ones: Gangsters of the '30s and Their Molls.* Greenwich, Conn.: Fawcett & Co., 1968.

Martin, Paul D. *Villains, Scoundrels, and Rogues.* Amherst, New York: Prometheus Books, 2014.

Matera, Dary. *John Dillinger: the Life and Death of America's First Celebrity Criminal.* Berkeley, California: Caroll & Graf, 2004.

Milner, E. R. *The Lives and Times of Bonnie and Clyde.* Carbondale, Illinois: Southern Illinois University Press, 1996.

Morgan, R. D. *The Tri-State Terror: The Life and Crimes of Wilbur Underhill.* Stilwater, Oklahoma: New Forums Press, Inc., 2005.

Newton, Michael. *Encyclopedia of Robbers, Heists, and Capers.* New York: Facts on File, Inc., 2002.

_____. *True Crimes: Gangsters Outside the Law.* Sywell, NN6 OBJ: Igloo Books Ltd., 2010.

Nickel, Steven and William J. Helmer. *Baby-Face Nelson.* Nashville, Tennessee: Cumberland House Publishing, Inc., 2002.

Peters, Robert. *What Dillinger Meant to Me.* Seahorse Press, 1983.

Preston, Hayten. *They Shoot to Kill: Secrets of the G-Men.* London: Readers Library, 1938, pp. 92-93.

Ramsey, Winston G. *On the Trail of Bonnie and Clyde: Then and Now.* London: Battle of Britain Prints, 2003.

Sanborn, Debra. *The Barrow Gang's Visit to Dexter.* Dexter, Iowa, Bob Weesner, 1976.

Schneider, Paul. *Bonnie and Clyde: The Lives Behind the Legend.* New York: Henry Holt and Company, 2009.

Simmons, Lee. *Assignment Huntsville: Memoirs of a Texas Prison Officer*. Austin, Texas: University of Texas Press, 1957.

Stewart, Tony. Dillinger: *The Hidden Truth—A Tribute to Gangsters and G-Men of the Great Depression Era*. Xibris Corporation, 2002.

Tresiniowski, Alex. *The Vendetta: Special Agent Melvin Purvis, John Dillinger, and Hoover's FBI in the Age of Gangsters*. New York: Public Affairs, 2009.

Underwood, Sid. *Depression Desperado: Chronicle of Raymond Hamilton*. Austin, Texas: Eakin Press, 1995.

Unger, Robert. *Union Station Massacre*. Kansas City, Missouri: Kansas City Star Books, 2005.

Wallis, Michael. *Pretty Boy: The Life and Times of Charles Arthur Floyd*. New York: W. W. Norton & Co., 1992.

Newspaper and Magazines

Arizona Citizen
Arizona Star
Chicago Daily News
Chicago Tribune
Coshocton Tribune (Ohio)
Dallas Morning News
Dallas Dispatch
Dallas Times-Herald
New York Times
Okmulgee Daily Times
Salmanca Republican-Press
South Bend Tribune
St. Paul Pioneer Press
Toledo News-Bee
Time Magazine
Van Wert Daily Bulletin
Waco Herald-Tribune
Warsaw Times (Ind.)
West Plains Daily Quill (Missouri)

INDEX